S 8/08

CW01096060

PERFORMANCE AND IDENTITY IN THE CLASSICAL WORLD

Performance and Identity in the Classical World traces attitudes toward actors in Greek and Roman culture as a means of understanding ancient conceptions of, and anxieties about, the self. The actor's ability to impersonate different characters might be considered a threat to a philosophical commitment to the stability of the self, or to a political commitment to the stability of the social order. Actors were thus often viewed as frauds and impostors, capable of deliberately fabricating their identities. Conversely, they were sometimes viewed as possessed by the characters that they played, or as merely playing themselves onstage. Numerous sources reveal an uneasy fascination with actors and acting, from the writings of elite intellectuals (philosophers, orators, biographers, historians) to the abundant theatrical anecdotes that can be read as a body of "popular performance theory." *Performance and Identity in the Classical World* examines these sources, along with dramatic texts, and addresses the issue of impersonation from the late fifth century BCE to the early Roman Empire.

Anne Duncan is assistant professor of Classics in the Department of Languages and Literatures at Arizona State University. She has published articles on Greek and Roman comedy, Greek tragedy, and English Renaissance drama.

PERFORMANCE AND IDENTITY IN THE CLASSICAL WORLD

ANNE DUNCAN

Arizona State University

CAMBRIDGE
UNIVERSITY PRESS

LIBRARY
NEWCASTLE COLLEGE
NEWCASTLE UPON TYNE

Class 792.08

BARCODE 0215692X

CAMBRIDGE UNIVERSITY PRESS
Cambridge, New York, Melbourne, Madrid, Cape Town, Singapore, São Paulo

Cambridge University Press
40 West 20th Street, New York, NY 10011-4211, USA

www.cambridge.org
Information on this title: www.cambridge.org/9780521852821

© Anne Duncan 2006

This publication is in copyright. Subject to statutory exception
and to the provisions of relevant collective licensing agreements,
no reproduction of any part may take place without
the written permission of Cambridge University Press.

First published 2006

Printed in the United States of America

A catalog record for this publication is available from the British Library.

Library of Congress Cataloging in Publication Data

Duncan, Anne.
Performance and identity in the classical world / Anne Duncan.
p.   cm.
Includes bibliographical references.
ISBN-13: 978-0-521-85282-1 (hardback)
ISBN-10: 0-521-85282-X (hardback)
1. Acting – History – To 500.   2. Performing arts – Greece – History – To 1500.   3. Classican
drama – History and criticism.   4. Theater – Greece – History – To 500.   5. Identity
(Psychology) in literature.   6. Theater – History – To 500.   7. Performing arts – Rome.
8. Self in literature.   9. Actors – Greece.   10. Theater – Rome.   11. Actors – Rome.   I. Title.
PA3203.D76   2005
792.08'0938'0901 – dc22   2005011726

ISBN-13   978-0-521-85282-1 hardback
ISBN-10   0-521-85282-x hardback

Cambridge University Press has no responsibility for
the persistence or accuracy of URLs for external or
third-party Internet Web sites referred to in this publication
and does not guarantee that any content on such
Web sites is, or will remain, accurate or appropriate.

CONTENTS

v

PREFACE

I WOULD LIKE TO THANK THE FRIENDS AND COLLEAGUES WHO READ
drafts or talked through ideas at various stages of this project: Edward
E. Cohen, Joy Connolly, Taylor Corse, Jennifer Ebbeler, Mary-Kay
Gamel, Lisa Rengo George, Alexa Jervis, Amanda Krauss, Kevin Lee,
Susan McCready, Jess Miner, Alex Purves, Ralph Rosen, and Keith
Sidwell. Some of them may not be aware of how helpful they were.
Sheila Murnaghan deserves special thanks for reading through the entire
manuscript several times, both during and after her tenure as my disser-
tation advisor. I would also like to thank the two anonymous readers for
Cambridge University Press, who saved me from many errors of fact and
judgment. I can say with both stock formulaicness and utter sincerity that
any remaining deficiencies are entirely my own.

This project was also supported by a number of institutions. It began life
as a dissertation at the University of Pennsylvania. Chapter 4 was written
with the assistance of a Women's Studies Summer Research Grant from
Arizona State University. I would also like to thank the Department of
Classics at Columbia University for making me a Visiting Researcher for
the summers of 2001 and 2002, the Department of Classics at Georgetown
University for making me a Visiting Researcher for spring–summer 2005,
and the Library of Congress for granting me research privileges in the
summers of 2003 and 2004. Finally, a research leave from Arizona State
University in the spring of 2005 made it possible to finish this book. I
am very grateful to all these institutions for their assistance and support.

Part of the Introduction appeared earlier as an article in *Helios* (Duncan,
2005a); part of Chapter 1 appeared earlier as an article in the *European
Studies Journal* (Duncan, 2001); part of Chapter 4 appeared earlier as a
chapter in *Prostitutes and Courtesans in the Ancient World* (Duncan, 2005b).
I am grateful to all of the publishers for permission to reprint.

Titles of ancient texts follow the abbreviations listed in the *Oxford Classical Dictionary*, third edition.

I am afraid I have followed no consistent principle in the transliteration of Greek names and words. Names and words that seemed too familiar in their Latinized version to change (Ajax, Plato) were kept in that form; less familiar names and words were transliterated more closely (*Thesmophoriazousai*, Kleon). All translations are my own, unless otherwise indicated.

This book is dedicated to Eric Berger.

INTRODUCTION

THE HYPOCRITICAL SELF

For a book that is filled with anecdotes, it seems appropriate to begin with an anecdote of my own, and so here it is.

Like many children, I was afraid of clowns. I remember the moment vividly when, as a seven-year-old, I was finally able to articulate the basis of this fear. My grandparents had taken my brother and me to the circus, and since we had arrived early, we were sitting and watching the roustabouts set up the equipment. A clown spotted us and approached me and my brother. As he drew closer, I was able to get a good look at him. He asked us if we wanted to be in a procession during the show with a bunch of other kids, some animals in cages, and – of course – a whole host of clowns. I said no, shrinking back into my seat. He was surprised and looked at my grandparents, asking whether I was sure I didn't want to be part of the fun procession. They smiled and said that I was shy, and the clown retreated, seeking out other children among the early-comers. But I suddenly understood my fear: the clown had a big smile painted on his face, but the real mouth underneath the painted smile *wasn't smiling*. Clowns could go through a whole performance without ever actually smiling, I realized. Clowns could actually be evil, and you'd never know unless you got up close. And by then it would be too late.

The uneasiness that many people have felt throughout the ages with theatrical impersonation provided the genesis of this book. The dissonance between actor and character, or actor and mask, in the case of the ancient world, has often provoked uncertainty about actors as a class of people and acting as an activity. What follows is an examination of Greek and Roman attitudes toward actors and acting, the anxieties and desires that theatrical impersonation aroused, at different moments in Greek and Roman history. Numerous Greek vase-paintings show actors holding their masks, sometimes studying them intently, sometimes carelessly dangling them from a hand; the artists often depict the actor's face and the mask as identical.[1] On the other hand, there are late Roman ivory carvings of theatrical masks that carefully show the actor's eyes, lips, and teeth behind the eye-holes and mouth-hole of the mask.[2] Are these images of terror, as they would have been to my seven-year-old self, or of fascination, even admiration? I mention desires, as well as anxieties; the conclusion of my circus story is that I watched the procession of exotic animals, children selected from the audience, and clowns, and despite feeling that I had narrowly escaped some horrible fate, I was envious of the children in the spotlight. I secretly wished the clown would come back and give me a second chance.

While drama enjoyed great popularity during many periods in the ancient world, theatrical impersonation was an activity that was viewed with a great deal of ambivalence at both the moral level and the practical level. On the moral level, some people questioned the ethical status of impersonation: was it essentially lying? What effect did it have on the people who engaged in it, and what effect did it have on the spectators? On the practical level, some people wondered how acting worked: was acting the use of a set of skills, or was it a submersion of the self through some mysterious process into the character(s) played?[3] Both sets of questions have to do with the ontological status of the self – that is, with the effect of mimesis on identity. Both sets of questions had profound implications for the way society viewed not just actors, but all selves.

For the purposes of this study, I am defining mimesis as the act of theatrical impersonation,[4] and identity as the sense of possessing a self that is an integrated whole, consistent over time and in different settings. Scholars who study the history of ideas differ about what term to

---

[1] Bieber (1961) 82 (actors studying masks); Pickard-Cambridge (1988) 187 (on what he calls the "melting" of the actor's face and character's mask); see also the famous Pronomos Vase for a satyr-chorus in various stages of getting into or becoming one with their costumes, including one actor whose face seems to resemble the female mask he is holding.

[2] Bieber (1961) 243.

[3] Wiles (1991) 110 describes anecdotal and artistic representations of actors studying their masks in attitudes of "observation rather than immersion" and argues that this is necessitated in a theatrical tradition where actors play multiple roles, but there is abundant evidence for the "immersion" theory as well; see chapter 5 below on Clodius Aesopus.

[4] Rather than defining it more broadly as the imitation of "real life" in literature, as Auerbach does in his classic work Mimesis (1974).

use to describe the notion of identity in antiquity, though they tend to
agree that a fundamental divide separates us from the ancients. Sometime
between the Renaissance and the eighteenth century, the story goes,
people became self-conscious, and the modern sense of self was born,
now usually termed "subjectivity."[5] The ancients, on the other hand,
were not blessed (or cursed) with this anxious self-consciousness, and so
their sense of identity was more communal, more rooted in family, clan,
gender, age, and status than in a Romantic or post-Romantic sense of
possessing a unique individuality.[6] The philosopher Amelie Oksenberg
Rorty, for example, traces four distinct stages in the development of
the sense of identity of persons. She labels the unreflective, reactive
people contained within Homer and other ancient literary and philosophical texts "characters"; she describes later ancients and medievals as
"persons" (based on the ancient use of the term *persona* in both theater
and law), because they played a variety of roles and were held individually accountable for their actions; she defines as "selves" the people who
lived after the advent of capitalism and the social mobility (and consequent
shifts in the basis of identity) it enabled; and finally, she describes self-
conscious, late-capitalist, post-Romantic folk like us as "individuals."[7]
The literary critic Lionel Trilling has a simpler system, speaking of persons living after the early sixteenth century as having a sense of self where
sincerity was the ultimate measure of value, while modern persons have
a sense of self where *authenticity* is the ultimate measure. Persons living
before the sixteenth century, he says, simply were not "individuals" in

---

[5] Rorty, "Introduction," in Rorty (1976), locates the origin of the contemporary sense
of identity in three major components: the philosophical component is the development of the sense of self from the Cartesian "I" through the works of Locke, Hume,
Kant, Sartre, and Heidegger; the historical component is the advent of the Refor-
mation and its push toward individual responsibility; the cultural component is the
influence of Romanticism and the invention of the novel of first-person sensibility.
Other scholars might include the Renaissance's insistence on individual authorship of
literary and artistic works.

[6] See, for example, Blondell (2002) 60; Csapo (2002) 139–40.

[7] Rorty, "Postscript," in Rorty (1976). Rorty acknowledges that her system is far tidier
than any application of it to reality. It should be noted that she does not seem to
envision only literary characters as "characters," though this is not exactly clear, and
that her discussion of "persons" is shot through with a good deal of Christianity: the
person is the legally liable subject, but this becomes the moral agent accountable to
God for his actions. These two factors make her historical perspective on personal
identity less useful for examining the ancient world than for contrasting the modern
world with the ancient one. On Rorty's fourfold division of personal identity, see
Alcorn (1994) 7–11.

the modern sense.[8] As with Rorty's history of personal identity, the distinction Trilling draws is between external and internal evaluation of the sense of self, with a historical development from external to internal – corresponding roughly to the transition between what anthropologists call "shame cultures" and "guilt cultures," and sometimes used as a code for referring to the supposedly natural and inevitable development of Protestantism.[9]

It should be noted that these schemas have a pronounced evolutionary aspect to them, which might make us question them.[10] If we attempt to put aside the twentieth-century evolutionary model of psychic development represented by Rorty's and Trilling's theories when we look at the ancient evidence, a somewhat different picture of ancient selfhood emerges. The various media which provide our evidence for ancient conceptions of identity – literary, historical, philosophical, medical, and rhetorical texts, funerary and other inscriptions, letters, law, portrait sculpture – present rather different views of the sense of self in antiquity, depending on their target audience, level of sophistication, and degree of self-consciousness as sources. There is evidence from the ancient world that could be used to suggest the existence of a postmodern conception of subjectivity as fluid, fragmented, constructed, or contingent: Hesiod's account of the literal construction of woman in the creation of Pandora in the *Works and Days*, for example, or Ovid's *Metamorphoses*, with its interest in physical change, dissolution of ego boundaries, and instability of gender.[11] The general ideal, however, was closer to what we would call a modern sense of identity rather than a postmodern sense of subjectivity,

---

[8] Trilling (1972) ch. 1. Trilling's concern is with literary characters, not with historical persons: "The sincerity of Achilles or Beowulf cannot be discussed: they neither have nor lack sincerity" (2). We might wonder what he thought of Cicero, on the other hand. It is interesting to note that both Trilling's and Rorty's systems are haunted by the concept of authenticity; this seems to be "our" problem, as moderns.

[9] Rorty and Trilling (and many others) rely heavily on Mauss' schema of the evolution of the concept of the person, which connected the sense of interiority which defines the "person" to the advent of autobiography in Augustine's *Confessions*. For an excellent analysis and critique of this schema, see Carrithers, Collins, and Lukes, eds. (1985), especially the essays on the ancient world by Hollis and Momigliano.

[10] Alcorn (1994) 10; see also Lape (2004) 97.

[11] The fact that certain postmodern literary theories have been applied with great success to these authors – structuralism and semiotics to Hesiod, Lacanian psychoanalysis to Ovid – is a hint that these authors' theories of the self mesh fairly comfortably with postmodern theories of subjectivity. On Hesiod, see, e.g., Pucci (1977); on Ovid, see, e.g., Murray (1998).

stressing consistency (over time, among different aspects of the self, and between soul and body), self-control, and unity; Ruby Blondell has recently labeled this ideal in ancient thought "harmonious homogeneity."[12] Some scholars would add that the ancient sense of self was not modern in terms of its relative lack of "inwardness"; the ancients, unlike us, were not concerned with self-scrutiny.[13] This seems to overstate the case; after all, one of the most famous inscriptions from the ancient world was the inscription at the Oracle of Delphi, symbolic center of the Greek world: ΓΝⲰΘΙ ΣΑΥΤΟΝ, "Know thyself." This motto (or mandate) presumes the existence of a self to be known, and a capacity for inward scrutiny in order to know it. It is another expression of the ancient conception of the ideal self.

We see this ideal expressed to different degrees in different media from the ancient world. If it is possible to generalize so broadly and so diachronically about the different kinds of evidence, most ancient literature is concerned to represent personal identity as coherent, stable, and often distinctive, with a character's appearance usually matching his or her inner nature.[14] Ancient histories and biographies tend to be interested in drawing the moral character of their subjects, which is usually seen as developing through childhood and more or less fixed and coherent by adulthood.[15] Philosophical writings on identity are the most prescriptive

---

[12] Blondell (2002) 60.

[13] See, e.g., Di Vito (1999). Foucault (1986) 41–3 discusses the older scholarly view that a sense of "individualism" began to develop in the Hellenistic period and was brought to full flower in the Roman Republic and Empire; Foucault both critiques and nuances this view with his discussion of the "care of the self" enjoined and practiced by certain Roman philosophical elites, notably the Stoics: 37–68 and *passim*.

[14] The "high" literary genres, such as epic and tragedy, have as one of their projects the revelation of the protagonists' characters. Some of the "low" literary genres, such as comedy, are uninterested in this project; there is no emphasis on consistency of character in Aristophanes, for example, or much of a sense of individuality in Plautus or Terence. (On the question of apparent individualism in Menandrian comedy, see Lape (2004, 96–9).) But other "low" genres, such as satire and epigram, do share this focus on depicting a stable character whose appearance matches reality. To those like Rorty who would exclude the earliest ancient literature, that is, Homer, from this description, one could point to the depiction of Odysseus in the *Odyssey*, who maintains his essential nature through many deceptions and disguises. See Murnaghan (1987).

[15] This is clearest in moralizing biographers such as Plutarch and Suetonius, but is also evident in the "serious" historians, as in Thucydides' depiction of Nikias, or in Tacitus' *Agricola*. See Gill (1983). This tendency is also evident in the *Vita* tradition, which assumes that the poet's personality is expressed through his work.

of all ancient sources, and they overwhelmingly depict the goal of a coherent, stable, integrated self subjected to reason.[16] Ancient medical texts treat identity as consisting purely of the basic social categories of sex and age, with each category requiring a certain balance of temperature and moisture, or a certain balance of the humors.[17] Rhetorical texts are exceedingly concerned to depict identity as coherent and stable, and therefore predictable and legally responsible, as are legal texts.[18] Epideictic rhetoric too focuses on the praiseworthy individual, and in this resembles biography.[19] Funerary inscriptions speak to a sense of personal identity informed by the broadest social categories – class, status, age, gender, ethnicity, familial relationships – but occasionally, they provide a glimpse of the dead person's sense of him- or herself beyond these broad categories.[20] Letters are coming under scholarly scrutiny now for what they reveal about new ways of imagining identity in relation to other people: the letter can replace the physical presence of the correspondent; correspondence can create "imagined communities," to borrow Benedict Anderson's phrase; the self authoring the letter is highly aware of its own self-presentation and willing to present different personas to different correspondents.[21] And portrait sculpture in the ancient world shows a fascinating mix of descriptive and proscriptive elements which could be taken to indicate a sense of identity as constructed, but which in fact indicates the same focus on moral character and role modeling that we see in ancient biography.[22]

Most sources from the ancient world, then, point – in both a descriptive and a proscriptive way – to a sense (an ideal) of personal identity as

---

[16] Gill (1983) 480: "In ancient ethical theory, excellence of character is often conceived as a kind of psychological stability or consistency, including the capacity to keep emotions in line with what reason approves, regardless of the impact of circumstances, which often invite rather different emotional reactions." The model of the "pagan notion of the person" as "benevolent dualism" of body and soul, described in Brown (1988) 26–34, is heavily influenced by pagan philosophical writings on the soul, especially Plato and the Stoics.

[17] See, for example, Dean-Jones (1992).

[18] Both theoretical treatises on oratory, like Aristotle's *Rhetoric* or Cicero's *De Oratore*, as well as forensic speeches, like Lysias 1 or Cicero's *In Catilinam* 1.

[19] Beck (2000) 15.

[20] We could say the same about victory and dedicatory inscriptions. For an interesting example of complicated self-presentation on a funeral monument from Roman North Africa, see Groupe de Recherches sur l'Afrique Antique (1993).

[21] Anderson (1991); on letters, see, e.g., Ebbeler (2003).

[22] See Blondell (2002) 60–61; D'Ambra (1996).

the possession of a stable, coherent, integrated self where appearance matches essence. A conception of identity as fluid or constructed, in particular, was something the ancients often attributed to actors, and not admiringly. For these reasons, I use the term "identity" rather than "subjectivity," because I am emphasizing the ancients' investment in the concept. We will see that there are places and moments and people in the ancient world who challenge this sense of identity as stable and coherent, just as there are others who reaffirm it. These challenges to the ideal were often made by the actor, whose occupation – pretending to be a variety of fictional selves – could be seen to call personal identity into question. Lucian relates an anecdote in his discussion of pantomime (*On Dance*) in which a barbarian saw a pantomime actor laying out the masks of the five characters he was about to play in his performance. The barbarian exclaimed, "My friend, I didn't realize that although you have one body, you have many souls!" ("ἐλελήθεις," ἔφη, "ὦ βέλτιστε, σῶμα μὲν τοῦτο ἕν, πολλὰς δὲ τὰς ψυχὰς ἔχων"; *De salt*. 66.) The joke in this anecdote is that the barbarian (naively? mock-naively?) assumes that the actor, like everyone else, should have one soul for his one body; his reaction, displaced onto a foreign, uncultured "other," is actually the voice of Greek and Roman ideology: bodies and souls are distinct, but they should match each other. Lucian's anecdote could be taken as one ancient definition of identity.

Thus it makes sense to begin a discussion of acting and identity with the body. The body is the most obvious candidate for the source of a sense of identity, whether identity is defined by the qualities of integrity, coherence, continuity, consciousness, or use of language. It is our first world as infants, and it can serve as a metaphorical map for all other bounded systems.[23] The body thus seems to present a reasonable ground for an essential, stable identity, and in particular, the ground of a sexed identity. If the body is the ground of an essential identity, it may be assumed to reflect that identity; we see this assumption at work in the ancient "science" of physiognomy, for example, which claimed to read a person's inner nature by examining his or her body.[24] Yet many problems arise with this assumption.[25] The body can harbor an inner nature that diverges from its outward form; the body can misrepresent its inner nature,

[23] Douglas (1984) 114–15.
[24] On ancient physiognomy, see Gleason (1995) chs. 2–3; Edwards (1993) 89–90; Evans (1935).
[25] Rorty (1976) 9 points out one problem: "We are, after all, bodily continuous with our corpses; and indeed with their decay or desiccation. If we were to treat bodily

whether through clothing, adornment, cosmetics, disguise, deformation, or a host of other means. The body, in this mindset, can lie.[26] One of the earliest examples of this concept in literature is Paris in the *Iliad*.[27] Hector comments on the discrepancy between Paris' looks and his behavior after Paris shrinks from battle with Menelaus:

Δύσπαρι, εἶδος ἄριστε, γυναιμανὲς ἠπεροπευτά,
αἴθ᾽ ὄφελες ἄγονός τ᾽ ἔμεναι ἄγαμός τ᾽ ἀπολέσθαι.
{καί κε τὸ βουλοίμην, καί κεν πολὺ κέρδιον ἦεν}
ἢ οὕτω λώβην τ᾽ ἔμεναι καὶ ἐπόψιον ἄλλων.
ἦ που καγχαλόωσι κάρη κομόωντες Ἀχαιοί,
φάντες ἀριστῆα πρόμον ἔμμεναι, οὕνεκα καλὸν
εἶδος ἔπ᾽, ἀλλ᾽ οὐκ ἔστι βίη φρεσὶν οὐδέ τις ἀλκή.

Evil Paris, beautiful, woman-crazy, deceiving,
would that you had never been born, or been killed unmarried.
Truly I would have wished it, and it would have been much better
than for you to be a disgrace in this way and viewed with
    suspicion by others.
Surely the long-haired Achaeans laugh out loud
thinking you are our foremost man, because you are beautiful;
but there is no strength in your breast, nor any courage.

(*Iliad* 3.39–45)

At the very beginning of the Greek (and Western) literary tradition, a central character displays the ominous consequences of a mismatch between appearance and inner nature: Paris *looks* like a brave warrior, but he *acts* like a coward – with fatal results for his people. Paris' mismatch between appearance and inner nature is seen by his brother not merely as an unfortunate example of cognitive dissonance, but as "deceiving" (ἠπεροπευτά); it is a moral problem. Already at the beginning of recorded Greek thought, we see the concept of the body as the basis of personal identity, and with it, the moral ideal of the body – that is, appearance – matching the inner nature. In Paris' case, these concepts are honored in the breach.

---

continuity bold and bare, our life histories would continue behind the horizon and beyond the grave." Yet we *do* treat our bodies as continuous with our corpses, at least to some extent – otherwise, we would not make grave markers for them. Montserrat's essay in Montserrat, ed. (1998) deals with mummies as liminal bodies, somewhere between living and dead, sexed and unsexed, subject and object.
26 See Montserrat, ed. (1998).
27 See Dyck (2001) 121.

The body of the warrior is what makes battle possible; the body of the actor is what makes drama possible. In fact, drama has been called both "the adventure of the human body" and "the misadventure of the human body."[28] It is the capacity of the body to "lie" – to appear other than what it "really" is – that enables mimesis to occur. Acting, not surprisingly, has thus aroused a great deal of anxiety throughout its history in people who oppose "lying" and wish appearance and reality to match exactly; they see the actor as a deceiver, pretending to be who he or she is not. Yet paradoxically, the *inability* of the actor's body to disappear entirely behind or into the character's costume has also proved to be a source of uneasiness. Jonas Barish, discussing the antitheatrical prejudice in D. H. Lawrence's *The Lost Girl*, puts his critical finger on one source of this uneasiness. Lawrence's novel is set during the period in the early twentieth century when movies were becoming popular enough to draw audiences away from traditional theater. Barish summarizes people's preference for movies in Lawrence's novel:

> In short, the very element of confrontation between performer and spectator that creates excitement in the theater, the human fire that attracts Alvina [the novel's protagonist] to the actors, disturbs her townspeople, who prefer not to be hotly scorched. It requires the onlooker to take account of another human being, distinct from himself, with a prickly otherness that can never be entirely soothing, as the image on the screen can be soothing, over whose unresisting flicker the watcher may pour without hindrance whatever he will of his own feelings . . . If Alvina is right, audiences sense this underlying self-assertion on the part of the players, and though exhilarated by it, find it alarming.[29]

At a fundamental level, theater is a confrontation between the actor and the spectator. No matter how well the actor plays the role, the spectator retains a sort of awkward awareness of the actor's "otherness," his or her body beneath and behind the costume.[30] Even in a theatrical tradition that uses full-head masks and full-body costumes, like ancient Greece, this confrontation between the audience and the actor's "underlying self-assertion" can produce uneasiness in some spectators.

---

[28] The first quotation is from Y. Belaval, "Ouverture sur le spectacle," 3–16, quoted in Zeitlin (1996) 349 n.18; the second quotation is Zeitlin's (349), modifying Belaval's quotation to describe tragedy in particular.

[29] Barish (1981) 398–9.

[30] See Ubersfeld (1980) 11–12; on the audience's "double consciousness," see Wiles (1991) 11, 26.

Another reason for that uneasiness may be the way in which theater makes the socialization process of a given society apparent and transparent. A society pressures its members to conform to norms of gender, class, age, and status, but makes its pressures seem to be the workings of a natural and inevitable development;[31] a play, on the other hand, shows actors reproducing those norms through conscious study and imitation. Gender norms are one especially interesting and transparent case of this necessary display. Karen Bassi, building on Judith Butler's theory of gender as *only* performance,[32] argues that "theater is precisely the place where the political regulations and disciplinary practices that produce an ostensibly coherent gender are effectively placed in view."[33] This is especially so in plays that address violations of gender norms, such as cross-dressing, or in theatrical traditions (ancient Greece and Rome, Elizabethan England) that use male actors to play female characters. If, as Rorty maintains, the ancients' sense of identity was much more confined to a sense of occupying a particular position within a series of broad categories – age, class, status, ethnicity, as well as gender – then we can generalize Bassi's observation a bit: theater is the place where the political regulations and disciplinary practices that produce an ostensibly coherent *identity* are placed in view. This effect of theatrical impersonation gets at one large component of the antitheatrical response in antiquity: it is motivated by a fear of upward social mobility, which theater is seen as somehow enabling. Trilling argues that the development of the concept of sincerity in the early sixteenth century was motivated by a rise in social mobility, which in turn produced anxieties about people from the lower orders dissembling or flattering their way up the social ladder; thus the character of the "villain" was born – originally the *villein,* or serf.[34] But earlier ages and other cultures also fretted about social mobility, including Athens and Rome. The chapters that follow will have much to say about this anxiety.

A third reason for the spectator's uneasiness with theatrical impersonation is the "deception" practiced by the actor. I place "deception"

---

[31] See Bourdieu (1977) 78–87 on the *habitus.*

[32] Butler (1990) *passim,* esp. 25, 128–41. I should note that I do not fully support Butler's theoretical position; I am unwilling to deny *any* biological ground to identity, even to gender identity, but Bassi's refinement of Butler's theory in terms of the reflective, representational aspect of theater is quite useful.

[33] Bassi (1998) 41.

[34] Trilling (1972) 14–16.

in quotation marks because, as Anne Ubersfeld notes (herself quoting O. Mannoni), "the theatrical illusion is an illusion: no one is fooled."[35] Yet the pretense required by acting has disturbed some spectators nonetheless, supposedly from the time of Solon and Thespis onwards. The story Plutarch tells is that Solon watched a performance by Thespis, the first actor:

μετὰ δὲ τὴν θέαν προσαγορεύσας αὐτὸν ἠρώτησεν εἰ τοσούτων ἐναντίον οὐκ αἰσχύνεται τηλικαῦτα ψευδόμενος. φήσαντος δὲ τοῦ Θέσπιδος μὴ δεινὸν εἶναι τὸ μετὰ παιδιᾶς λέγειν τὰ τοιαῦτα καὶ πράσσειν, σφόδρα τῇ βακτηρίᾳ τὴν γῆν ὁ Σόλων πατάξας· 'Ταχὺ μέντοι τὴν παιδιάν,' ἔφη, 'ταύτην ἐπαινοῦντες οὕτω καὶ τιμῶντες εὑρήσομεν ἐν τοῖς συμβολαίοις.'

After the show [Solon] went to speak to Thespis and asked him if he was not ashamed to tell all those lies in front of such a crowd of people. Thespis replied that there was no harm in talking and acting like this in play. Solon thumped his stick heavily on the ground. "Yes, but it won't be long," he said, "if we hold this sort of 'play' in such high esteem, before it rears its head in our contractual engagements too." (*Vit. Sol.* 29)

Solon and Thespis, mythologized as foundational figures for the distinctively Athenian institutions of democracy and tragedy, also serve in this anecdote as foundational figures in the Athenian imagination for the antitheatrical tradition.[36] Each stakes out a claim about drama that is taken up by pro- and antitheatrical intellectuals throughout Classical antiquity. Solon speaks of "shame" at telling "lies," refusing to differentiate between falsehood and fiction, and warns that spectators will be encouraged to commit fraud in their financial dealings. (This is a Platonic "slippery

---

[35] Ubersfeld (1980) 11. See also Heiden (1993) 154, 162–3.
[36] Most scholars today agree that Thespis was invented or embellished as an Athenian foundational figure to counter Doric claims of having invented tragedy. This legend-making process parallels the elevation of Solon into an Athenian foundational figure to rival the Spartan Lycurgus. It is a process we see in full flower in Plutarch's text, but well before the Plutarch anecdote, Solon and Thespis were firmly fixed in the Athenian imagination; one has only to think of the innumerable references to "the lawgiver" in Athenian court cases, or of the way Thespis is literally inscribed into Athenian history on the Marmor Parium. See Wise (1998) 61–2, 87–8; Pickard-Cambridge (1988) 72, 93, 124, 130, 190, 196, 232, 251; Else (1957).

slope" argument against theatrical impersonation, which is not surprising considering Plutarch's Platonist inclinations;[37] see below on Plato.) Thespis, on the other hand, defends impersonation as "play," and suggests that spectators are capable of distinguishing between illusion and reality. And while Thespis has the last laugh in this anecdote – for as everyone knows, the Athenians *did* honor dramatic performance more and more throughout the Classical period, and thus by implication, mimesis (or fraud, depending on how one sees it) *did* enter Athenian "real life" – it is an uneasy laugh. One reason for the spectator's uneasiness with theatrical "deception," I suggest, is that the spectators are made to feel complicit in it: "This is Delphi, and I am the Pythia" says the male actor speaking the opening lines of Aeschylus' *Eumenides* in the theater of Dionysus at Athens, and the spectators are expected to accept this manifestly untrue statement. If a spectator resists the statement as a falsehood, that only makes things worse, because, as the sociologist Erving Goffman says, "it turns out that the study of how to uncover deception is by and large the study of how to build up fabrications."[38] In other words, deciding that theater is based upon lies can lead the spectator to decide that the "real life" that theater supposedly imitates from a distance is also based upon lies. The actor playing the Pythia is not really a seer – but the woman who is the (current) Pythia may not be either.

Spectators in the ancient world seem to have coped with the threat of theatrical deception in two different ways, each of which produced a *de facto* theory of acting. One approach was to assume that an actor playing a character was innately similar to the character: thus boorish men played soldiers, crafty men played rogues, and servile men played slaves.[39] Acting could be seen as simply "playing oneself" onstage; rather than fooling anyone, the actor would be revealing his nature. A modification of this view was to believe that the actor was "inspired" or "possessed" by the character he played, thus making him temporarily rather than permanently identical to the character. The other approach was to grant acting the status of a *techne*, a consciously acquired and deployed skill; thus the actor was like a craftsman, whose skill could be admired as long as one remembered that one was watching something created, something

---

[37] Here I must disagree with Wise (1998) 87–8, who reads this anecdote as indicating Solon's anger, not at theatrical impersonation, but at the revisionist mythology of so many tragic plots. See Bassi (1998) 188.

[38] Goffman (1974) 251.

[39] See Blondell (2002) 82–3.

artificial.[40] Acting could thus be seen as a skill potentially worthy of admiration as long as it was used properly and with the audience's full knowledge (that is, as long as it was used in good faith – a recurrent issue). We will see these two theories of acting manifest themselves over and over again: in our examination of the figure of Agathon (chapter 1), in the construction of the rivalry between Aeschines and Demosthenes (chapter 2), in the comic stock figures of the *alazon* and the *kolax* (chapter 3) and the *hetaira* or *meretrix* (chapter 4), in the contrast between the Roman actors Roscius and Clodius Aesopus (chapter 5), and finally, in the appeal of "extreme" forms of mimesis in the early Empire (chapter 6).

The moral set of questions about mimesis as a worthy activity are first taken up in a systematic way by Plato in the *Republic* and elsewhere (*Ion, Gorgias, Laws*). The practical questions about how to do mimesis are articulated early on by Aristotle in the *Poetics* and the *Rhetoric*.[41] A lack of other early discussions of mimesis has tended to confer on these two writers the status of foundational thinkers. While the tidy bifurcation of Plato and Aristotle into the founders of two "schools" of rhetoric has been called into question,[42] the discussions about acting that took place in the ancient world do tend to fall under one of these two headings. Plato's unwillingness to grant acting the status of a skill, a τέχνη, and his insistence that people should only do one thing (and thus should not impersonate different characters, if they engage in impersonation at all), was picked up by a number of antitheatrical thinkers in later ages. This attitude toward drama lies at the root of theories of acting as simply playing oneself onstage or as possession.[43] Aristotle's discussion of mimesis

---

[40] Lada-Richards uses the terms "Stanislavskian" and "Brechtian" to refer to these ancient ideas of engaged and distanced (or possessed and technical) performance styles, respectively. I find these terms to be not as helpful as they might be, since they must be hedged about with so many reservations in order to protect against anachronistic assumptions that they lose some of their descriptive force. Her discussion of these concepts in fifth-c. performance, however, is quite illuminating. See Lada-Richards (1997a), (2002).

[41] One particularly clear and concise summary of the genealogy of rhetorical theory is that by James Baumlin in his introduction to the collection of essays he has edited with Tita French Baumlin: (1994) xi–xix.

[42] Swearingen (1994) 116 argues against accepting the "reductive and tired disjunction between Plato and Aristotle, and dividing subsequent rhetorical traditions derived from each of them."

[43] For example, seventeenth- and eighteenth-c. French antitheatrical thought relied heavily on Plato; it was believed at that time that the actor must truly feel his character's emotions and must make the audience truly feel them as well. See Barish (1981) ch. 7: Carlson (1993) chs. 8 and 10.

skill

as a τέχνη, on the other hand, and his concern with effective dramatic and rhetorical practice set the terms of one side of the debate for people who believed that acting was a skill like any other. We will see the debate between different theories of acting recur throughout this book.

Plato's dour views on mimesis are familiar to many and thus require only a brief sketch here.[44] In the *Ion*, Plato refuses to grant mimesis the status of a *techne*, arguing instead that the rhapsode Ion is possessed by divine inspiration when he performs Homer.[45] In *Republic* 2 and 3, in the context of the education of the Guardians of his ideal *polis*, he argues that the Guardians should be allowed to engage in mimesis only of people like themselves, or of people who have the qualities to which they aspire: self-control, righteousness, courage, etc. The Guardians should not imitate slavish or unworthy people (in other words, they should not impersonate cowards, slaves, or women) because imitation over time can alter the "habit and nature" of people (395d). Furthermore, if a poet who could play more than one kind of character were to come to the city, he should be sent away to another city (398a), because in this city people should only be able to do one thing (397e). The only allowance Plato makes for poetry, and in particular mimetic poetry, is that Guardians may imitate the exact sorts of selves that they are supposed to become; the implication is that the habit-forming (or character-altering) potential of mimesis may be harnessed for the good in this instance.[46] In *Republic* 10, on the other hand, Plato banishes all mimetic poetry from his ideal city (595a), although eventually he allows hymns to the gods and encomia of good people to remain (607a).[47] He banishes poetry because mimesis "brings disarray into the soul"[48]: it imitates, not the true nature of a thing, but merely the appearance of that thing (597e); it encourages the

---

[44] The bibliography on Plato and the arts is enormous. Three clear and instructive studies are Halliwell (2002) chs. 1–4, Nehamas (1999) chs. 12, 13, 15, and Barish (1981) ch. 1.

[45] On Plato's views on mimesis in the *Ion*, see, e.g., Weineck (1998).

[46] On the prevailing (not just Platonic) ancient assumption that imitation causes everyone involved – spectators and actors – to try to become like the characters imitated, see Blondell (2002) 26, 81–3.

[47] On the issue of the conflict between books 2&3 and book 10 of the *Republic*, see Naddaff (2002); Nehamas (1999) ch. 12. Tarrant (1955) 84 reads Plato's banishment of the poets in *Republic* 10 as "not whole-hearted," based on Plato's own obvious engagement with drama and commitment to the dialogue form.

[48] The phrase is Nehamas's: (1999) 256.

audience to feel the excessive emotions of the tragic characters onstage (605c–e); it destabilizes the spectator's soul (605b, 608a–b).[49]

Aristotle's views on drama are often set against Plato's as a "correction."[50] In the *Poetics*, not only does Aristotle grant mimesis the status of a *techne*, he considers it a fundamental human impulse (1448b).[51] He is most concerned with techniques for creating effective plots, rather than with a consideration of the emotional effect of tragedy on its audience; when he does turn to that topic, he deals with it quickly in one enigmatic sentence about pity and fear producing the κάθαρσις of those emotions (1449b).[52] Nor does he discuss acting style *per se*; rather, he propounds his theory that the poet reveals the character's *ethos* through the moral choices he makes, as well as his theory that characters should speak "appropriately," that is, according to the genre of the play, as well as according to their age, sex, and status. We can infer that he preferred an acting style "free of the individual idiosyncrasies or shades of characterisation found in realistic dramatic dialogue."[53] In the *Rhetoric*, his concern is with the creation of an effective rhetorical persona, with no moral questions raised.[54] In fact, he mentions the fourth-century tragic actor Theodoros approvingly, noting his ability to make his voice sound like that of the character he was playing (1404b). This suggests a "value-neutral" conception of acting, but it is in line with the approach taken by rhetorical handbooks and orators throughout antiquity: acting is acceptable as a set of skills for orators to employ discreetly, while remaining suspicious in an explicitly dramatic setting. We will see the connection between acting and oratory in chapter 2 with Demosthenes and Aeschines, and, on the Roman side, in chapter 5 with Cicero, Roscius, and Quintilian.

Scholarly interest in ancient acting is on the rise, due in part to the "historical turn" observable in many fields of literary analysis in the humanities. In the 1980s and 1990s, interest in Roman theater practice

[49] Lada-Richards (1997a) 92–5 discusses this Platonic fear that imitation leads to a permanent alteration of the self, both for the theatrical performer and for the spectators.

[50] Many recent studies dispute this: see, e.g., Ford (2002) 210; Woodruff (1992) 73–4. On Aristotle and drama, see Halliwell (2002) chs. 5–8; Golden (1992) ch. 4; Rorty, ed. (1992).

[51] See Jones (1962) 51–2.

[52] For a useful overview of the immense bibliography on this topic, see Halliwell (1986); see also Golden (1992) ch. 2.

[53] Sifakis (2002) 155; see passim.

[54] See Baumlin (1994) xvi–xvii; Swearingen (1994) 120–23.

began catching up with longstanding interest in Greek drama through the publication of several much-needed studies of actors and stage conditions in the Roman world.[55] Eric Csapo and William Slater's compilation of testimonia about ancient theatrical practice has also been an invaluable tool to scholars of ancient acting.[56] In addition to books and collections of essays, a number of articles appeared that attempted to situate acting in its social and historical context. Two examples are Niall Slater's discussion of the emergence of the actor as a conceptual category in Classical Athens, and Bruce Heiden's analysis of the fifth-century actor's and audience's experience of dramatic performance from a ritual perspective.[57] Ismene Lada-Richards has been assembling a body of work on the emotional and ritual significance of acting in fifth-century Athens.[58] And the recent appearance of Pat Easterling and Edith Hall's collection of essays on ancient actors augurs well for rising interest in the people involved in ancient performance culture. In their Introduction, Easterling and Hall note that a history of the antitheatrical tradition in antiquity remains to be written; this book begins to fill that gap.[59]

I have written a selective history of ancient attitudes toward the effect of theater on the sense of personal identity, building on these bodies of work on ancient actors and performance criticism of ancient drama. By using evidence from rhetorical, philosophical, and biographical texts in addition to the texts of plays, I have tried to ascertain both elite and popular attitudes toward actors and acting and their effect on conceptions of identity. My hope is that this project will help to paint a fuller picture of the impact of drama on the ancient world, and elucidate what many of the ancients found so appealing and so alarming about it.

Throughout this project, I read dramatic, philosophical, and rhetorical texts against their historical and cultural backgrounds in order to gain a richer understanding of the cultural forces that shaped and were shaped by these literary expressions. In addition, I draw on a variety of New Historicist, feminist, anthropological, sociological, and performance-oriented

---

[55] Leppin (1992); Beacham (1991); Dupont (1985).

[56] Csapo & Slater, eds. (1995).

[57] Slater's article appeared in the volume edited by Winkler & Zeitlin (1990) historicizing sexuality; Heiden's article (1993) appeared in the volume edited by Sommerstein, Halliwell, Henderson, and Zimmerman historicizing Greek drama.

[58] Lada-Richards (1997a), (1997b), (1999), and (2002).

[59] Easterling and Hall, eds. (2002) xx.

approaches. I also make use of a number of anecdotes about ancient actors and particular performances as evidence of attitudes toward mimesis. The rich tradition of theatrical anecdotes from the ancient world has been underutilized in performance studies by classicists, due in large part to the fact that most of the anecdotes are found in late sources and are therefore presumed to be untrustworthy. Representative of this attitude is the dismissal by David Bain: "Unfortunately most anecdotes that we possess about actors and acting in the early Greek theatre are either of doubtful authenticity or of little relevance to the kind of inquiry here undertaken."[60] Furthermore, many of the anecdotes preserved in later sources concern post–fifth century performances, and scholars of ancient drama tend to be interested either (if they are more textually oriented) in recovering the author's original intent, or (if they are more performance-oriented) in recovering the original, fifth-century audience's experience of viewing the original, fifth-century performance.[61] These are not the only approaches taken to ancient drama, but nearly so, and they neglect much interesting material that could enrich our understanding of the history of one of the most popular, long-lasting, and (arguably) important genres of the ancient world.

To be sure, anecdotes present their own problems of interpretation: they may be recounted because they reveal the social norm – or conversely, the exception to the rule;[62] they tend to follow certain patterns (often with a "punchline" at the end[63]); and in the ancient world, anecdotes may appear in texts that were written centuries after the setting of the anecdotal story.[64] One anecdotal pattern, for example, depicts members of a theatrical audience mistaking theater for reality, or being overly impressed by theatrical effects. It is crucial to interpreting this type of anecdote to recognize that it tends to identify those audience members

---

[60] Bain (1977) 7. A more optmimistic view is taken by Pelling (2000) 46 and n. 9 and Dover (1988).

[61] Slater (1993) 2 notes that attempts to situate performance criticism (here, of Aristophanes) in a historical context "need not necessarily exalt the specific first performance in antiquity over other performances."

[62] See Garton (1972) 23–4.

[63] See Slater (1996) 35; Saller (1980) 74, 81.

[64] Dover (1988) 48–9 draws a distinction between two other kinds of ancient anecdote: the "detachable" anecdote, where the names of the characters may change because they are not essential to the point, and the anecdote about a famous individual, where the person's identity is the subject of the anecdote.

as "deficient" in some way – women, children, or rustics.[65] The *Life* of Aeschylus relates that his Furies in the *Eumenides* were so terrifying to the audience that children fainted and women miscarried[66] (a story often repeated by scholars stressing Aeschylus' supposed tendency toward spectacle[67]), but says nothing about the adult males' reactions.

It is an assumption of my approach that anecdotes do not (usually) originate with the source in which they are found, but rather are told and retold until they wind up in a text such as Aelian, Aulus Gellius, or Plutarch. Of course, it is always possible that a particular anecdote was invented by the writer in whose text it appears, or that it was invented by one elite writer and passed down through others until it landed in a compendium such as Gellius'. It seems highly improbable, however, that every theatrical anecdote contained in an ancient source is utterly disconnected from historical events, especially when theater was a cultural form that a broad cross-section of the population (Greek or Roman) saw and responded to, both in the moment and later.[68] As Easterling and Hall state, "anecdotes about actors can suggest ways in which the experiences of spectators coloured collective awareness and imagination at different periods."[69] The "punchline" feature of many ancient theatrical anecdotes, moreover, could be taken as evidence of oral composition – which is to say, oral formulation and circulation of a story shortly after the events transpired; as with jokes that circulate among large numbers of people, the punchline makes the anecdote memorable, and thus repeatable.[70] Even if some anecdotes are entirely fictional, they offer evidence of what the writer thought his audience would believe to be possible.[71]

---

[65] Garton (1972) 26. More modern examples of this anecdotal pattern include the cowboys who supposedly shot up the screen in attempts to shoot the villains of early Westerns and the shadow-puppet show attacked by a too-engaged audience of Maoris in the film "The Piano." See also Hall (2002) 36; Slater (1996) 34 and n. 3.

[66] See Lefkowitz (1981) 71, 158.

[67] On the history of this scholarly assumption, see Taplin (1977) 39–49. See also Csapo & Slater (1995) 260; Enders (2002) 75.

[68] See also Wiles (2000) 5.

[69] Easterling and Hall (2002) xx.

[70] Vansina (1985) 27 states that in the development of oral traditions, "any formulation that sharpens the punchline is readily appreciated" because it makes the story easier to remember. Saller (1980) 81 notes that the punchline is much more likely to remain unchanged in different versions of an anecdote than almost any other detail (though see his cautionary remarks on the reliability of ancedotes on 78).

[71] Dover (1988) 46; Saller (1980) 82.

Some New Historicists would argue further that the anecdote has been ignored or dismissed by traditional historians because it disrupts traditional historical narratives; it can allow the voices of those usually silenced to emerge, however briefly.[72] Joel Fineman, for example, argues that the anecdote is the momentary eruption of the Real into teleological historical narrative. Fineman's argument must be qualified by the patterning evident in some ancient anecdotes, but his observation that "the anecdote, however literary, is nevertheless ... the smallest minimal unit of the historiographic fact" gets at the dual literary/historical nature of the anecdote.[73]

The source in which the anecdote is embedded also must be taken into account. Each ancient author has his own agenda in using the anecdote, and each anecdote is situated in a discursive context. Plutarch, for example, whose *Lives* and *Moralia* are the source for many theatrical anecdotes, was a Greek writing under the Roman Empire and looking backward nostalgically to the time when Athens ruled the world, as well as a Platonist interpreting history according to certain moral categories.[74] But Plutarch's texts may be viewed as part of a "cultural database," in Karen Bassi's term; they offer evidence of attitudes and ideology, even if – or especially when – they are factually inaccurate.[75] The same can be said for Aelian, Athenaeus, Aulus Gellius, and Macrobius, all compilers of anecdotal material with a particular agenda or agendas, all "late," and all valuable sources nonetheless. The anecdotes embedded in these and other authors' texts may be grouped to make a certain point; they may use different names for the characters involved in different versions of a story, but there is a kernel of observation in any given anecdote that has survived through generations of oral and written transmission – and it has survived for a reason.[76]

Thus I argue that we can view the anecdotal tradition *in general* as a kind of "popular performance theory" because of the way in which anecdotes tend to be told and retold by many people in a given culture;[77] regardless of their historical accuracy, they strike a chord, or perhaps hit a

---

[72] See Gallagher and Greenblatt (2000) chs. 1–2 on the anecdote as providing "the touch of the real" and enabling "counterhistories" to be written.

[73] Fineman (1989) 57.

[74] See Lamberton (2001); Beck (2000); Pelling (1995); Russell (1995).

[75] Bassi (1998) 8.

[76] On Aelian, see Wilson's introduction to the recent (1997) Loeb edition of the *Varia Historia*. On Aulus Gellius, see Holford-Strevens (2003) esp. ch. 16; Baldwin (1975).

[77] Harris (1995) 17.

nerve, in the culture's self-image.[78] Anecdotes can serve as an important counterweight, supplement, or even alternative to the texts of elite intellectuals who wrote about drama; they can potentially give us access to the attitudes and opinions of a broad spectrum of ancient society toward actors, acting, and theatricality.

Because drama is one of the few literary genres that span the ancient world, and because so many sources for ancient attitudes towards drama come from the time of the Roman empire, it made sense to undertake a study that encompassed both Greek and Roman performance culture. This study traces certain themes that persisted over a period of several hundred years: the anxieties and stigmas generated by the gap between appearance and reality; the rise of the professional actor and his corresponding social marginalization, based on a fear of social mobility; the complicated coexistence of two or more different theories of acting at any given time. Like an ensemble cast, the various chapters in this book also have relationships among themselves, based on shared interests: the actor as a figure who arouses desire along with suspicion (chapters 1, 4, and 6); the symbiotic relationship between acting and oratory (chapters 2 and 5); certain stock characters as crystallizations of stereotypes about the actor in antiquity (chapters 3 and 4); the body as the ground of personal identity (chapters 1, 2, and 6). Read in order, each of the six chapters takes up a different aspect of the effect theatrical impersonation was thought to have on identity while pursuing a rough chronological trajectory from Athens at the end of the fifth century to the early Roman Empire. The overall picture that emerges is one of ancient antitheatricalism, terrified and fascinated by the potential for instability which the actor represents, finding various ways to manage this threat to the social and ontological order. Only when the social order changes radically, as it does in the early Roman Empire, is this threat re-imagined in a positive light.

Chapter 1 begins the investigation of attitudes toward mimesis and identity in the late fifth century BCE, when acting was just beginning

---

[78] One modern analogue is the "urban myth" – an anecdote about anonymous people in some unpleasant or threatening situation that speaks to our fears about modern life, which people happily tell and retell even if it turns out that the story is not true. Some typical patterns include dangerous/disgusting items found in fast food ("Kentucky Fried Rat"), dangerous animals lurking in urban settings (alligators in the sewers), and gangs preying on innocent victims through tricks (shooting at drivers who flick their headlights at night). Ronald Reagan's "Welfare Queen" anecdote is a famous example of someone influencing audiences by continuing to tell an urban myth after he learned it was not factually true. See Enders (2002) esp. xxv–xxvii, 8–11.

to become conceptually distinct from other aspects of dramatic performance. The chapter examines the figure of Agathon, the tragic playwright, both in his own words and in his depictions by other writers.
The fragments of Agathon reveal a playfulness with language and meter,
while the testimonia about him stress his innovation and his physical
beauty. Agathon appears as a character in both Plato's *Symposium* and
Aristophanes' *Thesmophoriazousai*; in both texts, he is mocked for resembling his flowery, effeminate verses too closely, and in both texts, he is
also an object of desire. He is thus a figure for the actor as an overly
mimetic creature, and for the actor as a man whose masculinity is in
question, both issues Plato is concerned with in the *Republic*. Agathon's
depiction in these two texts frames the issue of identification between
actor and text, and between actor and character, which will vex critics of the theater for hundreds of years. Interestingly, Aristotle mentions
Agathon in the *Poetics* as having written the first (and only) tragedy to
use entirely invented characters, and as having developed the completely
interchangeable interlude ode. In light of Plato's and Aristophanes' portraits of Agathon as too closely identified with his genre and texts, both
of these poetic innovations suggest a view of Agathon as self-creating,
self-authoring, an innovator of identity. His artful existence is seen as a
threat to the integrity of the self.

Chapter 2 examines the rivalry between the fourth-century orators
Aeschines and Demosthenes, as well as the construction and interpretation of that rivalry by later scholars and critics. Aeschines, a former
actor, is vilified by Demosthenes as a traitorous, unmanly coward, a liar,
and a hypocrite – all criticisms that would accrue to actors in general,
as they began to form a distinct professional identity in this century.
Demosthenes makes much of Aeschines' background as an actor, arguing that Aeschines is a rhetorically skilled manipulator while he himself
is a sincere patriot (a claim accepted by earlier generations of scholars);
yet Demosthenes makes use of many of the same theatrical techniques
that he imputes to Aeschines (as suggested in Plutarch's anecdote about
Demosthenes' being taught delivery by an actor). Their speeches point
to the formation of negative attitudes at Athens toward theatricality, a
growing sense of actors as inherent hypocrites, as well as to the infiltra-
tion of theatrical techniques into other arenas of public life dominated
by elite citizen males.

Chapters 3 and 4 form a bridge between Greek and Roman theatrical
traditions: both chapters look at the trajectories of various stock characters in comedy as a way of getting at popular attitudes toward acting and

identity, as actors in the fourth–second centuries BCE became increasingly professionalized and – not coincidentally – marginalized. Chapter 3 looks at the male stock characters of the *alazon* ("impostor" or "fraud") and the parasite in Greek and Roman comedy. Appearing as early as Aristophanes' *Acharnians*, the *alazon* is a pompous fraud, someone who pretends to know or be something he does or is not. He could appear as a doctor, lawyer, general, priest, or diplomat (it was during this period that famous actors served as ambassadors on important diplomatic missions). By the time of Menander, however, the *alazon* narrows into the "braggart soldier" type familiar from Roman comedy. The parasite, on the other hand, grows in importance from Old to New comedy and Roman comedy, regularly appearing alongside the protagonist as a flatterer and dissembler out for a free meal. The *alazon* can be seen as a figure for the actor in Greece, a self-important impostor, while the parasite can been seen as a figure for the actor at Rome, a servile hanger-on who lies to his audience in order to eat. Both characters are instantly recognizable, and thus never fool anyone; they are relegated to the margins of the plot as a way of managing the actor's threat to identity.

Chapter 4 investigates the female stock character of the prostitute as another figure for the actor. It looks at the *hetaira* in Greek New Comedy, Hellenistic society, and the Greek anecdotal tradition, and at the *meretrix* in Roman comedy, Republican Roman society, and the Roman anecdotal tradition. The comic prostitute combines stereotypes of the actor as hollow flatterer and the actor as fraud; even the occasional "hooker with a heart of gold," a stock subtype, is revealed to be a histrionic deceiver within the world of the play and is kept in her socially low status. The *pseudo-hetaira*, on the other hand, the girl in the position of a prostitute who is revealed to be a respectable girl of citizen birth, is never good at acting and deception, and is rewarded with the discovery of her true, higher status and marriage to a citizen. Yet the connection between prostitution and acting can have a more positive valence as well; Menander's beloved *hetaira* Glykera supposedly helped him select the masks to use in composing each play. I read the prostitute as what Stallybrass and White call a "low-Other," a figure of marginal social status who inspires both disgust and desire in members of the dominant class. Both of these reactions, I argue, are connected to her theatrical nature, much like the desire and disgust aroused by Agathon in chapter 1. The difference between the Roman *meretrix* and Agathon is that at Rome, prostitutes – and, it seems, actors – were *infamis*; the professionalization of acting in the fourth to second c. BCE was accompanied by increasingly stringent measures cordoning off the actor from respectable society.

Chapter 5 deals with Republican Roman attitudes toward acting by looking at the career of the most famous Republican actor, Roscius. Actors had a much lower social status at Rome than in the Greek world; there was a Roman law permitting public magistrates to beat actors at any time, whether performing or not, for any reason. While most actors at Rome were foreigners and were either slaves or freedmen, Roscius was a freeborn Roman; whereas most actors performed in only one genre, Roscius acted in both tragedies and comedies. He was knighted by Sulla and thus had to stop charging fees for his performances. Roscius' anomalous status as the only actor of his generation to transcend genre boundaries, as one of the few native Roman actors, and as the first superstar actor at Rome threw Roman anxieties about actors and acting into sharp relief. Plautus' *Captivi* provides one view of these anxieties, dealing as it does with issues of slavery and innate nobility. When the slave character "passes" as a free man, we can read concerns about the power of acting to override class and status, concerns that Roscius' being knighted also raised. Cicero's *Pro Roscio* brings these issues into focus by defending the actor against a symbolically loaded charge of fraud. Quintilian's early Imperial handbook on oratory, said to be influenced by Roscius' own lost handbook on acting, repeatedly contrasts the orator with the actor, even as it gives examples of effective delivery from the theater; it reveals the elite orator's dependence on the histrionic art, even as it must define itself against acting. These texts, together with anecdotes about Roscius, suggest a deep Roman anxiety about acting as enabling a threatening social mobility, or even as exposing the fundamental arbitrariness of Roman society. Finally, a comparison of the anecdotal traditions about Roscius' controlled, technical acting style and Clodius Aesopus' unrestrainedly emotional, eerie identifications with the characters he played gives additional insight into concerns about acting in the Roman Republic.

During most of Greco-Roman antiquity, then, the gap between appearance and reality which the actor created was perceived as a threat to the stability of the self, and societies took various measures to contain this threat. One impulse was to marginalize the actor in society, whether by creating negative stereotypes about him (as insincere, arrogant, or typecast), which made him easy to identify and thus exclude, or by assigning him to a legally marginal status category (*infamis*). This strategy was not applicable in all time periods, however, and even when it was, it did not solve the problem of the actor, because elite males needed (or wanted) to avail themselves of the art of the actor in various ways – especially in the other major arena of public performance: oratory. Another strategy for managing the actor's threat to identity, therefore, was to marginalize the actor within the world of theater itself. Certain kinds of low-status characters could be read as figures for the actor (the fraud, the flatterer, the boaster, the prostitute), and dramatic plots over and over again demonstrate that these characters deserve the station they inhabit, whereas other characters who seem too good for these stations (the sincere prostitute, the noble slave) are revealed to be legitimate citizens.

Chapter 6 contrasts the way theatrical impersonation was regarded in earlier periods with the ways in which it worked in the early Roman Empire, where comedy and tragedy gave way to mime, pantomime, and various theatrical spectacles. Especially under the "bad emperors," ancient historians and biographers suggest, the Roman public developed an insatiable taste for what I call "extreme mimesis"; political absolutism gave rise to other kinds of power displays. Instead of attempting to minimize the gap between appearance and reality, actors and other performers began to emphasize it; the gap between appearance and reality, previously focused on anxiously as the sign of insincerity, was reimagined positively as a survival strategy, while a complete coherence between appearance and reality was reimagined as a fatal ontological collapse. Superstar pantomime actors acted out famous scenes from tragedies solo, playing all of the roles in dizzying, virtuosic succession. Public executions of criminals were presented as scenes from famous tragedies or myths, with the criminals costumed as characters fated to die in particularly unpleasant ways (e.g., Orpheus); the difference, however, was that these "characters" were actually killed onstage. The theater-mad Nero even got into the act himself, performing the roles of various heroes from mythology whose stories were analogous to incidents in his own life; confounding the distinction between actor and character even further, Nero performed these roles wearing a mask of his own face. All of these theatrical activities pushed hard at the limits of Greco-Roman mimetic conventions, and indeed at the limits of mimesis itself in some cases. They suggest that as the public (and the emperors) found traditional mimetic pursuits dull, the impulse to seek more radical forms of mimesis caused a theatricalization of "real life." The self, under the Empire, was revealed as a theatrical role, or even roles.

CHAPTER ONE

DRAG QUEENS AND IN-BETWEENS: AGATHON AND THE MIMETIC BODY

I N THE FIFTH CENTURY BCE, DRAMA WAS AN ENORMOUSLY IMPORTANT cultural institution, which makes it easy to forget that many significant aspects of dramatic performance were still becoming codified or standardized over the course of the entire century. The *Vita* tradition credited Aeschylus with the introduction of the second actor (the deuteragonist) and Sophocles with the introduction of the third (the tritagonist), implying that Greek tragedy as we know it only took shape by the middle part of the fifth century or so. Like the members of the chorus, the actors in a given play in the fifth century were amateurs. Once a prize was developed in the mid-fifth century to reward the best lead actor (protagonist) in a play, as distinct from the best playwright, we could say the profession of acting was born. It seems to be the case, however, that acting did not become a profession proper until the very end of the fifth century, or possibly the beginning of the fourth, when the first performance circuit outside Athens began to appear; the first actors' unions did not appear until the Hellenistic period.[1] During most of the fifth century, then, the actor playing a role onstage would have been imagined by the audience to be an ordinary citizen of the democracy – a citizen who might equally as likely have served on a jury or been selected by lot to serve as a magistrate for a year and who most likely would have had some previous experience serving as a member of a dramatic or dithyrambic chorus. Actors were not yet conceptually or legally distinct from other citizens; a member of "the best people," the *kaloi kagathoi*, was theoretically just as likely to perform onstage as a poor citizen.

Yet the introduction of the prize for acting in 449 was having an effect on popular perceptions of performance. Already in the fifth century

---

[1] See Csapo & Slater (1995) 221–4; N. Slater (1990); Lefkowitz (1981).

the Athenians were inscribing the names of victorious actors on victory monuments, and making jokes at the expense of inept actors.[2] The actor was beginning to compete with the playwright for fame (although it would take another century before Aristotle would complain in the *Poetics* that actors were more important than playwrights). Actors were also beginning to compete with playwrights for a less positive distinction in the popular imagination: being identified with the plays they performed. Aristophanes' *Frogs* (405 BCE) shows the extent to which, even at the end of the fifth century, tragic playwrights were identified with the kind of plays they wrote: Euripides is an airy sophist who, like his most notorious characters, swears by Aether, while Aeschylus is a brooding, angry figure right out of one of his own prologues. Another tragic playwright who seems to have been strongly identified with the style of plays he wrote was Agathon, a contemporary of Euripides. Agathon is different from other tragic playwrights, however, in that he is depicted as changeable and indeterminate, rather than having one fixed style. In this way, Agathon represents the emerging figure of the actor, rather than the older figure of the playwright: he seems to have no single self, no coherent identity.

As a character in literary texts and as a historical figure, Agathon embodies the tension between two conceptions of the actor's identity prevalent in the ancient world: the actor as someone who simply plays himself onstage, and the actor as someone who lacks any core identity whatsoever. At times, his innate nature seems to dictate his actions, and he fools no one; at times, he seems to manipulate his appearance and behavior with disconcerting ease, suggesting that his "identity" is a role, or set of roles, he simply puts on and takes off. Agathon crystallizes the debate between the two theories of acting: it is the old essentialist-constructionist debate.[3] As a character in other people's texts, playwright

---

[2] Inept actors: in his performance as protagonist in Euripides' *Orestes* in 408, Hegelochus flubbed a line - which was remembered, and mocked, for years afterwards. (His error was a tiny but catastrophic mistake in accentuation: during Orestes' mad scene at the beginning of the play, Orestes begins to emerge from his temporary insanity with the line, "After the storm, once again I see the calm (γαλήν)," but Hegelochus said γαλῆν ("weasel") instead of γαλήν, making the mistake unintentionally hilarious.) For the testimonia, see Csapo & Slater (1995) 267–8.

[3] Dollimore (1991), chs. 1 and 6, provides a stimulating and refreshingly original analysis of the essentialist-constructivist debate in the context of "gay identity." He argues that the essentialist position has been mistakenly equated with a conservative political stance by contemporary gay activists and politically engaged scholars. For another attempt to analyze the debate (again in the context of "gay identity") without falling into the trap of its binary logic, see Sedgwick (1990) 40–44.

in his own right, gender- and genre-bender, and supposed "drag queen," Agathon foregrounds the anxieties about mimesis and identity that will haunt the ancient world for a thousand years. He serves as an early figure for the actor, and thus as a starting point for our discussion.

AGATHON AS TRAGEDY

Plato's *Symposium* ends, famously, with the narrator waking to find Socrates trying to persuade the sleepy and drunk Agathon and Aristophanes that the same man could write both tragedy and comedy (223c-d). Generic identity is linked with personal identity, just as in Aristotle's *Poetics*, which states that naturally serious men write tragedies, while naturally base and vulgar men write comedies (1448b). Plato's choice of Aristophanes to represent Comedy in the *Symposium* is by no means haphazard, of course; Aristophanes was not the only comic poet working at Athens (a fact that is easy to forget, given his dominance in surviving manuscripts), but he was one of the preeminent ones. The choice of Agathon to represent Tragedy may seem a bit less obvious, since he is not one of the "big three" tragedians and we have no extant plays of his. One explanation we could call historical (or contextual): Plato has set his text at Agathon's victory celebration in 416 BCE, which determines the choice of tragic playwright for this argument.[4] It is also possible that Plato is alluding to the other literary text that brings the two playwrights together, Aristophanes' *Thesmophoriazousai*, where Agathon is a character Aristophanes deploys to mock tragedy. Even if we do not allow that Plato is making that allusion, the choice of Agathon to represent Tragedy, alongside Aristophanes representing Comedy, makes a striking statement about the nature of the two dramatic genres. The playwrights, and the genres, are complementary opposites, as revealed in their bodies and in their speeches on Love: the beautiful Agathon delivers a flowery tribute to the divinity of Love, while Aristophanes gets the hiccups, loses his turn in the speaking order, and then talks about navels and genitalia. Agathon is the High, the ambitious reach of drama toward the realm that philosophers inhabit. Aristophanes is the Low, the derisive mockery of that higher realm, the interruption of parody. It is understandable that they would not, could not, believe Socrates' claim.

---

[4] I agree with von Blanckenagen (1992) 52–3 that we should read the *Symposium* as "a historical novel or play," rather than as a strictly accurate record of a long-past dinner party. See also Nehamas (1999) 304.

But Agathon is as unforgettably embodied as Aristophanes. Every ancient testimonium that describes Agathon remarks on his stunning beauty, a beauty that did not fade with age.[5] Plato portrays the effeminately beautiful Agathon as embodying the seductive lure of tragedy, his flowery, Gorgianic language the drug that keeps the seeker from the truth of philosophy.[6] He inspires desire both in his person and in his poetry. Agathon represents Tragedy taken to what Plato sees as its extreme form: astonishingly beautiful, but ambiguous and deceptive, it (he) seduces its viewers and leaves them with nothing substantive. It (he) is a tease. In short, it (he) operates under the sign of the feminine.[7] We will see this association of tragedy with the feminine throughout the history of Greek and Roman drama.

In using Aristophanes and Agathon as representatives of their respective genres, Plato is making the same identification of author with work/genre that we see in the *Vita* tradition on the poets, as well as in Aristophanes' parodies of tragedians. His body comes to stand for his poetry, and vice versa. In Aristophanes' *Thesmophoriazousai*, Agathon lounges about in women's clothing and owns many personal grooming tools appropriate to women (mirror, comb, razor), all of which Euripides and his kinsman ask to borrow. Agathon is so effeminate that he seems the logical choice to "go undercover" as a woman in Euripides' plan – but Agathon rejects this logic, explaining that he is actually so effeminate that women are suspicious of him because they fear he will steal boyfriends away from them. Euripides and his kinsman use Agathon as a costume and prop supplier and go on to start their covert operation. Aristophanes, meanwhile, uses Agathon to represent one extreme end on the spectrum of masculinity; he is what the gruff, hairy kinsman could never be, a man who completely "passes" as a woman. He is a καταπύγων (200), and his servant describes how he "bends" his verses over (κάμπτει, 53), using language that "connect[s] musical innovation with sexual corruption."[8]

In different ways, then, Agathon is a scare-figure for both Plato and Aristophanes. (Each author produces a "real man" as a foil to

---

[5] For a complete discussion of the sources, see Lévêque (1955) 35–40.

[6] "Hasty and conceited, in the hour of intoxication more with victory than wine, this gracious host of the symposium, after falling prey to his own craving for applause, masked his fallacy with the best of perfumed flowers": Anton (1996) 221. Anton does not question the motive behind Plato's depiction; rather, he seems to replicate it in his own description.

[7] On the identification of the mimetic with the feminine, see Zeitlin (1996) 341–74.

[8] Muecke (1982) 46.

Agathon: Plato provides Socrates as the foil, and Aristophanes provides the kinsman.) In his person and in his poetry, Agathon represents what Tragedy can do to a man – an elite man, at that. He is a figure for several kinds of identification: the identification of the poet with the genre, and of the poet with the roles he writes. As depicted in literature, Agathon is always a site for the investigation of identity, and in particular for investigating the degree to which the self has an essential and stable nature. On the one hand, he is totally identified with what and how he writes: he dresses like a woman and writes women's roles in the *Thesmophoriazousai*; he delivers a flowery speech about Eros that makes the god sound suspiciously like himself in the *Symposium*.[9] On the other hand, that identification always crosses a seemingly insurmountable boundary: masculine-feminine, or perhaps even male-female (*Thesmophoriazousai*), human-divine (*Symposium*). Does he have a nature that he simply performs, however perversely, or does he assimilate himself, chameleon-like, to every new situation? In raising this question, Agathon anticipates another kind of identification: that of the actor with the role, an identification that later ages were to make quite strongly. Finally, being an object of desire as well as a poet, he is a figure for the operation of desire in theatrical performance.

Agathon's depiction in literature reveals a great deal about how fifth-century Athenians conceived of theater practitioners, still officially "amateurs" at this point, but rapidly becoming recognized as a distinct category. Spectators were wrestling with whether the actor was really just another citizen male – and thus one whose identity was no more, or less, unstable than anyone else's – or whether the actor was a special category of person, who could be imagined to be safely distinct from others. In other words, fifth-century spectators were anxious about whether they should identify with actors or distance themselves from them. Later spectators were much more emphatic in rejecting identification with the actor, as we shall see.

THE HISTORICAL AGATHON

Agathon's tragedies survive in a few short fragments.[10] Obviously, it is risky to analyze a poet's style or themes on such slender evidence, but

---

[9] Lévêque (1955) 38; Anton (1996) 218–19; see Clay (1983) 193.
[10] All fragments are from Snell, *Tragicorum Graecorum Fragmenta*, vol. I, 155–68.

judging from such lines as

τέχνη τύχην ἔστερξε καὶ τύχη τέχνην
skill loves chance and chance, skill
(fr.6)

and

γνώμη δὲ κρεῖσσόν ἐστιν ἢ ῥώμη χερῶν
thought is stronger than strength of hands
(fr.27)

we can see his Gorgianic love of rhyme, assonance, *sententia*, antithesis, and paradox, which Aristophanes and Plato witness by parody in the *Thesmophoriazusai* and the *Symposium*.[11] The two longest fragments of Agathon extant are from his *Thyestes* (fr.3) and his *Telephos* (fr.4). In the *Thyestes* fragment, the Kouretes ("Shorn Ones") explain the aetiology of their name as a reminder of their hair shorn in grief. The love of etymological explanations for names is well attested in Greek literature, especially tragedy.[12] The *Telephos* fragment is a description, presumably by a character who is illiterate, of the visual appearance of letters in a word ("the third resembles a Scythian bow"); this is a conceit borrowed from Euripides' *Theseus*.[13] Taken as a group, the fragments of Agathon's poetry hint at a self-conscious, playful, linguistically and metrically extravagant style.[14] An anecdote preserved in Aelian encapsulates Agathon's style in the very reply he supposedly made to a critic:

Πολλοῖς καὶ πολλάκις χρῆται τοῖς ἀντιθέτοις ὁ Ἀγάθων. ἐπεὶ δὲ τις οἷον ἐπανορθούμενος αὐτὸν ἐβούλετο περιαιρεῖν αὐτὰ τῶν ἐκείνου δραμάτων, εἶπεν 'ἀλλὰ σύ γε, γενναῖε, λέληθας σεαυτὸν τὸν Ἀγάθωνα ἐκ τοῦ Ἀγάθωνος ἀφανίζων.' οὕτως ἐκόμα ἐπὶ τούτοις ἐκεῖνος, καὶ ᾤετο τὴν ἑαυτοῦ τραγῳδίαν ταῦτα εἶναι.   (*VH* 14.13)

---

[11] For Gorgias' (presumed) influence on Agathon's style, see Philostr. vs. 1.9.3, Plato. *Symp.* 198c; see also Lévêque (1955) 34, 126–37, Roberts (1900) 46–8.

[12] Lévêque (1955) 95.

[13] The letters described in the fragment of Agathon spell out ΘΗΣΕΥΣ. This was apparently a common motif in late-fifth and early-fourth century tragedy, begun (it seems) by Sophocles' *Amphiaraos* (fr. 117 Nauck), in which the character dances out the shapes of the letters; continued in Euripides' *Theseus* (fr.382 Nauck); and imitated not only by Agathon but also by Theodectes (fr. 6 Nauck) – see Lévêque (1955) 97 (and n. 2), 98. It seems to be a variation on the "puzzle" theme.

[14] For a more detailed analysis of Agathon's poetry and meter, see Muecke (1982) 43–9; Lévêque (1955) 127–51.

Agathon used antitheses in great numbers and often. When someone attempting to correct him wanted him to remove them from his plays, he said, "But friend, in forgetting yourself you're taking the Agathon out of Agathon!" Thus he prided himself on those devices, and he considered his own tragedy to be made of these things.

In playing on the common use of an author's name to mean his body of work, this retort also suggests the playwright's awareness that his personal identity is equated with his poetry – a theme we will explore at length below.

The two Classical texts that mention Agathon at any length in a non-parodic context are Plato's *Protagoras* and Aristotle's *Poetics*. In the *Protagoras* (315d), Agathon is briefly mentioned in a list of other listeners to the dialogue as a very young and very beautiful boy, the companion of Pausanias. In the *Poetics*, Aristotle seems to regard Agathon as a first-rate tragic playwright; in discussing the advantages of a tightly focused plot, he mentions that "even Agathon" had been known to forget this rule and to try to cover as much material as an epic (1456a10–18). Agathon is singled out for comment because he was the first poet to write a tragedy, the *Anthos* (or *Antheus*), using entirely invented characters (1451b20–23) – that is, not using characters from the body of traditional Greek myth.[15] He is also the poet Aristotle regards as having developed generic, interchangeable choral odes, ἐμβόλιμα, which can be used in more than one tragedy (1456a28–29).[16] From these few notices, we can discern that Agathon was considered to be both remarkably beautiful and an innovator in the tragic form.[17] We will see how Plato's and Aristotle's accounts of the historical Agathon fit with the literary representations of Agathon in comedy and philosophy later.

Many of the other testimonia about Agathon concern his relationships with Euripides and Pausanias. Aelian recounts an anecdote (*VH* 13.4) in which Euripides and Agathon were banqueting in Macedonia with

---

[15] All MSS of the *Poetics* give the title as Ἀνθεῖ, but scholars disagree over whether the title is properly Ἀνθός (*Flower*) or Ἀνθεύς, a masculine name taken from the word for flower (*Mr. Flower*). See the discussion in Lévêque (1955) 105–11, and in Pitcher (1939), both of whom argue for *Anthos*. Halliwell's 1995 Loeb edition of the *Poetics*, however, gives *Antheus*. For one possible reconstruction of the plot of this lost and (as far as we know) unique play, see Pitcher (1939).

[16] On *embolima*, see Sidwell (2001).

[17] Roberts (1900) 52–4 argues that Aristophanes shares with Plato and Aristotle this positive view of Agathon as personally charming and artistically talented and innovative, based on his readings of Aristophanes' *Thesmophoriazusai* and *Gerytades*.

Archelaus, both playwrights having left Athens at the end of the fifth century for the court of the king. Euripides became drunk and embraced and kissed Agathon, who was at that point 40 years old. When Archelaus asked Euripides whether "even now he [Agathon] seemed to him to be an *eromenos*," Euripides replied, "Indeed yes, by Zeus; for the most beautiful time for beautiful ones is not only the spring, but even late autumn." The erotic relationship between Agathon and Euripides in the anecdote could symbolize their stylistic affinity, but it could also be a more straightforward insinuation about Agathon's sexual proclivities.[18] The point of the anecdote seems to be that Agathon is an eternal *eromenos*; he does not "grow out of" this role even by middle age. Most of the testimonia name Pausanias, not Euripides, as Agathon's lover,[19] but Agathon is always the *eromenos*, no matter who is named as the *erastes*. Another anecdote from Aelian (*VH* 2.21) set in Macedonia relates that Agathon and Pausanias quarreled often because, as they explained to Archelaus, making up after a quarrel was sweet and made their love feel new again. The thrust of this anecdote seems to be that someone involved in a lifelong pederastic relationship would need to resort to mental manipulation in order to sustain it. The anecdote about the drunken Euripides suggests that Agathon's natural beauty was unnaturally long-lived; the anecdote about quarreling Pausanias suggests that the lovers had to trick themselves to sustain their bond. We will see this same ambivalence about Agathon's eternal, youthful desirability, and whether it is natural or deceptive, in both of our parodic texts.

AGATHON IN THE *THESMOPHORIAZOUSAI*

In Aristophanes' *Thesmophoriazusai*, the women of Athens, infuriated by Euripides' too-accurate portrayals of lustful and treacherous women, are plotting against him. Euripides and his kinsman come up with a plan to dress the kinsman in women's clothes and send him into the women's meeting as a spy. In order to dress the kinsman up, they stop at the house of Agathon, a notoriously effeminate tragic playwright, and ask to borrow some of his women's clothing and personal grooming items. The "robing scene" with Agathon has often been taken to be straightforward, if devastating, mockery of a historical figure's peculiarities. The figure of

---

[18] On relationships between poets (usually conceived of as familial relationships, but not always) as an allegory of their poetic kinship, see Lefkowitz (1981) 114, 137.

[19] Snell T3, T11, T15, T25.

Agathon in this comedy, however, serves a far more complicated function: he is a figure for the actor, or more precisely, he serves as a screen onto which the playwright projects anxieties about actors and acting already common in the fifth century. These anxieties include the fear that the actor has no essential self, the fear that the actor has an essentially effeminate self, and the fear that the actor causes the selves of the audience to change to match his own.

Agathon is depicted in this play as fundamentally indeterminate: effeminate, neither fully male nor fully female, not grounded in a stable, recognizable body.[20] He puts into question the distinctions between poet and work, actor and role, masculine and feminine, body and costume. At the same time that he destabilizes boundaries and seems to point toward the idea of identity as constructed, however, he also insists on a kind of essentialism. The tension between the two theories of identity implied by Agathon's portrayal in the play is expressed within the play by Agathon's two theories of mimesis. As we will see, Agathon's "essentialism" proves to be as subversive of Athenian gender ideology as his "constructionism," and both turn out to be theories of acting as well as theories of identity formation.

In a reworking of the scene between Dicaeopolis and Euripides in the *Acharnians*,[21] Euripides and his kinsman in the *Thesmophoriazousai* go to Agathon's house to borrow a disguise from the playwright. The entrance of Agathon's servant sets the tone for the rest of the scene: he describes his master's poetic activity in elevated language, while the kinsman interrupts him with derisive comments about Agathon's sexual behavior (see 50, 57, 59–62). Agathon is wheeled out on the *ekkyklema*,[22] arrayed in women's clothing, singing the lines of a female character (or chorus leader) and a

---

[20] See Stehle (2002), esp. 379–84.

[21] Compton-Engle (2003) 521 5–16; Stohn (1993) 200; Muecke (1982) 41–2; Roberts (1900) 50–51. In the *Acharnians*, the robustly masculine Dicaeopolis goes to Euripides to borrow a raggedy disguise from one of his heroes in rags; in the *Thesmophoriazusai*, Euripides goes to the *kinaidos* Agathon to borrow some women's clothing. Euripides' own masculinity is relatively compromised in *Acharnians*, by comparison to Dicaeopolis, but relatively affirmed in *Thesmophoriazousai*, by comparison to Agathon. This reworking of the scene reveals that, although the occupation of playwright was not considered to be terribly manly, playwrights were not automatically considered *kinaidoi*; Euripides moves along a continuum, while Agathon is located at one end of it.

[22] On the question of whether the *ekkyklema* was in use in the fifth century, and specifically in this passage, see the discussions in Dearden (1976) ch. 4, esp. 55, 57–9; Dover (1972) 24–5, 162; Arnott (1962) ch. 5.

female chorus.[23] His lyrical performance throws the kinsman into a whirl of desire – and blunt comic confusion. The kinsman first compliments and then interrogates Agathon:

ὡς ἡδὺ τὸ μέλος ὦ πότνιαι Γενετυλλίδες
καὶ θηλυδριῶδες καὶ κατεγλωττισμένον
καὶ μανδαλωτόν, ὥστ' ἐμοῦ γ' ἀκροωμένου
ὑπὸ τὴν ἕδραν αὐτὴν ὑπῆλθε γάργαλος.
καὶ σ' ὦ νεανίσχ' ὅστις εἶ, κατ' Αἰσχύλον
ἐκ τῆς Λυκουργείας ἐρέσθαι βούλομαι.
ποδαπὸς ὁ γύννις; τίς πάτρα; τίς ἡ στολή;
τίς ἡ τάραξις τοῦ βίου; τί βάρβιτος
λαλεῖ κροκωτῷ; τί δὲ λύρα κεκρυφάλῳ;
τί λήκυθος καὶ στρόφιον; ὡς οὐ ξύμφορον.
τίς δαὶ κατόπτρου καὶ ξίφους κοινωνία;
τίς δ' αὐτὸς ὦ παῖ; πότερον ὡς ἀνὴρ τρέφει;
καὶ ποῦ πέος; ποῦ χλαῖνα; ποῦ Λακωνικαί;
ἀλλ' ὡς γυνὴ δῆτ'· εἶτα ποῦ τὰ τιτθία;
τί φής; τί σιγᾷς; ἀλλὰ δῆτ' ἐκ τοῦ μέλους
ζητῶ σ', ἐπειδή γ' αὐτὸς οὐ βούλει φράσαι;

(*Thesm.* 130–45)

By the goddess of my birth-hour, what a sweet song!
how effeminate, how french-kissing,
how lascivious, as I listened to it
a tickle went up my seat!
And you, O youth, I want to ask you who you are
as Aeschylus does in the Lycurgus plays.
"Whence comes this woman-man? What is its fatherland, what is
    its raiment?"
What is this disturbance of life? What does a *barbiton* babble
to a saffron gown? What can a lyre say to a hair-net?
What's an oil-flask doing with a breast-band? How incongruous!
And what association can there be between a mirror and a sword?
And you, boy, were you raised as a man?
Then where's your cock? Where's your cloak? Where are your
    Laconian shoes?
Or was it as a woman, then? Then where are your tits?
What do you say? Why are you silent? Or shall I find you out
from your song, since you yourself don't want to speak?

---

[23] It is impossible to be certain whether Agathon is speaking the lines of a female character or of the female coryphaeus; see Muecke (1982) 46–7.

Aristophanes presents Agathon as an ontological puzzle for the kinsman. He is dressed as a woman but has no breasts; he seems to lack the usual stage phallus of comedy as well; he has both "masculine" and "feminine" objects lying around him, both mirror and sword.[24] He is not, or not only, a drag queen, tempting though the label is to apply.[25] He is a disrupter of categories (masculine/feminine, poet/actor, actor/character), and thus less easily dismissed.[26]

In her influential study of the cultural significances of cross-dressing, *Vested Interests*, Marjorie Garber claims that the transvestite in literature often serves as a means of displacing another kind of category crisis (e.g., sexuality, class, race). She argues further, following Lacan, that the transvestite occupies the Symbolic; it *is* representation, and thus makes representation, culture, and language itself possible. In her words, *"transvestism is a space of possibility structuring and confounding culture*: the

---

[24] Lada-Richards (1999) 14, 33–6 argues that many of the objects the kinsman enumerates here are items with strong Dionysiac cult associations. As for whether the kinsman is describing props present onstage or naming items the audience is to imagine, I must disagree with Saïd (1987) 230, who feels that "Il serait donc absurde de penser qu'Agathon porte sur lui toutes les pièces de costume qui sont énumerées ici" because the passage partly parodies Aeschylus' *Lycurgus*. She seems to admit the necessity of taking these lines as exact prop descriptions, however, when she reads the same passage to indicate that the actor playing Agathon is not wearing a leather phallus (ibid).

As for the issue of Agathon's phallus, the lines spoken by the kinsman imply that Agathon does not have a phallus visible, as the other male characters onstage do. Whether the actor playing him was dressed as a typical male comic character, phallus and all, and then dressed in women's clothes over that costume, hiding the phallus (but not its outline under the dress?) from view, or whether he was simply dressed as a comic female character, is impossible to ascertain. Either way would be "funny," presumably. Stehle (2002) 380 and Pickard-Cambridge (1988) 221–2 think that the actor who played Agathon did not wear a phallus. Taaffe (1993) 81 seems to think that the actor was wearing a phallus; she writes that the kinsman's question ("Where's your dick?") "is even more amusing than his confusion, for it calls attention to the male under Agathon's costume while it highlights the apparent absence of Agathon's badge of masculinity." Unless she is speaking of the actor's maleness, rather than Agathon's, of course.

[25] von Blanckenagen (1992) 59: "In modern slang, Agathon is a drag queen." Taaffe (1993) 81 notes that Agathon's lack of false breasts indicates that "he is not clearly either female or male."

[26] An interesting comparison is with the figure of Joan of Arc, who dressed in men's clothing (in armor, with cropped hair) but did not attempt to *disguise* herself as a man. See Shakespeare's *I Henry VI*, Shaw's *Saint Joan*. See also Garber (1992) 217, who quotes various actresses who have played Joan in Shaw's *Saint Joan*; some of them explain away her wearing armor as merely "necessary" for her goal (what Garber calls "the progress narrative"), but others talk about the way clothes "dictate what you do."

disruptive element that intervenes, not just a category crisis of male and female, but the crisis of category itself."[27] Garber's insights about the way the transvestite can signal a cultural category crisis (what she calls "the transvestite effect") can help us read the representations of Agathon in ancient literature. As someone who literally embodies mimesis, Agathon, too, can be read as a figure who opens up a space of possibility in the sex–gender system of his time.

At this moment, Agathon seems to embody a postmodern theory of identity (and in particular gender identity) as constructed, contingent upon the clothing, gestures, and mannerisms – the style, if you will – that a person assumes and displays.[28] The fact that he seems to *embody* this theory, however, is crucial; as the play goes on to reveal, at other moments Agathon seems to espouse an essentialist theory of identity rooted in one's innermost nature and expressed naturally in one's body and appearance. Agathon's essentialism comes as a surprise to critics looking for subversion in this play, for essentialism has been repudiated for some time now as a philosophy that has been used to keep the oppressed in their place through, for example, theories of the "natural" inferiority of women. Yet essentialism, as Jonathan Dollimore reminds us, is not an inherently conservative philosophy, just as constructionism is not inherently radical; either can be used in either way, and subversion may or may not follow.[29] And as Diana Fuss has argued, essentialism lurks beneath the surface of even the most avowedly constructionist theoretical positionings; the two

---

[27] Garber (1992) 17 (original italics). See also her 151–2 on modern-day drag performers deliberately mixing "masculine" and "feminine" items of clothing or accessories: "onstage, this method is called, significantly, 'working with (feminine) pieces' – so that the artifactuality of the 'feminine' (or the 'feminine piece') is overtly acknowledged and brought to consciousness."

[28] Agathon "mingles evocation of male and female as though he were beyond gender, or rather, as though gender were entirely a matter of representation and practices": Stehle (2002) 383. Probably the best-known theorist of this position is Judith Butler: in *Gender Trouble*, she argues that "Gender ought not to be construed as a stable identity or locus of agency from which various acts follow; rather, gender is an identity tenuously constructed in time, instituted in an exterior space through a *stylized repetition of acts*" (Butler (1990) 140, original italics).

[29] See Dollimore (1991) chs. 1–4. Dollimore discusses Andre Gide and Oscar Wilde as homosexuals who subverted societal norms from opposite theoretical positions: Wilde, of course, was the proto-postmodern social constructionist, while Gide was an unconventional essentialist: "Indeed, to the extent that Gide's essentialist legitimation of homosexual desire was primarily an affirmation of his own nature as pederast or paedophile, some critics might usefully rethink their own assumption that essentialism is fundamentally and always a conservative philosophy" (71).

are mutually implicated.[30] Agathon's use of *both* subject positions is, in fact, the most subversive move he makes.

It is interesting to note that the kinsman expresses his erotic arousal at Agathon's performance *before* he questions Agathon's appearance; at some level, the kinsman finds the tragedian arousing regardless of whether he can make sense of his attire.[31] Even after Agathon begins to explain that he changes his clothes to suit the role he is composing, the kinsman offers to "collaborate with you, long and hard, from the rear" (ἵνα συμποιῶ σοὔπισθεν ἐστυκὼς ἐγώ; trans. Sommerstein, 158) if he should ever write a satyr play. Critics too often dwell on the kinsman's robust masculinity and his comic confusion about Agathon's appearance while failing to analyze his attraction to Agathon despite, or perhaps because of, that appearance.[32]

A great deal of recent scholarship has undertaken to delineate the practices and prohibitions surrounding love between men (and between men and boys) in Classical Athens. K. J. Dover's pioneering work on Greek homosexuality in the 1970s, and Michel Foucault's influential model of sexual relations in ancient Athens (building on Dover), argued that sexual relations were structured along power imbalances and around certain valorized or stigmatized acts, rather than between individuals with complementary "orientations."[33] Penetration was equated with masculinity, and thus women, boys, and slaves were all functionally equivalent sexual objects for the adult citizen male, who might penetrate any or all of

---

[30] Fuss (1989) ch. 1.

[31] Noted also by Bobrick (1997) 180.

[32] Muecke (1982) 48–9 provides a fine analysis of the way in which Agathon's song is musically arousing to the kinsman (an example of the "New Music," with voluptuous, eccentric rhythms), but there is little mention of Agathon's visual effect on the kinsman. Taaffe (1993) reads the kinsman's arousal in two different and mutually exclusive ways: "The scene provides an opportunity for an analysis of the spectator's gaze and the semiotics of theater, for the Relative sees the man underneath Agathon's female costume and jokes about thinking, at first, that he was seeing the prostitute Cyrene (97–8)" (80); "The spectacle of Agathon dressed and speaking like a woman, no matter how confused or incomplete the pretense of femininity, has aroused the Relative's desires and he, as an aggressive and masculine comic figure, voices them" (90). Her first statement suggests that "the man underneath Agathon's costume" is visible to the kinsman, while her second statement suggests that Agathon's "pretense of femininity" is what the kinsman finds arousing. Does the costume work, or doesn't it? The answer I would suggest is that Agathon's indeterminacy is, at least in part, what turns the kinsman on. Zeitlin (1996) 401 notes Agathon's indeterminacy and compares him to Dionysus, but she does not address the issue of the kinsman's desire directly.

[33] Dover (1978, rev. ed. 1989); Foucault (1985).

them without compromising his masculinity. Many scholars traced out the implications of this model of sexual relations in classical Athens, focusing especially on pederasty;[34] others raised valuable questions about the descriptive value of the model and about the degree to which Foucault's ideological agenda determined the conclusions of his scholarship.[35] One detail of Athenian male–male erotics that all scholars seem to agree on, however, is the taboo against relationships between two adult males. Athenians had varying reactions to the "institution" of pederasty, ranging from encomiastic (Plato) to coarse mockery (Aristophanes); boys and men engaging in romantic relationships had to maneuver carefully to avoid stigma, especially the boys, whose nascent masculinity was potentially imperilled by being assimilated to the woman's role in the relationship.[36] Virtually all Athenians, however, agreed that an adult male who was penetrated by another adult male forfeited all claim to his masculinity. These men were subject to the stigma that the term "homosexual" still carries in most parts of the world today; they were labeled *kinaidoi* ("[male] sluts") or *katapugones* ("wide-assholes"), considered to be effeminate, and regarded with horror.

This is precisely the portrait of Agathon that Aristophanes paints in the *Thesmophoriazousai* – and yet the kinsman is attracted to Agathon nevertheless.[37] Why would the kinsman, who is routinely taken to be the

---

[34] See Halperin (1990) especially chs. 1 and 5; Winkler (1990) especially chs. 1 and 2; Halperin, Winkler, and Zeitlin (1990). The most extreme statement of the "anti-orientation" position is Halperin's, who insists (in the face of some compelling evidence to the contrary) that no conception of sexual "orientation," no idea of "homosexuality" (or "heterosexuality") as we now define it, existed in ancient Greece.

[35] Boswell (1980) argues that "homosexuality" as we conceive of it did exist in the ancient world, and paints a relatively sunny picture of life for "gay people" during classical antiquity. Richlin (1993) and Taylor (1997) also argue that "homosexuality" was an identity category and argue that male homosexuals were a stigmatized and persecuted subculture at Rome. Without diving into the orientation question, D. Cohen (1991) ch. 7 presents compelling evidence that the Athenians were deeply conflicted over the licitness of pederasty, *contra* Foucault's depiction of an Athens in which pederasty was viewed positively as long as both parties obeyed certain rules. Hubbard (1998) argues that the Athenians found pederasty deeply problematic and discusses the orientation question at length.

[36] See D. Cohen (1991) ch. 7.

[37] Dover (1989) 140 reads line 35, in which Euripides answers the kinsman's questions about who this Agathon is with, "Well, you've fucked him, but perhaps you don't know him," as "implying that the effeminate Agathon has functioned as a male prostitute in the dark." The line could be read instead to mean that the kinsman has had sex with Agathon without knowing his name; or that he has only seen Agathon from behind, in the act; or that he thought Agathon was a woman when they had anal sex; or it

character onstage with whom the audience identifies,[38] find a *kinaidos* attractive? Or, to rephrase the question more generally, why are *kinaidoi* apparently attractive despite the horror they arouse when a man imagines being one himself? The proponents of the Foucauldian paradigm of Greek sexuality do not directly address this question; presumably, a hole is a hole to the man wielding the phallus, even if the hole belongs to a *kinaidos*. Since there was no such thing as a sense of sexual "orientation" or "identity," according to these scholars, penetrating a *kinaidos* would not compromise one's masculinity any more than penetrating a woman would. This explanation, however, does not address the issue of desire – or rather, the strange mingling of desire and horror that the specter of the *kinaidos* seems to arouse.

James Davidson's revision of the Foucauldian model of sexual behavior in Classical Athens may provide us with an answer to this question. Davidson argues that the *katapugon* and the *kinaidos* were figures who represented appetites out of control in general and points to evidence from comedy in which these supposedly "passive" figures are described as buggering other male characters. Calling someone a *katapugon* or a *kinaidos* is calling him lewd or insatiable, not calling him a "passive homosexual," as the terms tend to be translated since Foucault; this is why adulterers and animals such as the mouse and the wrasse were also called *katapugon*. Davidson dismisses the notion of "passive homosexuality" altogether as an ignorant fiction, an awkward compromise constructed by scholars to "reconcile a morality in which the most important thing is to avoid penetration with a morality centered on the necessity for self-control." Finally, he takes issue with the idea of "zero-sum" sexual relationships organized around power differentials and argues for a reacknowledgement of the pleasure of sex.[39]

If we are persuaded by Davidson's argument, then we need to reevaluate our ideas about Agathon. He is called a *katapugon* by the kinsman (200), who offers to bugger him whenever he should happen to write a

---

could simply be a cheap shot that does not try to make sense. In any event, the joke sets up the issue of the kinsman's arousal.

[38] Taaffe (1993) 78, 80 takes the kinsman to be "an intermediary through whom the audience's gaze is filtered" (yet she later calls him "a comic buffoon" (1993) 82, 84, which would suggest that the audience might not see him as their representative onstage). Henderson (1996) 96–7, in his introduction to his translation of the *Thesmophoriazousai*, sees the kinsman as nothing less than the embodiment of the robust, masculine spirit of Comedy itself, as does Sommerstein (1994) 9 in his introduction to his translation.

[39] Davidson (1998) 167–82; quotation from 174–5.

satyr play; what this means is that the kinsman sees Agathon as sexually insatiable, essentially lewd. At its most basic level, Davidson's argument calls for viewing the "passive homosexual" as an actively desiring subject, not as an object – and for seeing that the Athenians saw him that way too.

> Even passive sodomites are shown joining in [sexual activity] at every level, like the sausage-seller making his arse wide [*Knights* 720–21], and experiencing pleasure, as the *Problemata* show, not in sexual domination but in sex itself, a pleasure even greater than that of the penetrating partner, a pleasure like that of women: an itching kind of pleasure without end. The *kinaidos/katapugon* is not a sexual pathic, humiliated and make effeminate by repeated domination, he is a nymphomaniac, full of womanish desire, who dresses up to attract men and has sex at the drop of a hat.[40]

Agathon's effeminate clothing, then, points to his insatiable sexual appetite. He is dressed to seduce. Of course the kinsman wants him.

This rereading of the sexual mores of classical Athens should not blind us to the details of Aristophanes' presentation of Agathon, however. His effeminate costume[41] and incongruous props are both important, despite the fact that the best translation for *katapugon* may be "nympho" or "slut" rather than "faggot" (as Henderson and Sommerstein render it). Agathon is depicted in this play as fundamentally indeterminate: effeminate, neither fully male nor fully female, not grounded in a stable, recognizable body. He puts into question the distinctions between poet and work, actor and role, masculine and feminine, body and costume.[42] He is a

---

[40] Davidson (1998) 179. Pentheus' reaction to Dionysus' appearance in Euripides' *Bacchae* (453–9) supports Davidson's view of Athenian sexuality: Pentheus reads Dionysus' effeminate clothing and long hair as signs that he is a seducer of women, not that he is a "sex object." See Davidson (1998) 177 on Alcibiades. Aristophanes' myth of the halved sexes in Plato's *Symposium* also supports this view: the "androgynous" whole that was split into male and female halves produces men who are womanizers and adulterers (191d-e), presumably because they were once half-female and are thus still innately lustful.

[41] Muecke (1982) 50 believes that Agathon may be wearing long Ionian robes, like the poetic models he mentions, instead of women's clothing, although she admits that this "seems to eliminate the possibility of a visual assimilation of the poet to the female characters he is 'imitating'" – which is a major objection.

[42] He may also blur the distinctions between the supposedly rigid sexual roles for male–male erotic relationships: Hubbard (1998) 57–8 argues persuasively that Agathon in the *Thesomophoriazousai* is presented as both an effeminate, aging *eromenos* and as a potential *erastes* of younger boys: "Just as Agathon can slip in and out of gender roles

figure for the identity of the self because he opens up what Garber would call a "space of possibility," both physically and aesthetically (that is, in terms of both sex and gender). We need to look more closely at both the kinsman's and the audience's reaction to Agathon. The kinsman finds him laughable, horrible, but ultimately desirable; the audience, in turn, is encouraged to laugh at the thick-witted, lusty kinsman as much as at the effeminate, pretentious tragedian.

One reason for laughing at the kinsman's reaction to Agathon, of course, is that it masks anxiety: the kinsman is aroused by Agathon's music and costume, that is, by the dramatic spectacle Agathon presents. Agathon is performing a "women's play" when the kinsman observes him, as we remember, and the point of Aristophanes' mockery seems to be the effeminacy of Agathon's costume, music, and lifestyle. In Agathon's hands, Aristophanes is saying, tragedy is "women's plays." And the kinsman loves it in spite of himself. When the audience is invited to laugh at the kinsman's gushing reaction to Agathon's tragic performance, it suggests that the kinsman, as a kind of audience to Agathon, is doing something wrong.[43] The anxiety here is that the audience of a tragedy can become effeminate by watching (and hearing) it. Plato more or less spells out this anxiety in the *Republic*, arguing that watching actors impersonate "unworthy" characters (women, slaves, and cowardly men) leads the audience (and the actors) to fall prey to the same flaws as the characters have.[44] The kinsman is aroused by Agathon's appearance – both his physical appearance and his dramatic entrance – and then backs off, tries to figure out what Agathon is, tries to read his accessories, clothes, and body for clues to his identity. But Agathon has a sword as well as a mirror, and he lacks both breasts and phallus; he resists classification. His body is as mimetic as his clothes, and it "takes on what it needs." His body is a costume.[45] He has made sex, as well as gender, a theatrical construct.

---

as either man or woman, so also he has the capacity to alternate age roles as either man or boy."

[43] On the kinsman as an "interior audience," see Taaffe (1993) 80, 82–3, 88.

[44] *Resp.* 3.338d, 3.395c-d; 10.605c-606b; see Bassi (1998) 19–23. Similar anxieties existed in Renaissance England, another culture with a tradition of all-male theatrical troupes; see Levine (1994) ch. 1.

[45] Bassi (1998) 99–143 (published separately as Bassi (1995)) draws out the cultural logic by which "clothing is generally encoded as feminine in Greek culture," signifying the gap between appearance and reality, the essential deceptiveness of women – what she calls "the Pandora paradigm." Heroic male nudity is opposed to feminine clothing on Archaic pottery and in later discourse. This means that "disguise signifies compromised masculinity" for male characters in the *Odyssey* and elsewhere, and she suggests that

Agathon embodies mimesis. He explains this in response to the kinsman's puzzled questions:

Αγ. ἐγὼ δὲ τὴν ἐσθῆθ᾽ ἅμα γνώμῃ φορῶ.
χρὴ γὰρ ποιητὴν ἄνδρα πρὸς τὰ δράματα
ἃς δεῖ ποιεῖν πρὸς ταῦτα τοὺς τρόπους ἔχειν.
αὐτίκα γυναικεῖ᾽ ἢν ποιῇ τις δράματα,
μετουσίαν δεῖ τῶν τρόπων τὸ σῶμ᾽ ἔχειν.
Κη. οὐκοῦν κελητίζεις, ὅταν Φαίδραν ποιῇς;
Αγ. ἀνδρεῖα δ᾽ ἢν ποιῇ τις, ἐν τῷ σώματι
ἵνεσθ᾽ ὑπάρχον τοῦθ᾽. ἃς δ᾽ οὐ κεκτήμεθα,
μίμησις ἤδη ταῦτα συνθηρεύεται.

(*Thesm.* 148–56)

\Ag. I change my clothing along with my purpose.
For it's necessary that a poet-man have habits
according to the plays that he must write.
For example, if one is writing feminine plays,
one's body must participate in their habits.
Ki. Therefore you ride bareback when you write a *Phaedra*?
Ag. If you're writing about masculine things, that which you need
is there in your body; but if we don't have it,
then it must be captured by imitation.

He is a sort of "method writer," changing his outfits to match his compositions – or perhaps the reverse: writing his plays based on the outfit he is wearing. But Agathon also talks about his body, not just about his clothes: "one's body must participate in their habits [*tropoi*]." What are these *tropoi*? How does one perform mimesis on the body? Stohn decides that these *tropoi* consist of a feminine appearance and bearing, in addition to the wearing of women's clothing.[46] This seems like a reasonable reading, except for the follow-up question by the

the Proagon, the part of the Great Dionysia in which the poet and actors are thought to have appeared before the audience without their masks, really had the poet and actors appear nude in order to reaffirm their masculinity before donning costumes. While I do not follow all of her conclusions, Agathon, as a male character completely covered in feminine clothing, fits this "paradigm" nicely.

[46] "Zu den τρόποι, an denen er Anteil haben soll, gehört auch, abgesehen von der weiblichen Kleidung, ein feminines Aussehen und die entsprechende Haltung": Stohn (1993) 198. Muecke (1982) 55 agrees with this reading.

kinsman – "So when you write a *Phaedra*, you mount astride?" – and Agathon's answer. The kinsman understands Agathon's assertion much as Stohn does, albeit much more crudely: what it *must* mean for Agathon's body to participate in women's habits is that he has sex like a woman; he imitates the behavior of women. Agathon's coy answer, however, obscures the issue once again. He does not address the kinsman's blunt sexual reduction of his aesthetic theory, but instead "explains" that if he writes a play for men, then he already has what he needs, but if he is writing a play for women, his body must use mimesis. Is he talking about behavior or anatomy? Is he talking about the phallus, or isn't he? ("If you're a woman, where are your tits? If you're a man, where's your cock?") How could he use *mimesis* to capture those aspects of a woman's body that he lacks?

Our immediate impulse is to agree with Stohn that Agathon must be talking about behavior. The passage is reasonably clear this way, whereas introducing the idea of the physical body keeps everything much more confused. But I think it is important that Aristophanes has depicted Agathon in this way: clouding the issue, obscuring the kinsman's view of his bodily identity. The transvestite signals a crisis of category, Garber says. The transvestite onstage represents the category crisis of identity, both narrowly in terms of gender but also in a more existential sense: what, if anything, is under the costume? This is an ontological issue that drama faces at the beginning of its (Western) history, the crisis of illusion versus reality, or, more radically, whether there is any "reality" behind the illusion. Agathon's appearance raises these issues, and the uneasiness they provoke does not dissipate with mockery of the tragedian. Agathon is onstage to be laughed at, to be sure – we must never lose sight of this fact – but so is the kinsman. And if Agathon's appearance and song, his coy, teasing manner and his refusal to be classified, work on the kinsman, the internal audience, then they work on the larger audience too. Plato was right to be afraid. After all, a scare-figure must have some power in order to inspire fear. Part of Agathon's power is his ability to make blurring boundaries seductive. And sure enough, the kinsman's next action is to dress up as a woman.

After using the term *mimesis*[47] and adducing poetic role models for his effeminately luxurious dress (Ibycus, Anacreon, Alcaeus, Phrynichus), Agathon famously goes on to give a second and conflicting theory of art

---

[47] The first attested technical use of the term, according to Zeitlin (1996) 383.

alongside his earlier one:

αὐτός τε καλὸς ἦν καὶ καλῶς ἠμπέσχετο·
διὰ τοῦτ' ἄρ' αὐτοῦ καὶ κάλ' ἦν τὰ δράματα.
ὅμοια γὰρ ποιεῖν ἀνάγκη τῇ φύσει.

(*Thesm.* 165–67)

[And Phrynichus] was an attractive man and he dressed attractively,
and for this reason his plays were also attractive.
One writes according to one's nature.

The conclusion that the work reflects the poet's nature follows from
the assertion that the Ionian poets of yore were all attractive and well-
dressed men, but it does not square with Agathon's earlier claims about
dressing to suit the play he is writing. This second, essentialist claim about
the way mimesis works – outward, from the poet's nature to his writing –
uses the same logic as the ancient biographies of poets, which attributed
Sophocles' pleasant verses to his pleasant personality, for example.[48] The
first, constructionist claim about mimesis – that it works inward, from
the clothes to the poet's nature – is much more anxiety-provoking. It
suggests that the clothes we put on can change our natures, that we are all
actors, acting to suit our costumes. And Agathon refuses to disentangle the
two theories. When the kinsman finally comprehends his theory about
creating work that reflects one's nature ("That's why ugly Philocles writes
ugly plays!" 170), Agathon replies, "It's utterly inevitable, and knowing
this, I gave myself this treatment" (171–2). Because he recognized that his
nature determines the kind of poetry he writes (and how he dresses), he
dressed himself that way. In other words, because he realized the second,
constructionist theory about mimesis was correct, he implemented the
first, essentialist theory. Both cannot be true, seemingly – and yet Agathon
insists on keeping both in play. He will not be categorized. He is self-
creating: "what we lack, we capture by mimesis."

Euripides asks Agathon at this point to help him by going undercover, as a woman, to the Thesmophoria where the women are plotting
Euripides' downfall. Agathon refuses, giving two reasons: a quotation of a
line from Euripides' *Alcestis* ("You love life; do you think your father does
not?" 194) and the explanation that the women would treat him even
more harshly than Euripides if he were discovered. The use of Euripides'
verse against him makes Agathon a parodist in his own right, a fact which

---

[48] Lefkowitz (1981) 80. Of course, this "logic" is based on reading backward, inferring
the playwright's personality from the tone of his verses.

is not usually noted; it is another way in which he is able to turn the tables on those who mock him. His "explanation" is vaguely worded and has been translated various ways:

> δοκῶν γυναικῶν ἔργα νυκτερείσια
> κλέπτειν ὑφαρπάζειν τε θήλειαν Κύπριν.
> (*Thesm.* 204–05)

> I'd look to be stealing the nocturnal doings of women
> and absconding with the female Kypris
> (Henderson)

> ... they think I steal women's *knock* turnal business,
> and rob them of the female's natural rights
> (Sommerstein)

By "female Aphrodite," Agathon probably means "female sexual enjoyment," as Henderson thinks; thus these lines mean something like "they think I steal the nighttime business of women / and filch away their feminine pleasure." This reading seems most likely based on the kinsman's response: "'Steal'? You mean get fucked!" I would argue, however, that Agathon's lofty tone and euphemistic, vague words are significant not only as an Aristophanic parody of his high-tragic style, but as another example of how he keeps himself mysterious. Aristophanes consistently portrays Agathon as someone who is difficult to read, both visually and verbally; it seems possible that this trait had a real-life referent.

After Agathon refuses to go undercover for Euripides, the kinsman volunteers instead. Euripides proceeds to singe the kinsman's anus and then dress him in women's clothing, a bit of metatheatrical stage business that calls attention both to the artifice of femininity and to the costuming that all actors must go through. It also makes the kinsman look more like Agathon, of course. Agathon supplies all of the props needed to disguise the kinsman as a woman: razor, torch, breast-band, dress, wig, cloak, shoes.[49] The kinsman's drag is very different from Agathon's, as different

---

[49] Ferris (1989) 28 reads this play as reducing all women to this list of props, while male characters are "real" because they have phalluses over and in addition to any costume. While I think the issue is more complicated than this reading allows, Ferris' reading of stage women as *only* clothes meshes nicely with Bassi's analysis of the essentially feminine (i.e., deceptive, theatrical) nature of clothing, and with Zeitlin's argument that woman was seen as inherently mimetic. Stehle (2002) reads this play, conversely, as reducing the phallus – previously naturalized in Aristophanes' plays as the guarantor of masculinity – to the status of prop.

as the unshaven, deliberately sloppy drag of a frat boy is from the seam-less, illusionistic drag of a cabaret performer. The kinsman and Agathon occupy opposite poles of masculinity; according to the standard interpre-tations of this comedy, the kinsman's masculinity is so overwhelming that it is the reason that his female disguise fails.[50] Yet we do see the kinsman embrace his female role: he wants to make sure his hem hangs straight (256), he swears by Aphrodite (254), he is concerned about the fit of his wig and shoes (260, 263).[51] Even on the kinsman, it seems, clothes do "dictate what you do." Once he volunteers to go on Euripides' mis-sion, the kinsman proves quite comfortable with the idea of costume, disguise, impersonation, and parody, changing personas multiple times in his attempts to cue Euripides' rescue. Watching Agathon perform has had a measurable effect on this spectator: as Plato feared, he has become an actor.

In Agathon, we have playwright, actor, and character in one figure onstage. Aristophanes uses him to suggest the dangerous potential of watching tragedy: seeing him and listening to him make the audience resemble him. Agathon is in this way a figure for the operation of desire in theatrical performance. He is an object of desire, dressed up to seduce, performing for an audience. The audience (that is, Euripides and the kinsman, and by extension, the festival audience) finds him horrifying, laughable, in his effeminacy – "I thought he was Cyrene the courtesan!" – but also attractive to watch. And attraction, as we have seen, leads to imitation; spectatorship leads to mimesis of the person watched. That is, wanting to *watch* him becomes wanting to *have* him, which in turn

---

[50] See Henderson (1996) 97; Sommerstein (1994) 9; Taaffe (1993) 84, 90–91; Zeitlin (1996) 385.

[51] Taaffe (1993) 87 notes that once he is among the women at the festival, the Rela-tive "tries hard to speak correctly as a woman, and for the most part he succeeds," slipping up only once (θύειν ἔχουσιν, 288, a masculine expression). Compton-Engle (2003) 515–24 argues that the kinsman's masculinity is compromised by his inabil-ity to control his costume in this play, as part of her argument that control of cos-tume is linked to both masculinity and poetic control in Aristophanes. She does not address the successful tragic poet Agathon's control of his effeminate costume, however.

The parallels between this scene of transvestic disguise in the *Thesmophoriazousai* and the so-called Robing Scene in Euripides' *Bacchae* (810–976) are fascinating. In both plays, a seemingly virile man is dressed as a woman, somewhat against his will, and then he finds that his clothes change him: "Is my hem straight?" they both ask. The two scenes taken together suggest a deep anxiety about theatrical spectatorship: it seems to lead, over and over, to effeminacy and humiliation. See Bobrick (1997) 193.

becomes wanting to *be* him. As another fragment of Agathon says,

> ἐκ τοῦ γὰρ ἐσορᾶν γίγνετ' ἀνθρώποις ἐρᾶν
> love is born out of looking with admiration
> (fr. 29)

Just as Agathon refuses to disentangle his two conflicting theories of artistic composition [the clothes one wears determine the play one writes (constructionism); one writes according to one's nature and thus dresses that way (essentialism)], the desire he inspires confounds the distinction between having and being, between possession and identity. The transvestite onstage signals the crisis of identity not only for the actor ("is there anything under the costume?"), but for the audience ("what does watching a play make us?").[52] The *kinaidos* signals the crisis of identity inherent in the phenomenon of desire: his attractiveness threatens to overwhelm the distance between the two poles of Athenian masculinity. Desiring the *kinaidos* blurs the line between wanting and being, between object and subject, between Self and Other.

AGATHON IN THE *SYMPOSIUM*

There is a well-known anecdote about Plato and tragedy: Plato, in his youth, aspired to write tragedies. He wrote a tragic tetralogy, which Socrates persuaded him to burn in front of the Theater of Dionysus.[53] Regardless of its historical value, this story gets at many of the issues surrounding Plato's thought on theater: his obvious fascination and familiarity with the genre; Socrates' hostility to it (or Plato's hostility, projected onto the figure of Socrates); the sense that being a playwright and being a philosopher are fundamentally incompatible occupations. When Agathon appears in the *Symposium*, then, we might expect Plato's portrayal of him to be quite hostile. Plato's depiction of Agathon in the *Symposium* has been interpreted as everything from good-natured parody to devastating ridicule.[54] In fact, though, Plato's portrait of the tragedian is surprisingly

---

[52] See Garber (1992) 75 for a Lacanian analysis of the transvestite as the "space of desire."

[53] Aelian *VH* 2.30 (= Diogenes Laertius 3.5). Swift Riginos (1976) 43–51 argues that this anecdote (along with an anecdote that Plato dabbled in painting as a young man) must have been inspired by Plato's critique of poetry (and painting) in the *Republic*. See also Blondell (2002) 15; Tarrant (1955) 82 and *passim*.

[54] von Blanckenagen (1992) 61, for example, finds Agathon to be the subject of "good-natured banter, ironic but never malicious," while Ludwig (1996) 551 sees "derision"

nuanced; the flowery, rhyming, parodic speech put into Agathon's mouth is offset to some extent by the way the other characters interact with him.[55] As in the *Thesmophoriazousai*, Agathon in the *Symposium* is, despite everything unflattering in his presentation, an object of desire. He embodies the seductive beauty of tragedy, which enchants the spectator into forgetting himself. Agathon is also Desire incarnate, Eros himself. As this dual role may suggest, Agathon proves to be just as difficult to pin down in this text as in Aristophanes' play. And with the idea of a "dual role," of course, comes the corollary idea of Agathon as an actor – that is, someone capable of falsifying his identity. Plato uses Agathon to raise the same questions about the nature of the self that Aristophanes does: does Agathon have a nature that determines his actions, or does he change to suit his environment? Is there anyone, or anything, underneath the beautiful surface?

The setting of the *Symposium* is a victory celebration at Agathon's house in approximately 416 BCE. Agathon has just won first prize in the tragic competition.[56] Socrates and a friend go to Agathon's house, where the assembled guests conduct a series of speeches in praise of Eros. Aristophanes is present; so is Agathon's boyfriend Pausanias. But it is Socrates and the narrator who have the most to say about Agathon.

in the way Aristophanes refers to Agathon, and Anton (1996) discerns a great deal of implicit contempt for the tragedian.

[55] Nehamas (1999) 308, sees Agathon as "indulging in an unrestrained parody of Gorgianic style and sophistic argument" in his speech, a reading that makes Agathon a parodist in his own right, as in the *Thesmophoriazousai*, rather than an instrument of Platonic parody.

[56] At which festival, and with which play? Athenaeus thought that Agathon won at the Lenaia (*Deip.* 217a–b), as does Anton (1996) 209n2, but Socrates mentions him winning in front of 30,000 Hellenes (*Symposium* 175e), which suggests the seating capacity and pan-Hellenic audience of the City Dionysia. Lévêque (1955) 57 supports the latter interpretation. (Of course, Socrates could be flattering Agathon by exaggerating the size and composition of his audience, as Anton (1996) 212 thinks.) As for the play, Lévêque (1955) 55–6 thinks that Agathon won with *Anthos*, based on a passage from Agathon's speech in the *Symposium* (196a-b) that uses four versions of the word ἄνθος. This is possible but by no means necessary; it seems unlikely that the tragedian would have won his first victory with his most unusual play – or, for that matter, that he would have gone from writing a successful play in which all the characters were invented to writing the rest of his tragedies with standard mythological plots. If the *Antheus* won, why not attempt another "new" plot? It seems more likely that his artistic development (to use an unfashionable term) would have proceeded in the other direction, from derivative to innovative. But, of course, we cannot be certain either way.

Agathon's boyish beauty is stressed throughout the dialogue. Although he is around 30 years old, he is called νέος (by Socrates, 175e), νεανίσκος (by the narrator, 198a), and μειράκιον (by Socrates, 223a). Some scholars take these terms to be ironic banter, gentle hints Agathon's friends are dropping that he should act his age.[57] After all, he is past the age of a typical *eromenos*, who was thought to lose his attractiveness with the growth of his facial hair,[58] and yet he seems to be carrying on as the *eromenos* of Pausanias.[59] But it is Socrates and the narrator who call him "young," and while Socrates' sense of irony is notorious, the narrator seems less suspicious. Furthermore, as mentioned earlier, all of the testimonia that describe Agathon mention his great beauty.[60] Many of them, in fact, recount stories of his beauty remaining even in middle age. Considering the fact that the relationship between Agathon and Pausanias seems to be accepted without stigma by this group of elite friends,[61] it seems possible that Agathon was exceptional in several ways: in his physical beauty, in his long-term relationship with another man, in his ability to transgress social norms without scandal (at least within his own circle of friends). Most critics assume that the Agathon who is depicted here is a creature who has continued to try to look youthful, trimming his beard extremely close, perhaps shaving or depilating his body.[62] Whether meant ironically or not, Socrates' and the narrator's comments about Agathon's youthfulness

---

[57] Anton (1996) 209 n. 2 thinks the terms "youth" and "young man" are applied to Agathon "in jest." Yet he then (213) describes all of the symposiasts except Socrates as "conspicuously young."

[58] Ferrari (2002) 127–38 (and see all of ch. 6) provides a nuanced, rigorous analysis of Athenian pederastic ideology as it concerns the growth of facial hair. She argues convincingly that the Athenians made much more subtle distinctions concerning the facial hair of *eromenoi* – and thus, concerning whether an *eromenos* was still in his *hora*, or "bloom" – than merely noting its presence or absence. Ferrari's arguments help explain why Agathon's friends tease him about his appearance: he is on the verge of being too old, or past his *hora*, but the line separating "old enough" from "too old" was blurry, and perhaps intentionally so.

[59] According to the seating arrangments, Agathon shares a couch with Socrates, which playfully suggests that he is Socrates' *eromenos* as well: von Blanckenagen (1992) 61.

[60] See Lévêque (1955) 36.

[61] von Blanckenagen (1992) 61 identifies Agathon as "an aging, effeminate beauty, Pausanias' beloved, a passive homosexual," but notes that "There is not the slightest sign of the customary Athenian contempt for such a person" anywhere in the dialogue; see also 63.

[62] "Agathon's beardlessness is a mere counterfeit of youth": von Blanckenagen (1992) 61; Taaffe (1993) 92; see Lévêque (1955) 35–40. But see Ferrari (2002) ch. 1 (noted above).

establish Agathon's personal appearance, and its possibly deceptive quality, its counterfeit youth, as one of his defining characteristics.

Socrates and Agathon engage in some playful banter before Agathon's speech on Eros, each accusing the other of trying to make him nervous. Socrates compliments Agathon on his poise and composure in front of the crowd during the Proagon (194b).[63] Agathon replies that "a small critical audience is far more daunting than a large uncritical one" to anyone with sense (194b). Socrates then engages in a brief dialectic with Agathon about whether he feels shame in front of the uncritical masses or before a small critical elite; in a sense, the question is whether his true audience is the Athenian *demos* or the select group of literate friends that make up the *Symposium*. Anton reads this exchange as evidence that Agathon is two-faced, hypocritical, even doubled:

> Whereas Socrates, who was a member of yesterday's multitude and one of today's sensible few, remains the same person, Agathon does not. There are two Agathons; and each behaves differently, depending on what each addresses, the multitude or the sensible few. . . . The characters of the two Agathons differ significantly: one is shameless, the other shameful.[64]

This reading does not question Socrates' statements or motives, but replicates Socrates' (and Plato's) antitheatrical bias in finding Agathon to be a hypocrite. "Can the art of dramatic poetry from the pen of a bifurcated person be good and true, edifying and useful?"[65] Anton's question seems to come straight from the *Republic*'s vision of a carefully fashioned, controlled, unified self under attack from theater's corrupting effect on both actors and audience.[66] Yet Socrates himself is doubled, a member of both of Agathon's audiences. It is only his assertion that he was a member of the large audience and should not be put in the category of the elite few (a typically Socratic gesture of ironic mock humility)

---

[63] The Proagon was a part of the festival before the presentation of plays, in which the poet would appear with his unmasked actors and announce the subject matter of his plays. See Pickard–Cambridge (1988) 67–8. Bassi (see n. 45 *supra*) argues that the actors actually appeared nude in the Proagon, to counteract the effeminizing effect of their costumes later. Lévêque (1955) 63–6 discusses earlier scholarly notions, based on this passage, that Agathon acted in his own plays.

[64] Anton (1996) 15.

[65] Ibid., 216.

[66] See Clay (1983) 197.

that enables Anton to read him as unified and whole.[67] What is at stake here is the issue of hypocrisy: Socrates tries to suggest that Agathon is a dissembler, someone who adapts his reactions to his audience, an actor. Perhaps inadvertently, however, Plato must show Socrates engaging in a slippery denial of hypocrisy himself.[68] Theater seems to force this doubleness or dissembling upon not only its performers, but its audience as well; all must adapt their responses to the performance context. This inherent hypocrisy of the theatrical situation is at the heart of the antitheatrical response, from Plato onward.[69]

Agathon is thus a sort of doubled figure, playing to two different audiences. He is doubled in other ways as well: in the Proagon, he is a playwright setting forth the story of his tragedy, but he is also onstage with the actors. His speech on Eros, and the discussions around it, suggests still other ways in which he is doubled: he is subject and object of Eros, lover and beloved, god and man, man and boy, victor and vanquished.

Agathon begins his speech with a description of the god Eros: he is the most beautiful and the youngest of the gods, delicate and soft, supple, and fond of flowers; he is gentle, virtuous, courageous, just, and wise; he is, in fact, a poet (195a–197c). As has often been remarked, Agathon makes Eros sound very much like himself: a beautiful, young, delicate poet, loved by all.[70] Agathon describes Eros as an *eromenos*, as a young, beautiful object of desire[71] – but this *eromenos* only visits those resembling him. He is young and lives among the young (195b); he is tender and seeks out the tender-hearted (195e); he loves flowers and dwells only

---

[67] Anton (1996) 227 argues away this problem by claiming that "we may also entertain the possibility that there is not one Socrates but two, *in this case without the self-contradiction of Agathon*" (emphasis added): (1) Socrates the teacher/narrator (expressed as Diotima, a move that erases her problematic presence altogether; see Halperin (1990) 113–51) and (2) Socrates "the pupil of himself." This solution seems like special pleading; Socrates is still a member of the two opposed audiences, which suggests that a kind of flexibility was demanded from at least some audience members, an ability, perhaps, to suspend critical judgment, which would make Plato very nervous indeed.

[68] See Gagarin (1977) on Socrates' famous irony as a kind of "false pretense" in the *Symposium*.

[69] See Barish (1981) ch. 1.

[70] Anton (1996) 218–19; Arieti (1991) 103, Lévêque (1955) 37–8; von Blanckenagen (1992) 62–3; see Clay (1983) 193.

[71] Nehamas (1999) 308–9 notes that Agathon (and Socrates, before his reeducation by Diotima) "conceived of [eros] on the model of the beloved, who is the object of desire and is thus young, beautiful, and good and not – *as would have been correct* [emphasis added] – on the model of the lover, who lacks these features but is still close enough to them to recognize and appreciate them (204c)."

within those who are in their flower of youth (196a); he is a poet and he makes others poets (196e). Like is drawn to like. Agathon is talking about Eros as a god who makes people desirable, not about Eros desiring people, but he does not actually describe the results of this enhanced desirability. In his speech, Eros visits those who are *already* desirable. He may look like an *eromenos*, but he behaves like an *erastes*. If Eros is a doppelgänger of Agathon, then two boundaries have been crossed in this identification: Agathon is both man (himself) and god (Eros), and thus he is both boy (*eromenos*) and man (*erastes*). Furthermore, he is both subject (as Eros) and object of desire (of Eros), both lover and beloved. Making the god resemble himself is not simply a move of vanity, as some critics have suggested;[72] it is a radical reformulation of the mechanism of desire, from a model of difference (*erastes/eromenos*) to one of likeness, of blurred distinctions, of shared identity.

Interestingly, the other speech in the *Symposium* that posits a model of desire based on shared identity is Aristophanes' myth of the halved human beings. Humans, Aristophanes tells the group of symposiasts, were once four-legged and four-armed, with two heads and two sets of genitals. When Zeus grew angry at them, he cut them each in half. The halves sought each other, desperate to reunite, but they died in fruitless embraces until Zeus had pity and moved their genitals around to face each other, so that in embracing they might satisfy their sense of longing, and in some cases, reproduce. There are three races of humans, descended from three original sexes of whole beings: the race of men who desire other men, descended from the original male; the race of women who desire other women, descended from the original female; and the race of what we today would call heterosexual people, descended from the original hermaphrodite (189e–191e). Aristophanes' myth points to his theory of desire: "we love what we are."[73] But at this point, there is a telling slippage in Aristophanes' theory. He states that those descended from the original male are the most manly; they have lovers (*erastai*) when they are young and have beloveds (*eromenoi*) when they are older (192a). Yet his myth clearly implies that the pairs of lovers should be the same age; how could

---

[72] Arieti (1991) 4 points out that "Each character [in the *Symposium*], including Socrates, describes love as a reflection of himself"; see also 102–3, 106–7.

[73] Ludwig (2002) 54–7 argues this theory is "selfish"; Ludwig (1996) 554–6 argues that Aristophanes reduces it to absurdity. This seems to me to minimize the playfulness and creativity of Aristophanes' myth as an attempt to "explain" desire. Hubbard (1998) 59 notes that Aristophanes' myth is an essentialist theory of identity.

half of a body be younger than the other half? Athenian social norms have intruded into the theoretical symmetry of Aristophanes' model.[74] Plato's Aristophanes thus articulates a theory of desire that is based on likeness, in fact on sameness, but then undermines it with reference to social norms of desire based on difference. Agathon's implicit theory of Eros is much more radical, as is his enactment of this theory in his personal life.

Agathon and Pausanias are lovers in the *Symposium*. They correspond to Aristophanes' myth of the halved male selves who find each other and live together their whole lives (193b). As far as we know, a lifelong relationship between two men of roughly equal age was quite rare in Classical Athens, and usually stigmatized. Yet Pausanias and Agathon, perhaps five years apart in age, seem to have spent their lives together: they appear together in Plato's *Protagoras* (315d-e) when Agathon is a young teenager, and Pausanias seems to have accompanied the middle-aged Agathon into exile at Pella (Aelian *VH* 2.21).[75] Some scholars see tension between them in the *Symposium*,[76] and the anecdotes about their propensity to quarrel in Macedonia could be taken support this view, but there is no evidence of a break in their relationship.

One small detail complicates this picture of Agathon's private life: Eryximachus' dismissal of the flute-girl at the beginning of the *Symposium*. Agathon says that she may go play for the women in the women's quarters (176e). The symposiasts are in Agathon's house. It is commonly observed that the great discussion about Eros takes place without any women present, and everyone dwells on Agathon's relationship with Pausanias, while no one pauses over these women: who are they? Are they servants? Are they relatives? Could Agathon possibly be married?[77] The presence of these women in Agathon's house and in Plato's text suggests that Agathon's private life may have been both more complicated and more traditional, in a way, than has been previously thought. Once again, the tragedian escapes easy classification.

---

[74] Noted in Halperin (1990) 21.

[75] See Edmonds (2000) 280 n. 48.

[76] Ludwig (1996) 557: "Agathon has begun beforehand to flirt openly with Socrates (175c 6-e 10), and it must be evident to all present that the young man's recent triumph in the tragedy contest (175e 5-7, 174a 6-7) has gone to his head and that he will now attempt to leave Pausanias for bigger game." I see this "flirtation" as foreshadowing and paralleling the exchange between Alcibiades and Socrates later, in keeping with Plato's agenda of depicting Socrates' wisdom as the correct goal of Eros.

[77] Thanks to Edward E. Cohen for pointing this out to me.

Agathon speaks next to last, immediately before Socrates. He is placed in this position in order to be refuted immediately by Socrates.[78] Socrates begins by saying that he once thought about Eros as Agathon does, but that a wise woman named Diotima corrected his ideas. Diotima told him that Eros is not quite the opposite of Agathon's description, but somewhere between the description and its opposite: he is neither beautiful nor ugly, neither wise nor ignorant, neither good nor bad, but something in between. He is not a god, but a δαίμων, a spirit between heaven and earth, a mediator of polarities. He lacks almost every attribute that Agathon ascribes to him. He is, in fact, the son of Lack (mother) and Abundance (father). He is poor, hard, unkempt, barefoot, and homeless, like his mother, but has an appreciation of beauty and wisdom, like his father. Finally, he is a philosopher! (201e–203e) Socrates' Eros looks as much like Socrates as Agathon's Eros looked like Agathon.[79] Many scholars read this last speech on Eros as the key to the whole dialogue: Socrates is Eros, and thus a δαίμων, and thus the mediator between all of the polarities brought up in the *Symposium*.[80]

This interpretation fits in with readings that argue that it is Socrates, not Agathon, who is crowned by Alcibiades at the end of the dialogue.[81] This makes Agathon both victor and vanquished within the *Symposium*, another boundary blurred. But Socrates is not an unambiguous figure himself. As we have mentioned, he is doubled, and he is also disguised: he is like one of those icons, Alcibiades says, that are rough and dark on the outside but golden when you open them up (216e). Socrates is the one whose appearance and essence do not match.[82] Plato makes

---

[78] The applause that Agathon receives at the end of his speech has been read as an indication of Plato's disapproval of his speech; see Mooney (1994) 17.

[79] Edmonds (2000) 273. See Arieti (1991) 4, 105–7, 110, who is virtually alone among contemporary scholars in arguing that Plato does not privilege Socrates as the "correct" or "true" speaker in this dialogue. Arieti reads the elaborate and obviously fictional mouthpiece of Diotima, in particular, as evidence that Socrates' eloquent, inventive speech is no more to be believed than Aristophanes' inventive myth, or Agathon's flowery eloquence.

[80] Clay (1983) 200; see Blondell (2002) 74, Nehamas (1999) 312.

[81] Anton (1996) 213 n.13; Clay (1983) 190; Bacon (1959). Alcibiades enters the symposium wearing a wreath of flowers with which he intends to crown Agathon, but when he sees Socrates, he removes some of the flowers and ribbons to make a crown for him as well (212e-213e). I would point out, as Arieti (1991) 108 does, that Alcibiades crowns *both* men, not just Socrates.

[82] See Blondell (2002) 70–73; von Blanckenagen (1992) 65; Clay (1983) 197–8; Gagarin (1977). Edmonds (2000) argues that it is Socrates who is the innovator in erotics in the *Symposium*, rather than Agathon, as I have been arguing. Edmonds traces out the

the incongruity between Socrates' inside and outside less threatening, however, by locating Socrates' good qualities on the inside, reassuring us that his essential self is golden. Agathon's external appearance, his (possibly artificial) youthful beauty, on the other hand, seems to be his most golden quality. He is all glowing surface and beautiful-sounding language, Plato seems to be saying.[83] All Tragedy has to offer is a seductive façade, a costume, a stage set, a lie; Philosophy is the pure gold, the real thing. Despite Socrates' tricky doubleness, or perhaps because of it, it is Agathon who is set up in this text to bear the weight of theatrical hypocrisy.

In this way, Agathon is a figure for the actor in Plato's text. The actor puts both himself and his audience at risk by engaging in mimesis of "low" characters (cowards, slaves, women), according to Plato's theories in the *Republic*; both stand a fair chance of being corrupted by imitation. The actor's imitation of unworthy people can lead to taking on their traits; the audience, watching, begins to forget itself, to sympathize with the low characters onstage, and possibly even to imitate them as well. In Plato's view, drama destabilizes identity. But Plato was not alone in his apprehensions about the power of drama's spell. The anecdote about Solon and Thespis mentioned in the Introduction speaks to this anxiety as well. Solon reproaches Thespis for lying (i.e., playing a character in a drama); Thespis replies that it is not harmful to act thus "in play" (μετὰ παιδιᾶς); Solon retorts that this sort of "play" will infiltrate regular life if people are encouraged to approve of it onstage (Plut. *vit. sol.* 29.5). Solon, the Athenians' culture-hero, expresses their own fear that acting, lying, could infect the daily life of people who go to the theater. This anecdote, along with Plato's ideas, provides some evidence for a widespread sense of anxiety about drama in theater-mad Athens.[84] Drama has both a didactic

---

ways that Socrates consistently confounds the roles of *erastes* and *eromenos* in order to create reciprocal relationships based on philosophical dialogue. While this argument is intriguing, it passes over the uncomfortable mismatch between Socrates' appearance (he looks like an old, ugly, bald *erastes*) and his inner essence (he plays the philosophically pure *eromenos*), which, in any other character in a Platonic dialogue, would be loaded with moral censure – and which, Edmonds concedes, the other characters in the dialogue find "unnerving" (276).

[83] Anton (1996) 211 reads Socrates' initial response to Agathon's speech – "who could fail to be astonished at hearing the beauty of its words and phrases?" – as ironic.

[84] Choricius' "Speech on behalf of those who live by acting plays of Dionysus" 32.73 provides evidence for the continuation of this anxiety into the period of New Comedy. He says, "Is it really the case that, of the masks [*prosopa*] created by Menander, 'Moschion' has taught us to rape virgins? 'Chairestratos' to fall in love with harp girls? That 'Knemon' has made us cantankerous? And 'Smikrines' has turned us into

and an erotic aspect, and thus has the power to instill proper attitudes and behavior into spectators by making them desire to be like the characters onstage. At the same time, of course, this power has a negative potential: didacticism can go wrong, desire can be perverted, and spectatorship can turn everyone into actors. Agathon, as the glittering, deceptive, seductive face of Tragedy in the *Symposium*, is the character Plato fears we the audience will desire to imitate. That is why he insists on Agathon's doubleness, his duplicity, and why he immediately refutes Agathon's speech with Socrates'.

THE FIGURE OF AGATHON

Agathon's two theories of poetic composition in the *Thesmophoriazousai* are (1) the performance of one's true nature and (2) the impersonation of what one is not, the appropriation of what one lacks. These two mimetic theories, interestingly enough, correspond to the two theories of desire set forth in the *Symposium*: (1) Eros as like drawn to like (Aristophanes' myth of the halved whole; Agathon's identification of/with Eros as young and desirable), and (2) Eros as lack (Socrates' refutation of Agathon). The two theories of mimesis and the two theories of desire are concerned with a tension between identity and difference. Their parallelism suggests the way desire is aroused through drama: it is an oscillation between same and different, presence and absence, that provides the mechanism for both the experience of desire and the actor's craft.[85]

Agathon's doubleness in the *Symposium* is like his indeterminacy in the *Thesmophoriazousai*: by means of it he identifies himself with a role, an actor, or a genre; by means of it he crosses boundaries, puts identity into question, arouses desire, and opens a space of possibility. In each text, he is parodied and mocked, but each text must also portray him as seductive. In both texts – and perhaps in "real life" – Agathon raises questions about mimesis and identity, about the stability of the self within and outside of the theater.

We will never know how closely Aristophanes' and Plato's portraits of Agathon resembled the real person. One tantalizing connection between the fictional Agathon and the historical Agathon (as represented in

misers – Smikrines who is afraid that smoke may have stolen something from his house and made his getaway?" (trans. Wiles (1991) 92). The defense of acting suggests the nature of the attacks that were made on it: that its didactic power is potentially immoral.

[85] On desire as a dialectic between presence and absence, see Halperin (1992) 120.

Aristotle's *Poetics*) does exist, however. As we remember, Aristotle mentions Agathon as the inventor of *embolima*, interchangeable choral odes that could be used in any tragedy. He also credits Agathon with writing the first tragedy with entirely fictional characters, the *Anthos* or *Antheus*. If we bear in mind the strong identification the Greeks made, correctly or incorrectly, between the poet and his works, then both of these innovations suggest interesting ideas about popular perceptions of Agathon's own identity. The *embolima* suggest a kind of fragmentation, an ability or willingness to see wholes as composed of reusable parts. The *Anthos* or *Antheus* speaks to an enormous creativity, an ability to create characters, selves, out of nothing. Taken together, his two innovations in the tragic form suggest that Agathon was self-authoring, able to construct (and continually reconstruct) his own self, like his tragedies, out of common parts and his own ideas. In this sense also, Agathon is a proto-actor figure, someone around whom early anxieties about actors as duplicitous, malleable selves could coalesce. We will see how these anxieties were exploited in the next chapter on the rhetorical battle over character (in both the moral sense and the theatrical sense) waged by Aeschines and Demosthenes.

CHAPTER TWO

DEMOSTHENES VERSUS AESCHINES: THE RHETORIC OF SINCERITY

THE FOURTH CENTURY BCE USED TO BE THOUGHT OF, INFORMALLY, AS the century of oratory – as opposed to the fifth century, which was the century of drama (read: tragedy). This was understood to be a matter at least in part of the survival of texts, since we knew there to have been drama in the fourth century, and we knew there to have been trials in the fifth century (indeed, famous ones – Kleon's supposed prosecution of Aristophanes for slander, and, straddling the turn of the century, the trial of Socrates). But each century was thought to be marked, in some sense, by its dominant surviving textual tradition. Nowadays, scholars who work on performance issues are turning increasingly to the fourth century as a period which has much to tell us about the rise of the professional actor, the expansion of dramatic performance from Athens into the larger Greek world, the creation of a canon of dramatic texts and a repertoire of "old tragedies" and "old comedies" for performance, and the continuing production of new tragedy and new comedy.[1] Moreover, scholars have begun to trace the interactions between drama and oratory as competitive and at times complementary speech genres.[2] In this chapter, I will read four speeches – Aeschines 2 and 3, Demosthenes 18 and 19 – as historians have done with Greek oratory for a while now: to read between the lines and behind the assertions for evidence of daily social life, habits, attitudes, and practices.[3] These oratorical texts have much to tell us about acting,

---

[1] Lightfoot (2002); Easterling (1993); Xanthakis-Karamanos (1980); Ghiron-Bistagne (1976).

[2] See Easterling (1999); Scafuro (1997); Hall (1995); Graf (1991); Ober (1989) 152–5.

[3] This has proved to be a productive approach in many subfields of history: e.g., Davidson (1998), Halperin (1990), Winkler (1990), Dover (1989) for the history of sexuality; Cohen (1992) for economic history. For some cautionary remarks in the context of Demosthenes, see Golden (2000).

and although we might expect that the former actor Aeschines' orations might have more to say, we will find that Demosthenes' speeches are also extremely revealing of fourth-century attitudes toward actors and acting. Both orators use the language of theater as a flexible tool – to accuse their opponents of hypocrisy and fraud, and to depict themselves as sincere, truthful speakers. Both, as we will see, dwell on perceived gaps between appearance and reality as a sign of deceit, and both try to use the body as the ground of a sincere, consistent self.

Dramatic performance and oratory share some uncomfortable similarities – "uncomfortable," at least, from the perspective of orators. Both employ skillfully arranged language (often arranged by a writer who is not the speaker), vocal delivery, and gesture to induce a kind of belief in the speaker's emotions and character, his *ethos*.[4] In classical Athens, moreover, both dramatic performance and oratory were subject to a popular vote.[5] Of course, there are also clear differences; both seek to persuade an audience through the creation of a believable persona, but political oratory can produce real-life consequences that theater, presumably, cannot. Politics, as an arena officially open to any citizen of the Athenian democracy but still dominated in reality by the moneyed elite, had an interest in distancing itself from acting as a way of maintaining a status boundary.[6] ("You performed on stage, I was in the audience," says Demosthenes to Aeschines in the midst of a catalogue of their respective family statuses.) There was, in fact, a fine line that many orators routinely attempted to draw between political and forensic speechmaking, with its need to be taken as sincere, and acting, which was understood to be feigned. In attempting to draw this line, often with reference to an oratorical opponent, speakers had to take up the issue of sincerity in self-presentation, a move that had the potential to backfire. And when it does backfire, we see, for a moment, how accusations of hypocrisy – or protestations of sincerity – depend, for their significance, on their opposite. The concept of sincerity implies the concept of dissembling, and it can never completely eradicate the kernel of doubt that it plants.[7] Or, as one scholar has put it, describing Aristotle's theoretical discussion of oratorical self-presentation in the *Rhetoric*, "Aristotle's depictions of imitation and the

---

[4] See Scafuro (1997) 59.

[5] See Hall (1995) for an extended and fascinating treatment of this "isomorphism." See also Easterling (1999), esp. 159, 165.

[6] Ober (1989) 112–18.

[7] For a theoretically informed discussion of this concept in the context of Roman rhetorical handbooks, see Gunderson (2000).

deliberate construction of character (*ethos*) within rhetoric promote the illusion of naturalness and ordinary speech, an emphasis that can only have been propaedeutic to an awareness that authenticity can be a construct or a contrivance."[8]

DEMOSTHENES VERSUS AESCHINES: ORATORY, ACTING, AND SINCERITY

In their disputes about diplomatic embassies and civic honors, Demosthenes and Aeschines both call attention to the fine line between oratory and acting by contrasting themselves with each other. Each suggests that his opponent is a dissembling actor who manipulates the audience. Demosthenes warns the audience not to be swept away by Aeschines' fine voice and empty phrases; Aeschines makes it seem that the weak-voiced Demosthenes is jealous of his natural talent. Demosthenes, whom the ancient biographies depict as having achieved oratorical success through ferociously hard work in spite of his lack of talent,[9] suggests that Aeschines is using the same talents to win over his audience as an orator that he had used as a (bad) actor. Aeschines, the former actor who claims to use natural talent instead of sophistry, suggests that Demosthenes is just as covetous of applause as any actor. Briefly, Demosthenes depicts himself as a sincere citizen and Aeschines as a bad actor, while Aeschines attempts to debunk Demosthenes' sincere persona. For both, the claim to sincerity is a double-edged sword.

Both orators tap into broadly based sentiments about drama and its effect on the self, sentiments that are at times contradictory. Demosthenes tries to exploit popular suspicion of actors and acting, of the power drama has to make an audience believe a lie. The power of drama to inspire "false" emotion (or real emotion inspired by a false situation) is the point of an anecdote from Aelian (*VH* 14.40): the fourth-century tyrant Alexander of Pherai, while watching the tragic actor Theodoros, was so moved to pity that he jumped up and left the theater, exclaiming that it would be a terrible thing for him to be seen weeping over the sufferings of Hecuba and Polyxena when he had caused so many

---

[8] Swearingen (1994) 121–2. Trilling (1972) 86 notes that the conscious self-fashioning Aristotle requires of the "great-souled man" makes him into an actor.

[9] Plut. *Vit. Dem.* 5–8. Cooper (2000) demonstrates that this depiction was originally constructed by the Peripatetics, who were hostile to Demosthenes and considered it an insult, although it was later given a positive spin; see below. See also Gunderson (2000) 100–07 for Roman accounts of Demosthenes that stressed his relentless hard work and "self-mastery."

deaths. The anecdote presents the tyrant's emotional reaction to dramatic illusion as morally inadequate at best – rather than act on his compassionate feelings, he flees – and depraved at worst. But other anecdotal evidence suggests the existence of the opposite pole in popular thought: a level of comfort with drama's pretense, an appreciation of feigning without confusing it for reality. This is the attitude toward theater that Aeschines plays on, and it could be summed up in an anecdote about the late–fourth century comic actor Parmenon from Plutarch's *Moralia* (18c, 674b): Parmenon imitated a pig's squeal in a kind of mimicry competition. Parmenon's enemies brought a live pig into the theater to show up his imitation, and when the pig squealed, the audience shouted "Good, but not as good as Parmenon's" – which became a proverb! The development of this proverb suggests a widespread conception that artistic enhancement often "improves" reality, rather than threatening it; this is, after all, the orator's job in turning everyday speech into persuasive, aesthetically pleasing argumentation. Both of these anecdotes represent attitudes about acting that were current in the fourth century, I suggest, even if they contradict each other. And our orators make use of both positive and negative attitudes toward acting at critical moments in their speeches, to arouse the emotions vital to their success in their audience. Consistency of argument was not as important as consistency in the construction, by whatever rhetorical means possible, of an *ethos* that was trustworthy, honest, and above all, sincere.

The terms of Aeschines' and Demosthenes' oratorical and political rivalry have carried over into scholarly debate. Critics and commentators routinely employ a rhetoric of sincerity when they contrast Demosthenes' and Aeschines' political programs; the estimation of sincerity also seems to form part of their estimation of literary quality for these two orators. Demosthenes, the argument goes, truly believed in the political program he urged on the Athenians (at least once he made up his mind to oppose Macedon), and his oratory, partly as a result of this sincere conviction, attains true sublimity.[10] (Notice the use of "true" on both sides of the equation, as it were.)

---

[10] G. L. Cawkwell, in his *Oxford Classical Dictionary* entry, sums up a fairly even-handed treatment of Demosthenes with this statement: "His claim to greatness rests on his singleness of purpose, his sincerity, and his lucid and convincing exposition of his argument" (*OCD*, third ed. (1996) 458). Sincerity is evidently a prerequisite of greatness. See Worthington (2000) 3 for a quick synopsis of the scholarly view of Demosthenes as a statesman-hero. See also Badian (2000) and Cawkwell (1969) for debunking views of his political and moral heroism.

Aeschines' oratory is considered to be inferior to Demosthenes' because it feels shallow and insincere, lacking in profundity and sublimity; it is inferior to Demosthenes' because Aeschines' political convictions were not genuine and unwavering, as Demosthenes' were.[11] Even Dyck, who stresses more than most scholars the calculated nature of the emotions presented by both Aeschines and Demosthenes, argues that Demosthenes' vilification of Aeschines in *On the Crown* did not necessarily arise out of "inauthentic" emotion.[12] Aeschines was an actor before he was an orator, which, I would suggest, critics tend to read back into his oratory. Edith Hall, in an excellent article on theatrical aspects of Greek oratory, reveals this perception when she describes a speech of Aeschines:

> Aeschines, histrionic as ever, titillates his audience by unusually offering to let his slaves be tortured in court during his allotted time (although this may have not been a serious possibility): he caps this offer with the invitation to his fellow citizens to rise up and execute him on the spot if the slaves should not corroborate his testimony (2.126).[13]

Aeschines' style as well as his content here seems to be labeled "histrionic"; his offer is dramatic and, it is also assumed, delivered in a dramatic way. Furthermore, he "titillates" his audience with his histrionic performance, suggesting that Aeschines' appeal lay in cheap thrills. Interestingly, Hall reveals the common scholarly blind spot when she goes on in the next paragraph to discuss other "dramatic" threats of violence in forensic speeches: "In one Demosthenic speech the jurors are begged to acquit the defendant, for the sake of his mother; if they do not, he will kill himself (57.70): conviction in this case would have meant being sold as a slave."[14] Aeschines is "histrionic" because he offers himself for immediate capital punishment if his slaves do not corroborate his testimony,[15] while the threat of immediate suicide in the speech written by Demosthenes is called "dramatic," but Demosthenes himself escapes such labeling.

---

[11] One of the very few modern studies of Aeschines' oratory begins with this sentence: "Aeschines cannot be regarded as one of the greatest orators in the history of Greek rhetoric." Kindstrand (1982) 15.

[12] Dyck (1985) 46.

[13] Hall (1995) 43. For a similar analysis of Aeschines' "histrionics," see Scafuro (1997) 64.

[14] Ibid.

[15] Gagarin (1996) argues compellingly that the βάσανος had become a "legal fiction" by the time of the orators, although see Mirhady (2000) 198 and n. 32 for the opposite view.

There are several reasons for this blind spot: Demosthenes' speech was delivered by someone else, thus allowing the logographer to distance himself from the performance of the speech; Aeschines' past profession as an actor marks him as a "histrionic" self, apparently for all time and in all settings; and as we will see, Demosthenes works especially hard to distance himself from theater in speeches he himself delivers. A vicious scholarly circle has arisen in which both Aeschines' and Demosthenes' characters and words are read through the filter (*ethos*) Demosthenes constructs of ostensibly sincere, authentic feeling.[16]

Demosthenes' moral lapses are also sometimes excused based on his sincere persona. Both Aeschines and Demosthenes deliver vicious personal attacks on each other, but Demosthenes' are often excused, to some extent, because he is felt to be attacking Aeschines out of concern for a larger goal. Similarly, Demosthenes is also often excused, albeit uneasily, for possibly writing two speeches on opposite sides of the same private suit (36, *For Phormion*, and 45, *Against Stephanus*); often the attribution of the latter is questioned. Murray's introduction to *Against Stephanus* in the 1936 Loeb lays out the reasoning on each side of the debate over the authenticity of the speech, noting that one side has little but "admiration for Demosthenes as orator and patriot" to recommend its denial of authenticity, while the other side takes the speech as genuine but excuses it on the grounds of political expediency.[17] Aeschines does not let his opponent off the hook so easily.[18] Sealey's recent study of Demosthenes accepts *Against Stephanus* as genuine and insists that the supposed ethical lapse was not an issue for the Athenians, who understood that Demosthenes was a paid speechwriter and continued to hire his services.[19] Undoubtedly this is in the main part true, but Sealey dismisses Aeschines' use of the issue far too quickly, saying that he tries to *make* it into an issue in order to get a response from the Athenian public. Surely Aeschines would not waste his time trying to arouse the jury's indignation over an action that everyone agreed was perfectly moral. Even aspects of Demosthenes' career that have traditionally aroused admiration can be read negatively: Demosthenes' constant involvement in

---

[16] On (mostly positive) perceptions of Demosthenes as orator and statesman throughout the ages, see the synopsis in Harding (2000).

[17] Murray (Loeb) (1936) 175. See also Badian (2000) 10; Mirhady (2000) 182.

[18] Aeschin. 3.64, 75.

[19] Sealey (1993) 136. The same argument is often used to excuse Demosthenes' opportunistic use of diametrically opposed arguments in different speeches, although see Badian (2000) 22.

political affairs, for example, could be read more as a sign of his ambitions than of his sincere political convictions, as Aeschines points out. Reading Aeschines against Demosthenes demonstrates that every claim they make about themselves or each other can be turned on its head. It also reveals that both orators use a fairly "histrionic" style to win over their audiences.

By reading their pairs of opposed speeches together (Demosthenes 19, *On the False Embassy*, and Aeschines 2, *On the Embassy*; Demosthenes 18, *On the Crown*, and Aeschines 3, *Against Ktesiphon*), we find that their rivalry returns again and again to certain accusations: bribery, cowardice, and bad acting. All three reflect stereotypes of the actor that were current from the fourth century BCE.[20] For example, Ps.-Aristotle *Problems* 30.10.956b12–16 wonders:

Διὰ τί οἱ Διονυσιακοὶ τεχνῖται ὡς ἐπὶ τὸ πολὺ πονηροί εἰσιν; ἢ ὅτι ἥκιστα λόγου σοφίας κοινωνοῦσι διὰ τὸ περὶ τὰς ἀναγκαίας τέχνας τὸ πολὺ μέρος τοῦ βίου εἶναι, καὶ ὅτι ἐν ἀκρασίαις τὸ πολὺ τοῦ βίου εἰσίν, τὰ δὲ καὶ ἐν ἀπορίαις; ἀμφότερα δὲ φαυλότητος παρασκευαστικά.

Why are the Artists of Dionysus [members of the actors' guild] for the most part worthless men? Is it because they have the least share of reason and wisdom, because the majority of their life is taken up with skills necessary for their livelihood, and because most of their life is spent in incontinence, and sometimes in poverty? Both of these conditions tend to produce meanness.

We can also see, from another angle, the saturation of Athenian culture by drama. It is a dominant metaphor, but beyond that, it is coming to be a dominant reality; for no other reason does Demosthenes desire so fiercely to be crowned in the Theater of Dionysus – and Aeschines desire to prevent it.

Demosthenes' *On the False Embassy* and Aeschines' *On the Embassy* bring out the themes of bribery, cowardice, and bad acting brilliantly. The two speeches are our best historical sources for the Athenian embassies

---

[20] Ghiron-Bistagne (1976) 191–2 argues that the actor's prestige began to wane in the fourth century (although "stars" were always highly regarded). She also claims that venality was a common complaint against actors. Her only evidence, unfortunately, is the quotation from ps-Aristotle and Demosthenes' allegations that Aeschines and other actors accepted Macedonian bribes.

to Philip in 347/6, but they paint such differing pictures of the events that historians "have not the faintest idea of what actually happened."[21] What the two speeches do corroborate is the ambition of both speakers for public recognition of their speaking ability, as well as their desire not to be perceived as frauds.

DEMOSTHENES 19: *ON THE FALSE EMBASSY*

Throughout his speech, Demosthenes depicts Aeschines as a corrupt, venal actor, someone who plays the patriotic orator at home but accepts bribes from Philip while visiting his court.[22] Demosthenes sets up his use of the theatrical metaphor from the outset of his speech: early on, he says Ischander was Aeschines' "supporting actor" (δευτεραγωνιστής) in an address Aeschines made to the Boule (10). When Aeschines wanted to display himself to Philip's ambassadors, he derided those who were trying to shout the ambassadors down, crying "Many shouters, but few fighters, when fighting is needed!" – "Being himself, I suppose," Demosthenes adds sarcastically, "such an incredible fighter, O Zeus!" (113) A little later on (120), Demosthenes claims that Aeschines picks up a new prosecution as easily as he studies a new play. Demosthenes warns the audience that his opponent will "tragedize" (τραγῳδεῖ) his defense (189) and chides him for a supposed melodramatic outburst –ἰοὺ ἰού! (209) In listing dishonorable, hired positions that Aeschines has held, Demosthenes includes his having been a τριταγωνιστής.[23] He characterizes Aeschines not simply as an actor – for to vilify actors in general might alienate his

---

[21] Todd (1990) 173. See also Buckler (2000) 117–40 and Appendix; Pelling (2000) 7; Harris (1995) 63–77.

[22] See Easterling (1999) 155.

[23] Based largely on this passage and its supercilious tone, many scholars have argued that the term τριταγωνιστής already meant "third-rate actor" by the fourth century BCE, as well as "actor who plays all the roles not played by the protagonist or deuteragonist." But see Pickard-Cambridge (1988) 132–5, who concludes that πρωταγωνιστής and δευτεραγωνιστής acquired metaphorical uses of "leader" and "seconder or supporter" early on, while "τριταγωνιστής, whenever it first came into use, gained an indelible colour from its use by Demosthenes as a weapon with which to beat Aeschines" (134). Furthermore, the pejorative tone of the word cannot come from its meaning "third-rate actor," but from its implication that the tritagonist was presumably the least talented in the troupe (135). Aeschines did not perform with "roarers," but with some of the finest actors of his day, including Theodoros, Aristodemos, and Thettalos: see Pickard-Cambridge (1988) 135 n. 1; Dover (1976) 32.

theater-loving audience – but as a *bad* actor, someone who will take on any role for money, and perform it poorly.[24]

Demosthenes makes a peculiar argument at one point (243–50), when he criticizes Aeschines both for quoting lines of drama (in his speech *Against Timarchus*) that he never spoke onstage and for failing to quote lines that he did speak onstage. Demosthenes has the clerk read lines that Aeschines supposedly spoke when he was a tritagonist, playing the stock tyrant Kreon.[25] Aeschines failed to use these lines in his oration, Demosthenes says, because he knows they make him look bad: in them, Kreon denounces the man who puts private interests above his country (*Antigone* 175–90).[26] Demosthenes is making a connection between the roles Aeschines has played onstage and his "real character"; it is as if Aeschines is only allowed to quote lines he has actually spoken in character, as if he must continue to play that character in his oration – unflattering speeches and all. It is a level of consistency that no orator would wish to be held to, of course, but Demosthenes' comic exaggeration brings up an interesting point: a perceptible gap between character played and "true self" weakens credibility.

Demosthenes proves to be a master of comic abuse,[27] in fact, calling Aeschines "bribe-taker (δωροδόκος), flatterer (κόλαξ), guilty under the curse (ταῖς ἄραις ἔνοχος), liar (ψεύστης), betrayer of his friends (τῶν φιλῶν προδότης)" (201), many of which are terms, even titles, taken straight from comedy.[28] He repeatedly brings up Aeschines' previous profession and uses it to suggest that Aeschines is untrustworthy, a

---

[24] Harris (1995) 30 and Kindstrand (1982) 20 note this insistence on the poor quality of Aeschines' acting in Demosthenes 18 and 19. See also Easterling (1999) 155, 161; Dyck (1985) 45 (on Dem. 18); Pearson (1976) 172, 183. Wilson (2000) 93–5 attempts to quantify Athenian love of drama by estimating the amount of money spent by *choregoi* on tragedy, comedy, and dithyramb in the Classical period.

[25] North (1952) 24–6 notes that Demosthenes, like most Attic orators, rarely uses direct quotation of poetry in his speeches. The exception is *On the False Embassy*, in which he himself reads three quotations and has the clerk read the fourth (mentioned above), from *Antigone*. Aeschines, on the other hand, quotes poetry freely and often, usually reading the shorter quotations himself and having the clerk read the longer ones. See Scafuro (1997) 158 n. 11; Kindstrand (1982) 22.

[26] See Easterling (1999) 157 n. 14.

[27] See Perelman (1964) 170–71.

[28] Rowe (1966) notes that Demosthenes' abuse of Aeschines in this speech is evocative of Greek comedy; I would suggest that Demosthenes does the same thing in *On the False Embassy*. Dyck (1985) 43–4 disputes Rowe's emphasis on the comic tone of the invective, arguing that most of Demosthenes' attacks are meant to provoke moral outrage, not laughter; I see no reason that they cannot provoke both.

swindler – yet at the same time he has to insist that Aeschines' treachery is easily detectable, or he has no case. He makes repeated assertions that Aeschines accepted bribes from Philip, without producing any hard evidence.[29] Aeschines' treachery is as obvious as his bad acting; in fact, it is obvious *because* of his bad acting.

Demosthenes concludes his speech with an exhortation to the audience not to vote for Aeschines, who has a beautiful voice but an evil soul; he urges the audience to remember when they hissed Aeschines offstage in a tragedy about Thyestes, forcing him to give up being a tritagonist (337–40). The analogy is clear: vote him down again and force him to give up being a politician this time. But it is more than an analogy, as Demosthenes himself would admit: Aeschines' orations are rather close to drama, which suggests that Demosthenes' speech is potentially a dramatic performance as well. It is because he is attempting to contrast himself with Aeschines that he has the clerk read the quotation from the *Antigone* instead of reading it aloud himself – as Aeschines might.

AESCHINES 2: *ON THE EMBASSY*

On the Embassy, Aeschines' reply to Demosthenes, turns Demosthenes' accusations about bad acting back on himself. He paints a picture of a Demosthenes consumed by professional jealousy, who uses sophistry solely for personal advancement and chokes under pressure. He is also a coward (79, 148) and a taker of bribes (3, 141). Aeschines begins his speech by voicing a concern that the audience has been "beguiled by Demosthenes' antitheses" (4), a typical oratorical move that calls attention to the eloquence of the other side in order to discredit it as merely fine rhetoric.[30] Aeschines then works to show that far from despising actors and their talents, Demosthenes was eager for the assistance of actors on the

---

[29] Buckler (2000) 135. Harvey (1985) 106 notes that allegations of bribery were often made against ambassadors dealing with foreign monarchies, suggesting that perhaps they stemmed from a misinterpretation of ξενία. In addition, he cautions that "When a speaker says, not that he has been unable to find any witnesses, but that it is so obvious that money changed hands that it is unnecessary to produce witnesses, we ought to be very suspicious indeed" (94). He goes on to cite examples of this tactic in Demosthenes 19.120, 19.331, 19.111, 19.119, 19.9, and 19.116–17; he cites no examples, interestingly enough, from Aeschines.

[30] Kindstrand (1982) 18 lists a number of passages in Aeschines' three extant orations "which seek to convey the impression that his own oratory is natural, while Demosthenes' is artful, referring to the latter's τέχναι (*Or.* 1.117, *Or.* 2.1, *Or.* 2.156, *Or.* 3.35, *Or.* 3.37, *Or.* 3.193) and even calling him τεχνίτης λογῶν (*Or.* 1.170 and *Or.* 3.200)."

embassy. He was so eager for the famous tragic actor Aristodemos to go on the embassy, in fact, that he moved to have envoys travel to the cities that had acting contracts with him and beg to have him released from those contracts, in order that he could participate in the diplomatic mission.[31] Once the embassy was completed, Demosthenes voted Aristodemos a crown (15–19). It was only later, says Aeschines, that Demosthenes tried to discredit the other ambassadors; having dared the rest of them to return to Athens and say something in praise of Philip, he then pounced on Ctesiphon's praise, saying, "He [Philip] seemed to Ctesiphon to be brilliant in appearance, but to me not better than Aristodemos the actor" (52).[32] Aeschines' allegation is clever: by his account, Demosthenes is the true hypocrite, setting up his colleagues and then turning on them in order to score points with the Athenian public.

Aeschines' account of Demosthenes' failure in front of Philip is equally adroit: Demosthenes had promised his fellow ambassadors a flood of eloquence when it was his turn to address Philip, but when the moment came to speak, he froze. Philip supposedly encouraged him by saying that he should not think that his pause was an irreparable calamity, *as if he were an actor onstage* (34–35; italics mine). Demosthenes remained frozen (ἐκπίπτει – a theatrical term[33]), silent and ashamed. Not only do Demosthenes' actions fail to live up to his words in Aeschines' account (just as Demosthenes accused Aeschines of failing to live up to Kreon's lines), but Aeschines is able to liken Demosthenes to an actor – and a bad one, at that – without being the one to call him that.

Aeschines' peroration finishes off the inversion of Demosthenes' accusations, suggesting that Demosthenes is a histrionic sophist and a hypocrite, one who condemns actors while attempting to conceal the fact that he is the biggest (and worst) actor of all:

Τῶν μὲν μαρτύρων διομνυμένων καὶ μαρτυρούντων ἀκούετε· τὰς δ' ἀνοσίους [τῶν λόγων] ταύτας τέχνας, ἃς οὗτος πρὸς νέους ἐπαγγέλλεται καὶ κέκρηται νυνὶ κατ' ἐμοῦ, ἆρα μέμνησθε, ὡς ἐπιδακρύσας καὶ τὴν Ἑλλάδα κατοδυράμενος καὶ Σάτυρον τὸν κωμικὸν ὑποκριτὴν προσεπαινέσας, ὅτι ξένους τινὰς ἑαυτοῦ

---

[31] Beginning in the fourth century, famous actors sometimes served on important diplomatic missions; see Csapo & Slater (1995) 243–4; Ghiron-Bistagne (1976) 156.

[32] Easterling (1999) 162 interprets this remark as Aeschines' insinuation that Demosthenes was "under the spell of Aristodemus" as well as the others, but this seems to ignore the context of the remark.

[33] Easterling (1999) 164.

αἰχμαλώτους σκάπτοντας ἐν τῷ Φιλίππου ἀμπελουργείῳ καὶ
δεδεμένους παρὰ πότον ἐξῃτήσατο παρὰ Φιλίππου, ταῦθ᾿ ὑποθεὶς
ἐπεῖπεν ἐντεινάμενος ταύτην τὴν ὀξεῖαν καὶ ἀνόσιον φωνήν, ᾿ὡς
δεινόν, εἰ ὁ μὲν τοὺς Καρίωνας καὶ Ξανθίας ὑποκρινόμενος οὕτως
εὐγενὴς καὶ μεγαλόψυχος γένοιτο, ἐγὼ δ᾿ ὁ τῆς μεγίστης πόλεως
σύβουλος, ὁ τοὺς μυρίους Ἀρχάδων νουθετῶν, οὐ κατάσχοιμι
τὴν ὕβριν, ἀλλὰ παραθερμανθείς, ὅθ᾿ ἡμᾶς εἱστία Ξενόδοκος τῶν
ἑταίρων τις τῶν Φιλίππου, ἕλκοιμι τῶν τριχῶν καὶ λαβὼν ῥυτῆρα
μαστιγοίην αἰχμάλωτον γυναῖκα.᾿   (Aeschin. 2.156–7)

You have heard the witnesses speak under oath and testify. But these
unholy arts of rhetoric, which he [Demosthenes] proffers to the young,
and has now used against me – do you remember how he wept and
grieved for Hellas and how he praised Satyros the comic actor, because
certain friends of his [Satyros'] were prisoners, digging in Philip's vine-
yard, and he [Satyros], drunk, begged Philip that they be released – how
after this he [Demosthenes] strained to lift up that sharp and unholy
voice of his and cried aloud, "How strange, that he who habitually plays
Karion or Xanthias has shown himself to be so noble and generous, and
that Aeschines on the other hand, the advisor of the greatest city, the
counselor of the Ten Thousand Arcadians, did not restrain his outrageous action, but hotly drunk, when Xenodokos, one of the retainers
of Philip, was entertaining us, he grabbed a captive woman by the hair
and took a whip and beat her!"

Demosthenes praises some actors but attacks Aeschines; he indulges in
theatrical groans and lamentations but has a weak and annoying voice.
He alternately glorifies and deprecates actors as he needs, but Aeschines
suggests that Demosthenes also depends on theater, on acting, for his
political survival.[34]

Aeschines ends his speech by underscoring the "reality" of his own
presentation: "My logos (μέν) is done; this my body (δέ) both I and the law
hand over to you" (Ὁ μὲν οὖν ἐμὸς λόγος εἴρηται, τὸ δὲ σῶμα τοὐμὸν
ἤδη παραδίδωσιν ὑμῖν καὶ ἐγὼ καὶ ὁ νόμος, 184). He uses his body as a
marker of this reality, displaying himself not as the actor behind the mask,
but the vulnerable person beneath the costume, onstage before his judges.
It is interesting that he splits himself into an "I" and a body here, with
the "I" handing over the body to be judged. The body is presented as the
ground of identity; the intellect, or soul (the "I"), may have produced
the logos, but it is only so many words without the physical embodied

---

[34] See Buckler (2000) 138–9.

presence to authorize and validate it. At the same time, however, the fact that the self is split into an "I" and a body suggests that there is some distance between those two parts. The "I" hands over the body as a guarantee, as a hostage; yet as we have already discussed, the body can lie. It seems impossible to rid the body of its theatrical nature, even when it is explicitly sought out as the ground of a stable identity.

THE VERDICT: AESCHINES' CHARACTER APPROVED

Aeschines was acquitted by a narrow margin, and the two had to wait for a number of years until an opportune moment came to challenge each other again. Demosthenes was in charge of the Theoric Fund in 337/6, and his associate Ktesiphon voted that he be crowned in the Theater of Dionysus during the City Dionysia in that year. Aeschines promptly challenged the motion as illegal, but due to more pressing political problems, the case did not come to court until 330. As plaintiff, Aeschines spoke first, delivering the speech we have as *Against Ktesiphon*; he based his legal argument on laws requiring the awarding of crowns to take place in the Pnyx or the Assembly and after the εὔθυνα, or formal audit at the end of an official's term, but he used the opportunity to attack Demosthenes' political career in general. Demosthenes refused to answer his opponent's charges in order, as required, and instead gave a masterful, general defense of his services to the state, mingled with vicious attacks on Aeschines' character and background. *On the Crown* is generally regarded not only as Demosthenes' masterpiece, but as the finest extant piece of Greek oratory. It won over the jury so completely that Aeschines failed to get even the requisite one-fifth of the votes necessary to avoid banishment, and he retired from Athens, perhaps to teach rhetoric in Rhodes.[35] A close examination of the two speeches has led many scholars to conclude that Aeschines, legally speaking, was in the right.[36] They also seem to accept,

---

[35] Kindstrand (1982) 75–84 provides a thorough discussion of the sources for this bit of biographical information. He concludes that it is most likely true but cautions that going into exile after losing a competition is a common *topos* in the ancient biographies of Greek poets; see Lefkowitz (1981) 43–4, 71–2, 92, 129–30. In addition, Kindstrand (1982) 75 notes that Aeschines' supposed exile bears striking similarities to Apollonius Rhodius'; he, too, supposedly left Athens to teach in Rhodes.

[36] Buckler (2000) 147; Pearson (1976) 178; Rowe (1966) 405. On the legal merits of Aeschines' charges, see Gwatkin (1957), who finds that Aeschines was in the right on his two main objections to the crowning.

for the most part, Demosthenes' self-portrait as a noble-minded, coura-geous voice in the wilderness, even a tragic hero. The view of Demos-thenes as tragic hero is no accidental choice of metaphor; he uses the language of comedy consistently to characterize Aeschines and reserves tragic diction for himself.[37] Thus we see, once again, Demosthenes vil-ifying his opponent for being an actor while still availing himself of the power of the theatrical metaphor – and of real acting.

AESCHINES 3: *AGAINST KTESIPHON*

Aeschines' *Against Ktesiphon* lays out his objections against the motion to crown Demosthenes clearly and carefully. In doing so, he also reveals the extent to which politics has become (or has always been) a theatri-cal business. Laws were enacted that forbade being awarded a crown in the theater, Aeschines argues, because many people were using the the-ater as the site for making proclamations, freeing slaves, and receiving crowns from demes and foreign cities. As a result, those citizens who were awarded crowns legitimately in front of only the Assembly on the Pnyx, were less honored than those awarded crowns in the theater in front of all of Athens and foreigners. Furthermore, he asserts, the actors, *choregoi*, and spectators were all irritated by the awarding of crowns in the theater; presumably, the actors and *choregoi* at least were irritated because the awarding of crowns was drawing attention away from the performance (41–3). That people were choosing the theater as the site for public recognition of political actions, largesse, or honors bestowed, suggests that a "theatricalized" event was felt to have more clout, more impact – in Bourdieu's term, more symbolic capital.[38] It also suggests the motive for Ktesiphon's motion to crown Demosthenes in the theater.

Aeschines' speech brings in the motifs of bribery, cowardice, and bad acting to suggest that Demosthenes is deeply unworthy of being awarded a crown at all, much less in front of foreigners at the theater. In a series of unflattering stories about Demosthenes, Aeschines mentions "that story about Meidias and the knuckle sandwich that Demosthenes took in the orchestra when he was *choregos*, and how for 30 minas he sold both the outrage to himself and the vote of condemnation that the people had voted against Meidias in the Theater of Dionysus" (52). Aeschines sug-gests that Demosthenes has been physically assaulted in the same theater

---

[37] See Rowe (1966).
[38] Bourdieu (1977) 179.

previously, in direct contravention of the Athenian citizen male's prerogative of physical inviolability, and that rather than demand satisfaction, Demosthenes was willing to swallow the insult like a coward in exchange for money. In effect, Demosthenes undergoes public humiliation twice in this account: he is struck in front of an audience, and he settles out of court for money with everyone's knowledge. This story sets up an association among Demosthenes, the Theater of Dionysus, and bribery that leads to humiliation. The association comes up again in a later anecdote about Demosthenes' treatment of Philip's ambassadors: Aeschines reminds the audience how they hissed Demosthenes when he brought the ambassadors into the theater, seated them on cushions, and generally fawned on them (76).[39] Once again, Aeschines suggests, Demosthenes is willing to be humiliated in the Theater of Dionysus, as long as he is paid enough. Aeschines' account of Demosthenes being hissed in the theater forms a kind of reply to Demosthenes' earlier story of Aeschines being hissed out of his acting career; both allege that the other's bad acting has incurred public disfavor.

Aeschines uses theater in other interesting ways in this speech. He suggests that Demosthenes is a histrionic orator who will attempt to manipulate the audience's sympathies: "For he [Ktesiphon] will bring in besides this wizard and thief and constitution-shredder. This man weeps more easily than other men laugh, and he perjures most easily of all" (207). Moments later he addresses Demosthenes directly (if with rhetorical questions): "In a word, why the tears? Why the shouting? Why this straining of the voice? Is it not Ktesiphon who is the defendant?" (210). Another tactic is to suggest that awarding Demosthenes a crown would be a real tragedy, or, put another way, that Demosthenes is not a fit tragic hero. Aeschines asks his audience to imagine two different scenarios:

γένεσθε δή μοι μικρὸν χρόνον τὴν διανοίαν μὴ ἐν τῷ δικαστηρίῳ, ἀλλ' ἐν τῷ θεάτρῳ, καὶ νομίσαθ' ὁρᾶν προϊόντα τὸν κήρυκα καὶ τὴν ἐκ τοῦ ψηφίσματος ἀνάρρησιν μέλλουσαν γίγνεσθαι καὶ λογίσασθε πότερ' οἴεσθε τοὺς οἰκείους τῶν τελευτησάντων πλείω δάκρυα ἀφήσειν ἐπὶ ταῖς τραγῳδίαις καὶ τοῖς ἡρωικοῖς πάθεσι τοῖς μετὰ ταῦτ' ἐπεισιοῦσιν, ἢ ἐπὶ τῇ τῆς πόλεως ἀγνωμοσύνῃ.

(Aeschin. 3.153)

---

[39] Theophrastos Characters 2.11 describes "The Toady" (Κόλαξ): "And in the theater, snatching the cushions from the slave, he himself spreads them out [for his patron]." On the κόλαξ, see ch. 3.

Please pretend for a little while that you are not in the courtroom, but in the theater, and imagine that you see the herald coming forward to make the proclamation from the measure passed by the vote; consider whether you believe the relatives of the dead will weep more over the tragedies and the sufferings of the heroes soon to be presented on the stage after this, or over the folly of the city.

καὶ εἰ μέν τις τῶν τραγικῶν ποιητῶν τῶν μετὰ ταῦτα ἐπεισα-
γόντων ποιήσειεν ἐν τραγῳδίᾳ τὸν Θερσίτην ὑπὸ τῶν Ἑλλήνων
στεφανούμενον, οὐδεὶς ἂν ὑμῶν ὑπομείνειεν, ὅτι φησίν Ὅμηρος ἄναν-
δρον αὐτὸν εἶναι καὶ συκοφάντην· αὐτοὶ δ᾽ ὅταν τὸν τοιοῦτον ἄνθρ-
ωπον στεφανῶτε, οὐκ <ἂν> οἴεσθε ἐν ταῖς τῶν Ἑλλήνων δόξαις
συρίττεσθαι;   (*Aeschin.* 3.231)

And if some one of the tragic poets who bring on their plays after the crowning were to represent in a tragedy Thersites crowned by the Greeks, none of you would endure it, for Homer says he was a coward and a slanderer; but when you yourselves crown this sort of man, do you not think that you would be hissed in the opinion of Hellas?

The first quotation plays on the false-yet-real nature of the emotion engendered by a theatrical performance, as brought out in the anecdote above about Alexander of Pherai watching Theodoros. Aeschines suggests that, as powerful as the tragedies will be, the relatives of slain Athenian soldiers will find it more grievous that Demosthenes is awarded a crown – and implicitly, that "real" pain ultimately outweighs that experienced while watching a theatrical production. The second quotation shifts the terms slightly in anticipating Demosthenes' self-presentation as a tragic hero. Far from being the equivalent of a tragic hero, Demosthenes is a Thersites: a cowardly, ignoble, slanderous, quarrelsome fool.[40] You would not stand for this in art, Aeschines says; do not stand for it in real life. His final use of the theatrical metaphor is fascinating: if Demosthenes should be crowned by Athens, the rest of Greece will hiss the city – offstage, perhaps. Politics is a drama performed in view of the whole world.

---

[40] Easterling (1999) 164 traces "hints" that Aeschines drops in his two speeches against Demosthenes – hints about his weak voice, his stage fright, and his poor acting – that "when it comes to images of failed actors Demosthenes fills the bill better than Aeschines."

DEMOSTHENES 18: *ON THE CROWN*

In his reply, *On the Crown*, Demosthenes does indeed portray himself as a tragic hero, with Athens as his supporting chorus. By reminding the citizens of their role in approving his policies, Demosthenes implicates all of Athens in his failures – but he also salves their sense of defeat with his ennobling rhetoric. Throughout the speech, Demosthenes works the political and military setbacks of the last sixty years into the Tragedy of Athens, transmuting the anguish of real defeat into an aesthetic appreciation of the city's (and his own) heroic struggle. Aeschines is cast, not surprisingly, as the villain, but Demosthenes portrays him as both comic buffoon and bombastic would-be tragedian. Demosthenes has it both ways; he uses the resources of comedy and tragedy for himself as well as his opponent, ridiculing him with coarse invective one moment and arrogating the language of high pathos for himself (and the citizens of Athens) the next moment.

Demosthenes' basic argument is that he deserves to be awarded a crown (in the Theater of Dionysus, incidentally) because his policies, while unsuccessful, were morally right. He waves off the allegation that he wants to be crowned illegally in the theater because of a desire for greater glory, claiming disingenuously that the person crowned is happy to be crowned anywhere, but that the award of a crown in the theater inspires a greater number of spectators to greater virtue and civic service (120).[41] He also dismisses the charge that he cannot be awarded a crown before undergoing his εὔθυνα, arguing loftily that he has been accountable to the city during his entire lifetime of service (111). Since they have approved his policies, they have by implication officially approved his conduct in office. This is the move by which Demosthenes implicates the city in his failures[42]; the next move is to translate political failure into art.

He achieves this translation by invoking Fortune. It is Fortune, not Demosthenes, who is responsible for the failures of his policies; all he could do was point out the only honorable course for the city to take

---

[41] Dyck (1985) 42–3 notes that one reason Demosthenes attacks Aeschines' character so harshly in this speech is that it enables him to avoid appearing to praise himself excessively; by vilifying Aeschines the foil, Demosthenes implicitly appears heroic. Dyck also notes that Plutarch cites *On the Crown* as a superlative example of skillfully executed self-praise (*Mor.* 542b, 543b).

[42] Pearson (1976) 171 points out that Demosthenes does a similar thing in *On the False Embassy* 218–20, only in that passage he gives the city a choice between blaming itself for the Peace of Philocrates and blaming Aeschines. Dyck (1985) 45 reads Dem. 18 as implicating Aeschines in the city's defeat.

(69–72, 189–94, 199–200, 271). This is the plot of tragedy, and Demosthenes creates a tragic narrative of his role in the city's affairs in his
speech.[43] Perhaps the clearest example of this move comes in Demosthenes' description of the city thrown into turmoil by the news that
Elatea had been taken by Philip (169). He begins the section vividly: "It
was evening. Someone brought a message to the prytanies that Elatea had
been taken...."[44] He proceeds to describe the Boule hastily convened,
a mob of anxious citizens swelling their ranks, and the repeated cries for
someone, anyone, to address the people. No one comes forward (169–
72) until Demosthenes does (173), and he goes on to repeat (supposedly)
the speech he made then (174–78). This speech-within-a-narrative is
reminiscent of the messenger speech in tragedy,[45] but it serves a different purpose here: if I may coin a term, auto-ethopoeia. Demosthenes
the orator gets to play Demosthenes the Champion of Athens' Independence, the Tragic Hero – the character he has been working hard
to create[46] – *within* this masterful speech. This self-contained episode
is as poetic, as stirring, as dramatic as any tragedy. Demosthenes makes
his role clear when he accuses Aeschines of casting himself as some legendary tragic hero, "a Kresphontes or a Kreon, or that Oenomaos you
once mangled terribly at Kollytos" (180) and of casting Demosthenes as
"Battalos," his vulgar nickname from childhood.[47] "Well, at that crucial
moment, I, the Battalos of Paeania, was seen to be worth more to the
country than you, the Oenomaos of Kothokidai" (180). His implication,
of course, is that Aeschines has duplicitously cast them in each other's
roles, while Demosthenes has matched up inner essence and dramatic role
correctly.

By co-opting the language and imagery of tragedy, Demosthenes
makes himself into a doomed, noble hero. The city may have been

---

[43] See Rowe (1966) 404. He argues that Demosthenes modestly represents Athens, and
not himself, as the protagonist in the tragedy.

[44] *On the Sublime* 10 includes this line (and what follows) in its list of awe-inspiring passages. The author also discusses Demosthenes' oath by those who fell at Marathon
(Dem. 18.208) as an example of the successful concealment of artistic ingenuity
through sublimity so as not to appear too tricky or deceptive (16). See also Buckler
(2000) 144 on the "stirring picture" Demosthenes paints here of Athens, heroic in its
isolation, which is "doubtless dramatically embellished."

[45] See Hall (1995) 53–4 and *passim.*

[46] Hall (1995) 49: "Winning a case required the adoption of a believable character. Every
litigant and every corroborative speaker needed to convince the jury that his character
(*ethos*) was authentic."

[47] Aeschin. 2.99; Plut. *Vit. Dem.* 4.

defeated, but in the person of its leading statesman it retains a kind of victory:

καὶ μὴν τὸ διαφθαρῆναι χρήμασιν ἢ μὴ κεκράτηκα Φίλιππον· ὥσπερ γὰρ ὁ ὠνούμενος νενίκηκε τὸν λαβόντα, ἐὰν πρίηται, οὕτως ὁ μὴ λαβὼν [καί διαφθαρείς] νενίκηκε τὸν ὠνούμενον. ὥστε ἀήττητος ἡ πόλις τὸ κατ' ἐμέ.   (Dem. 18.247)

And indeed, in terms of being corrupted by bribes or not, I conquered Philip; for just as the briber has conquered the one taking his bribe, so the one who refuses to be corrupted has conquered the briber. Thus the city was unconquered as far as I was concerned.[48]

Through Demosthenes, Athens has won a moral, if not a military, contest with Philip. His use of tragic imagery also transforms his audience from actors in their own political affairs into spectators of the city's fortunes. He enables them to find a kind of (cathartic?) pleasure in their experience of defeat and subjugation to a foreign power: the pleasure experienced by an audience watching a tragedy. And that pleasure is all the greater for them because it comes in contemplating their own (and his) heroic, doomed actions. It is a self-validating circle – one from which Aeschines is entirely excluded.

Demosthenes must use these arguments and this rhetorical strategy subtly, because he wants to appear as a tragic *character*, but to resist seeming like an *actor*. As always, he works to associate Aeschines with all of the negative stereotypes of the theater, and yet quietly to appropriate theater's power to himself. For example, after lambasting Aeschines for swearing melodramatic oaths ("as if he were in a tragedy crying out 'O Earth and Sun and Virtue' and that sort of thing" 127–8), Demosthenes goes on to utter some ponderous ones himself: the solemn invocation of all the gods and goddesses of Attica (141) and the famous oath by those who died at

---

[48] There is an interesting parallel here between Demosthenes' language about bribery and the Athenians' view, as is now generally accepted, of "passive homosexuality" (but see my discussion of this topic in Chapter 1). The man who purchases "defeats" the man who sells himself (compare Aeschines' portrait of Timarchus), while the man who refuses to sell himself remains "unconquered" in his person. According to Harvey (1985) 81, giving bribes was not necessarily dishonorable, as long as the bribes were thought to work in Athens' interest, but taking bribes was a frequent accusation made by politicians against each other. The same active/passive, zero-sum dynamic seems to be at work here that Foucault, Halperin, Winkler, et al. have traced in Athenian thought about adult males who engage in same-sex sex: to give is fine, but to receive, especially for pay, is shameful. This also brings up the association of actors with prostitutes, which we will see in chapter 4.

Marathon (208). Demosthenes' style, in fact, is at least as "histrionic" as Aeschines', if not more so, in *On the Crown*. He appeals directly to the audience quite often in this speech, broadening his language to include all of Athens (see especially 88).[49] He prompts the audience to shout the right answer to the question, "Which does Aeschines seem to you to be, a hired servant or a friend of Alexander?" (52).[50] These tactics resemble the address to the chorus in tragedy, or the direct audience address of a comic parabasis. He addresses his opponent directly as well, often with derogatory epithets, sometimes asking him questions to which, of course, no answer is given or expected.[51] In this way, he simulates dramatic dialogue – or rather, he performs a monologue masquerading as a dialogue with a recalcitrant partner. Other theatrical flourishes include his use of oaths, as mentioned above; his use of comic invective, as described below; his mimicry of Aeschines (while claiming that Aeschines was mimicking him); his highly wrought, poetic language; and his many rhetorical questions. One study of Demosthenes' rhetorical skill even imagines his stage gestures, as at 18.49: "Demosthenes says he has described these past events in order to cleanse himself of the 'stale dregs' of Aeschines' dishonesty, with which Aeschines has drenched him (one can see him, with an expression of disgust on his face, brushing at imaginary stains on his gown)."[52]

Demosthenes employs a remarkable amount of comic-style abuse in his speech.[53] He repeatedly maligns Aeschines' entire family, calling his

---

[49] "He addresses the jury as though they were not merely representative of the people, but the people itself": Loeb Introduction to *On the Crown* (1936) 16.

[50] See Bers (1985) and Hall (1995) 44 on this phenomenon. Both critics see it as "unscripted response" (Hall's words), but it certainly appears right on cue. To be fair, Aeschines uses it as well, in *Against Timarchus* (Aeschin. 1.159).

[51] 19, 22–3, 41, 51–2, 66, 69–70, 73, 82, 113, 117, 120–31, 140, 150, 162, 180, 191–3, 196–8, 200, 208–9, 217, 222, 233, 238–43, 245, 256–66, 270–73, 280–90, 297–8, 307, 309–20.

[52] Pearson (1976) 183–4. Pearson uses a fairly sustained theatrical metaphor to describe Demosthenes' art in *On the False Embassy* and *On the Crown*; see 158–99. Most interesting is his observation that Demosthenes tends to have only three characters "onstage" at any one time in his speeches (50, 192).

[53] Rowe (1966) 397–8 finds that "Out of 47 instances of derogatory epithet in the *Oration on the Crown*, 39 can be found in the plays of Aristophanes and in the comic fragments." He is quick to point out that this tally does not necessarily mean that those epithets are found only in comedy; they may not be "essentially" comic. But it does suggest that there is a correspondence between Demosthenes' language and comic invective. See Rowe (1966) passim for a detailed analysis of types of comic language to be found in this speech.

mother a whore and his father a slave. He alleges that Aeschines' mother led orgiastic religious rites in which she made the young boy play a part, preparing him for the life of a tritagonist (129, 259–60; see 19.199–200); her nickname was Empousa from her profession (130).[54] His father was a slave schoolmaster who also used to require Aeschines' assistance on the job (129, 258). Taken together, these insults suggest not only the usual dishonor for each sex (for a woman, being unchaste; for a man, being servile), but a particularly apt background for an actor to grow up in.[55] Objectively, an actor would have to possess literacy[56] and some training in performance; stereotypically, an actor would excel early on in shamming religious ecstasy, participating in licentious behavior, attending on richer people,[57] and performing behind-the-scenes menial tasks.

Demosthenes also uses derogatory comic epithets for Aeschines: κίναδος ("fox," 162), with an obvious pun on κίναιδος ("male slut"); αἰσχύνη ("shameless," 308; On the False Embassy 255), with a play on the name Aeschines;[58] βάσκανος ἰαμβειοφάγος ("malicious poetaster"; literally, "glutton of iambics" 139); αὐτοτραγικός πίθηκος, ἀρουραῖος Οἰνόμαος, παράσημος ῥήτωρ ("a born tragic ape, a rustic Oinomaos, a counterfeit orator," 242).[59] Shamelessness and bad acting, as always, are the charges. The effect of Demosthenes' repeated comic abuse is to cast Aeschines as the butt of his jokes, as a character from comedy with whom no one sympathizes. At the same time, as we have seen, Demosthenes

---

[54] Empousa was a familiar character from folklore and mime, a shape-changing female monster who sometimes ate children. It is tempting to infer that Demosthenes uses this name to suggest that Aeschines' mother, like her son, was also a hack actor, playing Empousa in crude mimes, but we cannot, of course, be certain.

[55] In On the False Embassy, Demosthenes alleges that Aeschines' brother-in-law "Kurebio" ("Offal") reveled unmasked (κωμάζει ἄνευ τοῦ πρόσωπου, 281; perhaps literally "he participated in a comic κῶμος"); Demosthenes attempts to connect nearly all of Aeschines' relatives to theater and shamelessness in some way.

[56] Harris (1995) 28 discusses the value of the traditional education which Aeschines' father, as a teacher, was able to give him; it was his one avenue of social mobility into the ranks of the kaloi kagathoi. Garton (1972) 59 suggests that one reason for the social mobility of Roman actors was their literacy, citing Cic. 2 Verr. 3.184, which implies that actors hope to climb the social ladder into the equestrian order by starting out as clerks.

[57] In fact, this may have been pure slander: Hall (1995) 45 assembles some evidence that actors in this period, at least the more famous ones, seem to have come from the same social class as logographers and politicians – that is, the upper class.

[58] Noted in Too (1995) 91.

[59] Connors (2004) 188–9 argues that "ape" was a term of abuse in Athenian culture that specifically connoted ugliness and/or deceit; see 188 on this passage in Demosthenes.

appropriates the language of tragedy to describe himself and Athens. Generically speaking, Demosthenes attempts to have it both ways: he pillories Aeschines for attempting to use tragic language, yet he uses it himself; he relegates Aeschines to the role of comic target, but – presumably – his use of comic invective brings him into the genre of comedy at some level. After all, his abuse of Aeschines must have gotten laughs for it to have been successful.[60] This last point, however, is never made by critics, who fall into the same blind spot concerning Demosthenes' comedy that also leads them to gloss over his potential ethical lapses and his shifting political career.[61] Demosthenes' speech is a masterpiece, in part, because it has persuaded even scholars to believe in the character of Demosthenes the Tragic Hero that Demosthenes the orator has fashioned within it.[62] No one remembers Aeschines' image of a crowned Thersites instead.

On the Crown has also fixed Aeschines' character, seemingly for all time, as a hack actor turned orator, while deflecting attention from Demosthenes' own histrionics. Demosthenes accuses Aeschines of "mimicking" (μιμούμενος, 232) his gestures and diction instead of criticizing his political agenda. Aeschines had attempted to show up Demosthenes as melodramatic, but with this deft maneuver, Demosthenes once again turns the tables on him. He reminds his audience that Aeschines entered the acting troupe of Simylus and Socrates, whom he dubs "the Heavy Groaners" (βαρυστόνοις, 262), as their tritagonist and claims that Aeschines made a better living from gathering the fruit thrown by the audience than by his acting ability.[63] Demosthenes' desire to distinguish himself (and his rather

---

[60] Demosthenes admits as much when he accuses the audience of wanting to see a show of good invective more than wanting to hear good policy from orators (138), which suggests that the audience for oratory is the same as, or at least similar to, the audience for comedy. Indeed, berating the audience is a comic trope (Aristophanes' *Knights, Clouds, Wasps, Frogs*; Cratinus, *PCG* F 360: "Hail, O greatly-laughing-at-stupidities-crowd, best of all judges at our wisdom on the days after the festival"). See also *On the False Embassy* 46.

[61] Rowe (1966) 401 notes that parody of tragedy is a specialty of comedy and that Demosthenes deflates Aeschines' pretensions to tragic grandeur (399), but he never connects the two; his conclusion is that Demosthenes successfully drives Aeschines into comic exile from the tragic world he has created.

[62] Again, after measured consideration of the events, including a critique of Demosthenes' policies, Cawkwell allows, "But the situation was tragic, and Demosthenes was certainly of heroic stature" (*OCD*, third ed. (1996) 458).

[63] Harris (1995) 31 argues that, contrary to Demosthenes' claims that Aeschines was driven from his acting career by hostile audiences, Aeschines most likely ceased acting

theatrical speechmaking) from Aeschines comes out most forcefully in his summary of their careers:

ἐδίδασκες γράμματα, ἐγὼ δ' ἐφοίτων. ἐτέλεις, ἐγὼ δ' ἐτελούμην. ἐγραμμάτευες, ἐγὼ δ' ἠκκλησίαζον. ἐτριτραγωνίστες, ἐγὼ δ' ἐθεώρουν. ἐξέπιπτες, ἐγὼ δ' ἐσύριττον. ὑπὲρ τῶν ἐχθρῶν πεπολίτευσαι πάντα, ἐγὼ δ' ὑπὲρ τῆς πατρίδος. (Dem. 18.265)⁶⁴

You taught reading; I was a student. You conducted initiations; I was initiated. You were an assembly-clerk; I was a speaker. You were a player of bit parts; I was in the audience. You broke down; I hissed. You have always served our enemies' interests in politics; I those of our country.

Demosthenes equates acting with poverty, worship of foreign cults, and political disloyalty, and sets himself up as the ideal Athenian citizen instead. Bad acting, he suggests, leads to treason. He positions himself as a spectator, in contrast to the actor Aeschines, and thereby aligns himself with the rest of the audience.

It is because Demosthenes is emphatically *not* an actor that he was chosen to deliver the funeral oration of 338: the Athenians preferred that the speaker should not "mourn their fate with his voice, acting, but feel their pain with them in his heart" (287). Here is the sincerity issue in its briefest formulation, framed by Demosthenes himself. "He [Aeschines] did not weep or feel this sort of thing at all in his heart, but, lifting up his voice and rejoicing and bellowing it was clear that he thought he was accusing me, but in fact furnished clear proof against himself that he did not feel the same way as the rest of them at those grievous events" (291).⁶⁵ While the term ὑποκριτής had a neutral moral significance in this period, "Demosthenes seems only to employ the words ὑποκριτής and ὑποκρίνεσθαι as terms of abuse, indicating that the oratory of Aeschines is characterized by both theatricality and hypocrisy."⁶⁶

---

because his advantageous marriage to a wealthier woman enabled him to stop working for a living and to enter politics instead.

⁶⁴ Wooten (1977) 261 asserts that "style is never simply an ornamentation in Demosthenes. It is always closely related to the thought which he wants to convey. It always reflects and reinforces that thought." In this climactic passage, the tight, paired contrasts, with the emphatic ἐγὼ always leading off Demosthenes' side, as it were, put Demosthenes literally on the side of right.

⁶⁵ Easterling (1999) 159 notes Demosthenes' "rather Gorgianic play on the contrast between 'soul' or 'heart' (*psuchē*) and 'voice' (*phōnē*) which is made twice (287 and 291, prepared for already in 280–1) in an impassioned passage a few paragraphs earlier."

⁶⁶ Kindstrand (1982) 20–21.

Aeschines is a feigning actor; Demosthenes is the authentic, sincere voice of the Athenian people's feelings. Aeschines only uses his acting talent to harm Athens, moreover: "Whenever there is something to be said against these people: it is then that your voice is at its most resonant and your memory at its best; then that you are the supreme actor, a tragic Theokrines [a notorious informer]" (313). Demosthenes makes even his own weak voice a mark of sincerity by associating Aeschines' famous voice with treasonous conduct[67]: just as Aeschines did in *On the Embassy*, Demosthenes here attempts to make the vulnerable, weak body (or its physical emanations) the ground of a true, stable, sincere identity.

The last contrast between the two speakers occurs toward the end of *On the Crown*, and Demosthenes presents it as Aeschines' ultimate offense:

Καὶ πρὸς τοῖς ἄλλοις, ὥσπερ αὐτὸς ἁπλῶς καὶ μετ' εὐνοίας πάντας εἰρηκὼς τοὺς λόγους, φυλάττειν ἐμὲ καὶ τηρεῖν ἐκέλευεν, ὅπως μὴ παρακρούσομαι μηδ' ἐξαπατήσω, δεινὸν καὶ γόητα καὶ σοφιστὴν καὶ τὰ τοιαῦτ' ὀνομάζων, ὡς ἐὰν πρότερός τις εἴπῃ τὰ προσόνθ' ἑαυτῷ περὶ ἄλλου, καὶ δὴ ταῦθ' οὕτως ἔχοντα, καὶ οὐκέτι τοὺς ἀκούοντας σκεψομένους τίς ποτ' αὐτός ἐστιν ὁ ταῦτα λέγων. ἐγὼ δ' οἶδ' ὅτι γιγνώσκετε τοῦτον ἅπαντες, καὶ πολὺ τούτῳ μᾶλλον ἢ ἐμοὶ νομίζετε ταῦτα προσεῖναι. κἀκεῖνο εὖ οἶδ' ὅτι τὴν ἐμὴν δεινότητα – ἔστω γάρ. καίτοι ἔγωγ' ὁρῶ τῆς τῶν λεγόντων δυνάμεως τοὺς ἀκούοντας τὸ πλεῖστον κυρίους.   (*Dem.* 18.276–7)

And in addition to these things, as if he himself were straightforward and he had made all his speeches with good will, he ordered you to guard against me and watch carefully that I do not mislead and deceive you, calling me a clever speaker and a wizard and sophist and that sort of thing, as if, when one man preemptively says things about another man which apply to himself, they are held to be so, and his audience will not examine what sort of man the speaker is. But I know that you all know him, and that you think that these charges apply to him far more than to me. And I know well that my eloquence – well, let that be. And yet I perceive that, for the most part, the audience is in control of the power of speakers.

Demosthenes depicts Aeschines as doing what *he* is really doing: claiming to make speeches out of a "disinterested and patriotic spirit," misleading the audience, and calling his opponent names that are more suitable for

---

[67] For a list of instances in which Demosthenes attempts to discredit Aeschines' fine voice, see Kindstrand (1982) 18. Easterling (1999) also focuses on the issue of Aeschines' voice and Demosthenes' attempts to neutralize its power.

himself. It is significant that he declines to discuss his own artfulness out of supposed modesty, and flatters the audience in so doing. Once again, everything one speaker says about his opponent can be turned on its head.

THE VERDICT: DEMOSTHENES THE TRAGIC HERO

Demosthenes won his audience over so completely that Aeschines failed to get one-fifth of the votes and was forced to withdraw from Athenian political life. It is interesting to note that in both cases we have examined, the jury voted to acquit the defendant, who spoke second. Both defendants, moreover, depicted their opponents as being motivated by spite and personal vendetta.[68] We could read the results of these two trials as votes against the jealous vendetta, or, perhaps, votes for the more likeable character. If the task of the orator is to create a winning character, then Aeschines in *On the Embassy* and Demosthenes in *On the Crown* seem to be engaged in creating the same stock character: the public-spirited politician, wrongfully accused by a jealous, vindictive sophist.[69] Similarly, the two orators appear to be playing the stock character of the spiteful, grudge-bearing enemy in *On the False Embassy* and *Against Ctesiphon*. Both times, the trial boils down to a contest between the tragic hero and the villain. The jury knows who to vote for.[70]

AESCHINES' BIOGRAPHY

The fourth century saw the rise of both the professional actor and the professional logographer. It also saw, in Athens, the beginnings of a more truly democratic kind of politician, in the sense that the leaders of the city were no longer solely members of the old, aristocratic families. The old snobbery of the *kaloi kagathoi* remained, but they had to admit a new generation of politicians with little or no illustrious heritage, men

---

[68] Aeschin. 2.139, 154, 180–83; Dem. 18.281–2; see Dem. 19.221–2. Badian (2000) 18–26 discusses the pronounced subtext of seeking revenge that structures even Demosthenes' early career.

[69] See Scafuro (1997) ch. 1 on the "staginess" of both informal dispute settlement and formal courtroom debate in fourth-century Athens.

[70] Pearson (1976) 179–81 notes some of the similarities between Aeschines' and Demosthenes' positions in the two cases.

who made their way up to the status of Assembly speaker by virtue of new money, new political connections, or simple oratorical talent.[71] Aeschines' life and career embody all three of these social trends. The son of free, citizen, but poor and unconnected parents, he worked as a clerk and as an actor, married well, and became a *rhetor*, a speaker at the Assembly, a political player.[72] His social mobility is one of the things Demosthenes, as a wealthy aristocrat, continually attacks. Both Aeschines' rise and Demosthenes' reaction speak to one component of ancient antitheatrical sentiment: it was motivated, at least in part, by the perception that skill in acting could lead to upward social mobility.[73] In Aeschines' case, his elevation in status seems to have been brought about by his marriage to a wealthy man's daughter, which some speculate he achieved by making social connections through military service;[74] it does not seem to have been a direct consequence of his acting career. But the easy applicability of Aeschines' acting skills to his political speechmaking, and his service as an ambassador, along with other actors, suggest that his career as an actor could have been seen as (ironically) good preparation for his move up the social and political ladder. The fear of social mobility led to prohibitions on actors playing certain kinds of roles in other theatrical

---

[71] Even in the later fifth century, there is evidence of anxiety about upward social mobility from both the elitist and the populist positions: the "Old Oligarch" grumbles about how in democratic Athens, anyone, no matter how poor, can address the Assembly ([Xen.] *Ath. pol.* 6); Strepsiades, in Aristophanes' *Clouds*, undertakes a pricey rhetorical education to pay off the debts his social-climbing son Pheidippides has incurred. One thinks also of the figure of Kleon in Aristophanes' comedies and Thucydides' history, the "son of a tanner" who became a leading political player.

[72] Harris (1995) 35. Ober (1989) 280–84 describes Aeschines' self-presentation in his speeches as a *kalos kagathos*, even as he admits to humble beginnings. Ober (1989) 112–18 emphasizes that even in the fourth century, politicians were members of the Athenian elite; he notes that those fourth-century public speakers who were not aristocrats by birth but (like Aeschines) married into the elite or made fortunes during their lifetimes tended to stress their aristocratic connections and pursuits. In other words, the ideology of the *rhetor* was still that he was *kalos kagathos*, even if he was a self-made *kalos kagathos*.

[73] It is in the fourth century that we begin to find anecdotes about actors being paid huge sums to perform, such as the one recorded in Aulus Gellius *NA* 11.9 in which an actor claims to be able to charge one talent for two days of performing; for other testimonia, see my ch. 3 n. 72. The fact that their fees were the subject of discussion suggests a certain level of anxiety about superstar actors. The fourth-century tragic actor Theodoros contributed 70 drachmas to the rebuilding of the Temple of Apollo at Delphi, while all other contributions recorded from private individuals are under 15 drachmas apiece: *FD* III 5.3.67.

[74] Harris (1995) 31–2, 36–40.

traditions.[75] We see the origins of this fear in the fourth century, but it will continue throughout the rest of this study.

DEMOSTHENES' BIOGRAPHICAL TRADITION

As for Demosthenes' life and career, the biographical tradition consistently associates him with acting and actors.[76] After a rocky start to his oratorical career, the story goes in Plutarch's *Life* of Demosthenes, the young Demosthenes happened to meet Satyros the actor, who taught him deportment and delivery.[77] The hardworking young orator promptly built an underground study and spent months at a time writing and rehearsing his speeches, shaving half his head to prevent himself from going out in public (5–8). He trained his weak voice by speaking with pebbles in his mouth, both while running and in front of a mirror (11). Eventually he grew so skilled and confident that he was able to give advice in turn: when a potential client came to him saying he had been assaulted, Demosthenes said, "On the contrary, you have suffered none of the things which you describe." When the man protested loudly and indignantly, Demosthenes replied, "Yes, by Zeus, now I hear the voice of someone who has been wronged and suffered" (11). There is also the famous anecdote from ps.-Plutarch's *Lives of the Ten Orators* (845a): when asked what the three most important components of oratory were, Demosthenes said, "Delivery, delivery, delivery."[78] Another anecdotal tradition emphasizes Demosthenes' connection with acting while at the same time contrasting the two occupations: an actor bragged to Demosthenes that he had been paid up to a talent for appearing in a single performance, and Demosthenes replied, topping him, "I have been paid more than that to keep quiet."[79] This anecdotal tradition, interestingly, hints at Demosthenes' association with bribery even as it suggests the intimidation he could arouse in his opponents.

Plutarch asserts that Demosthenes never grew skilled or confident enough to speak extempore, that he remained dependent on his habits of diligent preparation and (actorly) rehearsal (*Demosthenes* 8). One

---

[75] For Early Modern England, see Baker (1992).

[76] See Gunderson (2000) 120–24.

[77] Other biographical sources give different names for the actor who taught Demosthenes: see Easterling (2002) 333 and n. 23.

[78] See Cooper (2000) 231–2.

[79] See Easterling (2002) 331 and n. 14 for all the varied sources of this anecdote, which again give different names for the actor.

anecdote from another tradition may suggest he was capable of extempore speaking: while giving a speech for a defendant, Demosthenes perceived that the jurors were growing bored, and so he interrupted his defense with a story about two men who went to court over the shadow of a rented ass. Just when he was about to give the dénouement of the story, however, he left the *bema*. The jurors asked him what happened in the trial over the ass' shadow, and Demosthenes returned to the *bema* and rebuked them for caring more about an ass' shadow than about the life of the man whose fate they were actually judging.[80] Of course, this apparently spontaneous "digression" could just as easily have been a carefully planned part of Demosthenes' defense strategy – and its staginess is beyond question, whether spontaneous or rehearsed. Demosthenes' supposed inability (or unwillingness) to speak off the cuff is a fascinating aspect of his biographical tradition. We could read it as a defensive maneuver, akin to his abuse of Aeschines for having been an actor; refusing to speak on the spur of the moment could be a way of protecting himself from seeming "histrionic." Conversely, we could read it as a tacit admission that his speeches were studiously worked up to seem spontaneous, instead of being spontaneous, that he could not perform without a script. Demosthenes himself, of course, tried to have it both ways: he praises his own rehearsal of his speeches (21.191–2) while criticizing Aeschines for rehearsing his (19.255).[81] It is interesting to note that Aeschines was strongly associated with speaking extempore by ancient sources from Philostratus onwards, and that some later sources even regarded him as inventing it.[82]

Plutarch also raises the issues of cowardice and bribery. He rates Demosthenes as a great orator, instead of as a great public figure like Pericles, because Demosthenes was a coward in battle and accepted bribes from the Persians; he was better at exhorting others to virtue than at being virtuous himself (13). Far from living up to his speeches, Demosthenes threw away his shield at the Battle of Thermodon (20). When he accepted a bribe from the Persians, he came into the Assembly the next day with his neck wrapped in wool, pretending to have lost his voice; other politicians quipped that he had come down with silver quinsy (25).

---

[80] The anecdote is in Dem. fr. XIII B-S; it is recounted in Scafuro (1997) 57 n. 110, who cites it as evidence of Demosthenes' "theatricality."

[81] Scafuro (1997) 28 n. 14.

[82] Kindstrand (1982) 84–90. Because of his supposedly inspired and emotional delivery, Aeschines was also regarded as the founder of the Second Sophistic: Kindstrand (1982) 90–95.

After all this, it is not surprising that Demosthenes' death is presented as a tragedy, but Plutarch makes the metaphor literal: he dies at the hands of a tragic actor, taking refuge before an altar (which was the one fixed stage property of early tragedy). Demosthenes even "directs" the actor-assassin, scornfully showing himself to be above the dignity of a hack actor one last time. The story is as follows: Demosthenes fled Athens when Antipater was approaching, but Antipater sent Archias "the exile-hunter" after Demosthenes. This Archias was a former tragic actor who had worked with the famous Polos. In his new career as bounty hunter, he had cut out Hyperides' tongue. He followed Demosthenes to the temple of Poseidon in Kalauria. Demosthenes took refuge at the altar there, fell asleep, and dreamed that he and Archias were competing in rival tragedies for the actor's prize; in the dream he lost because Archias had greater resources. When he awoke, Archias entered the temple and attempted to persuade him to leave the altar with kind words. Demosthenes said, "O Archias, you never convinced me with your acting, and you do not persuade me with your promises now." Archias then became angry and began to threaten Demosthenes, at which Demosthenes said, "Now you speak the oracular truth [lit. 'the things from the Macedonian tripod']; before you were acting" (λέγεις τὰ ἐκ τοῦ Μακεδονικοῦ τρίποδος, ἄρτι δ' ὑπεκρίνου). He then asked Archias for time to compose a letter to his family. He covered his head, took out a tablet and a poisoned reed, and bit the reed as if in concentration until he knew the poison had entered his system. Then he uncovered his head and said, "Now you should not delay playing the role of Kreon from a tragedy and casting out this body of mine unburied." He then died (28–9).

This extended anecdote works in complicated ways to connect Demosthenes with theater and, at the same time, to reinforce his own projected image as superior to actors and acting. On the one hand, Demosthenes tries to deflate Archias' pretensions – to inspire terror, to project kindness – by pointing out that he is only an actor, and a bad one at that. (Sound familiar?) This is an attempt by Demosthenes to show mastery of a situation in which he is actually powerless, an attempt to deny the power (and "reality") of emotions aroused by theater. On the other hand, several other features of the story point to the "reality" of this tragedy. Demosthenes is pursued by a villain, takes refuge at the altar, refuses to leave it, and commits suicide in secret, just as in a tragedy.[83]

---

[83] What tragedy does he see himself playing in? The reference to casting out his body unburied suggests he sees himself as Polyneices, but Plutarch may be suggesting that

His dream also tacitly admits to what he refuses to acknowledge in his waking life: that his career is deeply indebted to drama, and that we can view his last days as a play – for he dreams that he is an actor, as well as Archias. Often, an anecdotal dream like this reveals a similarity between two different areas of human activity; compare the general Thrasyllus on the eve of the battle of Arginusae, who dreamed he and his generals were actors in one play, competing against enemy generals acting in another play.[84] That dream points out that acting and generalship have qualities in common. In Plutarch's story, however, Archias is already an actor, so that when Demosthenes dreams that he and Archias are competing for the actor's prize, the dream points out, not a hidden similarity on both sides, but a secret identity on one side.[85] Demosthenes *is* an actor.

The final indication of the "reality" of Demosthenes' tragedy is the repetition of a motif from earlier in the biography: Demosthenes provokes Archias into loud outrage, just as he earlier goaded a client into loud outrage. In both cases, Demosthenes' response is, "Ah, now you sound like a man who is truly ____" (injured/an assassin), but the implications seem opposed in the two anecdotes. When he prods Archias into dropping his wheedling talk, he claims that he has revealed the murderous intent under the kind façade. When he prods the client into sounding outraged, however, it sounds like he is coaching him. The echo of the earlier anecdote in the later account of Demosthenes' death creates a tension between Demosthenes' acknowledgement and denial of the power of acting. Plutarch's account of Demosthenes' tragic end has Demosthenes conquered by, and subsumed, into drama at the last.

The biographical tradition on Demosthenes provides us with another means of seeing the way Demosthenes' own concerns have infiltrated

---

he is playing Antigone instead. After all, Polyneices died in battle, while Demosthenes is supposedly a coward; Antigone is the one who defies the power of the new ruler after a war and commits suicide. This hint of a specific tragedy is especially tantalizing because it calls to mind Demosthenes' quoting from *Antigone* (Dem. 19.243–50) to rebuke Aeschines for stepping out of character – as Kreon.

[84] Diod. Sic. 13.97.6.

[85] Easterling (2002) 336–9 ("icon") has an interesting excursus on dreams involving actors in antiquity, which she states serve as clues to antiquity's "collective unconscious" (though she is mostly interested in them as prophetic). She interprets this particular dream as being fulfilled by Demosthenes' actions: he "is indeed a better actor than Archias, but he lacks the material resources to be successful in the 'competition'" (337) – having to resort to suicide by poisoned pen.

works that undertake to study him.[86] Plutarch depicts Demosthenes' life as entwined with theater and his death as a tragedy.[87] It is a kind of poetic justice for the orator who worked so strenuously to depict his opponent as histrionic, as a means of deflecting attention from his own melodramatic style. Drama had been a potent cultural force at Athens long enough for there to exist negative as well as positive images of actors, and the orator's job was similar enough to acting that those negative images could be used to browbeat an opponent in court, as Demosthenes did. Changing one's stance on political matters, failing to live up to one's promises on the battlefield, overacting in a lawcourt speech, dissembling in an address to the Boule – shamelessness, bribery, cowardice, bad acting – all these accusations speak to an ideal self that is consistent over time, and consistent within itself. As noted earlier, public perception of a gap between character played and "true self" weakened a speaker's credibility. Aeschines, on the other hand, while availing himself of the chance to ridicule Demosthenes' bombast and gestures, displays a comfort with drama that must also have been part of the Athenian audience's experience. Only a culture as in love with theater as Athens was could have produced plays that mocked theater, and a theater-mad audience, with such deadly comic accuracy. And only this sort of culture could have produced speeches such as *On the Crown*, a carefully crafted, melodramatic masterpiece disguised as a sincerely outraged attack on acting.

There is, in fact, something essentially theatrical about the Athenian democracy. Politicians and private individuals had to make speeches and win the vote from the jury, just as plays had to compete every year and win the vote from the audience at the dramatic festivals. Political heroes were crowned in the Theater of Dionysus. Politicians were expected to present a stable, predictable, consistent self – the exact opposite of an actor. Yet politicians were also expected to bring an actor's flair to their public speaking, while somehow avoiding the appearance of being

---

[86] For an excellent overview of the ancient biographical traditions about Demosthenes, see Cooper (2000), who argues that much of Plutarch's material comes from Hellenistic Peripatetic sources hostile to Demosthenes. Only in later centuries did Demosthenes' shortcomings, as viewed by the Peripatetics – his inability to extemporize, his hard work, his rehearsal, his melodramatic flair – come to be positively valued, as Demosthenes was canonized the greatest orator in antiquity (and his political opportunism was excused or ignored).

[87] More than one reader of Plutarch has gone so far as to compose a tragedy about the death of Demosthenes: see Sellén (1926) for an early twentieth-c. tragedy in Spanish, and see the discussion in Harding (2000) 263 for a nineteenth-c. tragedy in English.

histrionic. Changing one's political stance was a tense issue, often attributed by one's opponents to bribery;[88] the tension this aroused is evidence of an anxiety about the changeability of the self, or perhaps the gap between the appearance and reality of the self, which is evident in anecdotes about actors as well. Actors as well as politicians served as ambassadors, as we have seen in Demosthenes' and Aeschines' accounts of the embassy to Philip. Ambassadors were often accused of being bribed, and they were often portrayed in comedy as impostors, frauds, ἀλαζόνες. In the next chapter, we will explore the comic ἀλαζών as a figure for the actor in Greek society, and his counterpart, the κόλαξ, or flatterer–one of the names Aeschines calls Demosthenes (3.76) – as a figure for the actor in Roman society.

[88] Demosthenes (Dem. 19.303ff.) claims Aeschines changed his tune after he met with Philip because he was bribed. Aeschines 2.164 answers that by saying that the *demos* changed its mind as a whole. Aeschines (Aeschin. 2.165) says that Demosthenes wrote speeches for opposing litigants in the same court case, and in 3.64, 75, 79f., he charges Demosthenes with changing positions. In 2.152 he says, "It is not Macedon that makes men good or bad, but their own inborn natures; and we have not come back from the embassy changed men, but the same men that you yourselves sent out."

CHAPTER THREE

THE FRAUD AND THE FLATTERER: IMAGES OF ACTORS ON THE COMIC STAGE

S TOCK CHARACTERS ARE ONE OF THE FEATURES THAT DIFFERENTIATE
Old Comedy from Middle and New Comedy most clearly. Whereas
Aristophanes depicts recognizable public figures (Socrates, Kleon,
Euripides, Agathon),[1] Menander, Plautus, and Terence depict types (the
Grouch, the Young Man in Love, the Sweet Young Thing).[2] As scholars
have noted, however, there are stock characters lurking in the background
of many of Aristophanes' other stage personalities.[3] I am interested in
two of these characters, who survive well into Roman comedy and

---

[1] Socrates: Ael. *VH* 2.13, recounts that Socrates stood up in the theater of Dionysus during the performance of Aristophanes' *Clouds* so that the foreigners who were present
could figure out to whom the Socrates on stage was referring (and judge the likeness
of the mask). Kleon: *Knights* 230–33; see Pickard-Cambridge (1988) 218–19, who
recounts an ancient explanation for the disappearance of portrait-masks from Middle
and New Comedy: the fear of offending any Macedonian ruler by any perceived
caricature. Dover (1976) argues that portrait-masks would only have been feasible for
public figures with unusual and distinctive features, using the analogy of political car-
toons. He argues that the scholia are right in suggesting that a portrait-mask of Kleon
was not attempted, not, however, because of Aristophanes' fear of offending Kleon,
but because of the regularity of Kleon's features (16–24). Dover argues further that
Socrates would have presented the mask-maker with the unique challenge of making
a portrait of someone whose face already looked caricatured (26–8). On the mockery
of real individuals in Aristophanes, see Storey (1998).

[2] Pollux's list of mask-types, even though much later than Menander, provides indirect
evidence of the typing of character in New Comedy; see Green (1994) 154.

[3] Hunter (1985) 8–9. As Green (1994) 37 notes, it is possible that Aristophanes was
old-fashioned in his use of recognizable characters, or that we have an odd selection
of his plays, because the evidence from terracotta comic figurines suggests that stock
characters already existed by the end of the fifth century BCE. The "New York
Group" of terracotta figurines, dating from the late fifth century, even shows features
of Middle Comedy in its masks and characters: Green (1994) 63. See Wilkins (2000)
on the cook, who becomes a stock character in Middle and New Comedy but, he
argues, is present "in the wings" in Old Comedy.

extend even into other genres: the ἀλαζών and the κόλαξ. The Fraud, or Impostor, or Braggart, and the Flatterer, or Toady, or (as he comes to be known) the Parasite, have a significance beyond their brief appearances onstage in which they trouble the hero: they can both be read as meta-characters, figuring the Actor. They come to stand for related negative stereotypes of the actor in society: that the actor lays claim to a position or a relationship that he does not merit, that he is, by one means or another, a social climber. The *alazon* represents the Greek world's perceptions of actors, and the *parasitus*, those of the Roman world.

THE *ALAZON*: THE ACTOR AS FRAUD

As various professions developed in the late fifth and early fourth centuries BCE – for example, medicine, banking, acting, oratory, philosophy – so did the problem of people impersonating professionals.[4] One of the side effects of the proliferation of technical treatises on bodies of specialized knowledge was that anyone who could read could attempt to pass himself off as a member of a profession. It seems reasonable to assume that most people in ancient Greece would have preferred a "real" (i.e., highly trained) doctor to a "false" (i.e., thinly read and/or practically inexperienced) doctor. A good deal of anxiety arose in the fourth century over differentiating the genuine article from the impostor, as witnessed in philosophical texts from the fourth century. The sociologist Erving Goffman pinpoints one source of society's anxiety about the impostor:

> When we discover that someone with whom we have dealings is an impostor and out-and-out fraud, we are discovering that he did not have the right to play the part he played, that he was not an accredited incumbent of the relevant status. . . . Paradoxically, the more closely the impostor's performance approximates the real thing, the more intensely we may be threatened, for a competent performance by someone who proves to be an impostor may weaken in our minds the moral connection between legitimate authorization to play a part and the capacity to play it. (Skilled mimics, who admit all along that their intentions are unserious, seem to provide one way in which we can "work through" some of these anxieties.)[5]

---

[4] See, for example, Dean-Jones (2003) on individuals impersonating doctors beginning in the fourth century.

[5] Goffman (1959) 59.

Thus the stock comic character of the *alazon*, the impostor or fraud, provides a window through which both the general problem of impostors and the specific problem of the actor as a professional impostor can be viewed.

We can trace the development of attitudes towards impostors in the texts of comedy and philosophy, as well as in the anecdotal tradition, from the fifth through the second century BCE. The *alazon* in Old Comedy tends to be a minor character, often with a "blocking" function, who claims a high status he does not deserve in order to gain something. Fourth-century philosophical texts that address themselves to the "problem" of the impostor tend to describe him as a theatrical dissembler, a fraud who is a threat to the social, moral, and ontological order. The anecdotal tradition humorously describes self-important actors of the fourth century humbled by their social superiors. In Greek New Comedy and Roman comedy the *alazon* narrows into the stock character of the braggart soldier;[6] he is consistently held up to the audience's ridicule. This progression of the stock character mirrors the development of the acting profession in the Hellenistic world: the actor aspires to a high position in Greek society and becomes stereotyped as greedy and arrogant.[7] Exposing his true nature – his pretension, his ignorance, his corrupt motives – is the way to keep him from rising too high. This is the solution the Greek world offers to the problem of the impostor: to emphasize the gap between appearance and reality.

THE *ALAZON* IN OLD COMEDY

The *alazon* begins in fifth-century comedy as a negative type associated with sophists and public officials, but his qualities of pretension, deception, and foolish pride, his essential claim to know and be more than who

---

[6] Wilkins (2000) ch. 8 argues that the cook (*mageiros*) is an *alazon* character as well, and mentions in passing (402 n. 123) that the cook is sometimes likened to a comic actor, but does not pursue this line of inquiry. One might point out that the comic cook's characteristic boasting about his prowess with ingredients is often left unproven; characters might eat the feast he has prepared at the end of the play, but the audience typically does not hear whether the food has lived up to its billing. In this way, we might see the cook as another potentially "fraudulent" *alazon* character, like the braggart soldier.

[7] I do not suggest that this is the only way to read the stock character of the *alazon*; Lape (2004) passim, esp. ch. 6, offers an intriguing reading of the *alazon* as an allegory for Hellenistic kingdoms that threatened Athens' self-image as an independent democracy in the Hellenistic period. It seems likely that the *alazon* resonated with audiences on a variety of levels.

he really is, make him the perfect figure for the newly prominent actor of the fourth century and later. This is not to say that all *alazones* in comedy stand specifically and only for actors, but that they could always be read that way, in addition to standing for frauds in general. "The quack-doctor, a character who pretends to be what he is not, appears regularly as a comic type."[8] Diplomats are regularly *alazones* in comedy,[9] and as we have seen, actors were sometimes diplomats in real life. Aristophanes' *Acharnians* provides an early example of the *alazon* in the person of the Persian ambassador:

ΠΡΕΣΒΕΙΣ·   ἄγε δὴ σὺ βασιλεὺς ἅττα σ᾽ ἀπέπεμψεν φράσον
λέξοντ᾽ Ἀθηναίοισιν ὦ Ψευδαρτάβα.
ΨΕΥΔΑΡΤΑΒΑΣ·   ἰαρταμὰν ἐξάραν ἀπισσόνα σάτρα.
    Πρ.·   ξυνήκαθ᾽ ὃς λέγει;
ΔΙΚΑΙΟΠΟΛΙΣ·   μὰ τὸν Ἀπόλλω ᾽γὼ μὲν οὔ.
    Πρ.   πέμψειν βασιλέα φησὶν ὑμῖν χρυσίον.
            λέγε δὴ σὺ μεῖζον καὶ σαφῶς τὸ χρυσίον.
    Ψε.·   οὐ λῆψι χρῦσο χαυνόπρωκτ᾽ Ἰαοναῦ.
    Δι.·   οἴμοι κακοδαίμων ὡς σαφῶς.
    Πρ.·   τί δ᾽ αὖ λέγει;
    Δι.·   ὅ τι; χαυνοπρώκτους τοὺς Ἰάονας λέγει,
            εἰ προσδοκῶσι χρυσίον ἐκ τῶν βαρβάρων.
    Πρ.·   οὔκ, ἀλλ᾽ ἀχάνας ὅδε γε χρυσίου λέγει.
    Δι.·   ποίας ἀχάνας; σὺ μέν ἀλαζὼν εἶ μέγας.
                                    (*Ach.* 98–109)

AMBASSADOR: Now tell the Athenians what the King
    told you to say, Pseudo-Artabas.
PS-ARTABAS: Shattershmattergoldimatter.
    AM: Did you get what he said?
DICAEOPOLIS: By Apollo, I did not.
    AM: He says the King is going to send you gold.
          You, speak more clearly about the gold.
    PS-A: You no get gold, wide-assed Ionian.
    DI: Woe is us! That's pretty clear.
    AM: What's he saying now?
    DI: What's he saying? He says the Ionians are wide-assed if
          they're expecting any gold from barbarians.
    AM: No, he's talking about "wide masses" of gold.
    DI: What "wide masses"? You're a big fraud [*alazon*]!

---

[8] Rowe (1966) 400; see Dean-Jones (2003) 104.
[9] Rowe (1966) 402 and n. 15. See Demosthenes 19, Aeschines 2.

Sophists and priests are often called *alazones* as well in comedy. Characters who are called *alazones* in Aristophanes include the Athenian ambassadors and Pseudo-Artabas in *Acharnians*, the soothsayer in *Birds*, Socrates and Chairephon in *Clouds*, Aeschylus (by Euripides) in *Frogs*, Paphlagon (Kleon) in *Knights*, and the priest (ἱεροκλῆς) in *Peace*.[10] Kratinos fr.227 K-A has one character call Amynias an *alazon*, a *kolax*, and a *sykophantes*.

The connection between all of these occupational types – diplomats, priests, sophists, politicians, poets – is that they make their livings with words. Furthermore, they all occupy positions of some authority. An authority based on mere words opened up a public figure to the suspicion that he was a fraud, that his special skill or knowledge consisted of pretending to do his job and benefit the people while actually profiting himself. Over and over again, Aristophanes' *alazones* attempt to exploit their office or occupation for ulterior motives of personal gain, pretending to render a service as they try to cheat the hero. The ambassadors in *Acharnians* claim to have worked selflessly for Athens, describing as a "hardship" a diplomatic mission of leisurely luxury; Paphlagon (Kleon) in *Knights* sees himself as a loyal servant of the people, while the chorus reveals him to be a rapacious demagogue; Socrates and Chairephon are pompous hustlers in *Clouds*; Hierokles, the priest in *Peace*, tries to secure a share of the sacrificial meat for himself by "correcting" Trygaios' sacrifice; the soothsayer in *Birds* spouts "prophecies" demanding that he be given new clothes, food, and drink; and in *Frogs*, Euripides argues that Aeschylus the *alazon* duped the simple audiences of yore with his imposing, robed figures who never spoke a word. "The outward show (πρόσχημα) of tragedy," Euripides pronounces Aeschylus' Niobe or Achilles (913) – but not, he implies, *real* tragedy.

The suspicion of being an impostor was easily applied to actors as well, because their job, after all, was to impersonate. Plutarch, *Phokion* 19.2–3, recounts a story about a "prima donna" actor from the fourth century BCE: an actor playing a queen in a "new tragedy"[11] refused to come onstage unless he was accompanied by a retinue of lavishly dressed attendants. The audience was kept waiting until the choregos pushed the

---

[10] See Dean-Jones (2003) 106 n. 27.

[11] The Athenian victory-list inscriptions first record victors in the categories of "old tragedy" and "old comedy" in 386 and 339, respectively: Pickard-Cambridge (1988) 72. "Old tragedy" meant reperformances of plays by Aeschylus, Sophocles, and Euripides; "old comedy," on the other hand, seems to have meant what Classicists call "New Comedy" – reperformances of plays by Menander and his contemporaries: Csapo & Slater (1995) 188.

actor onstage, saying audibly, "Don't you know that Phokion's wife always goes out with a single maidservant, but you're making false pretensions (ἀλαζονεύῃ) and ruining the women?" The audience then vigorously applauded the choregos' speech. Plutarch's point is that Phokion's wife was modest and incorruptible even in a position of great power, just like her husband, but the anecdote incidentally reveals public disapproval of the actor's attitude. The actor aspires to all the trappings of the role he is playing; when he refuses to go onstage unless properly attended, he is impersonating someone important (literally, being an *alazon*) in order to be treated deferentially.[12] Another fourth-century text, [Pseudo-] Aristotle *Problems* 30.10.956b12–16, wonders: "Why are the Artists of Dionysus [members of the actors' guild] for the most part worthless men? Is it because they have the least share of reason and wisdom, because the majority of their life is taken up with skills necessary for their livelihood, and because most of their life is spent in incontinence, and sometimes in poverty? Both of these conditions tend to produce meanness."[13] Stereotypes about actors, as well as about politicians and priests, kept the *alazon* a vital character type as comedy changed during the fourth century. In another anecdote from Plutarch, the Spartan king Agesilaus reveals his scorn for the self-important actors of the fourth century.

ἃ δὲ τοὺς ἄλλους ἑώρα θαυμάζοντας ἐδόκει μηδὲ γινώσκειν. καὶ ποτε Καλλιππίδης ὁ τῶν τραγῳδιῶν ὑποκριτής, ὄνομα καὶ δόξαν ἔχων ἐν τοῖς Ἕλλησι καὶ σπουδαζόμενος ὑπὸ πάντων, πρῶτον μὲν ἀπήντησεν αὐτῷ καὶ προσεῖπεν, ἔπειτα σοβαρῶς εἰς τοὺς συμπεριπατοῦντας ἐμβαλὼν ἑαυτὸν ἐπεδείκνυτο νομίζων ἐκεῖνον ἄρξειν τινὸς φιλοφροσύνης, τέλος δὲ εἶπεν· "Οὐκ ἐπιγινώσκεις με, ὦ βασιλεῦ;" κἀκεῖνος ἀποβλέψας πρὸς αὐτὸν εἶπεν· "Ἀλλὰ οὐ σύ γε ἐσσὶ Καλλιππίδας ὁ δεικηλίκτας;" οὕτω δὲ Λακεδαιμόνιοι τοὺς μίμους καλοῦσι.   (*Vit. Ages.* 21)[14]

He [Agesilaos] seemed not to notice the things that other people looked at with wonder. Once Kallipides the tragic actor, who had a name and reputation among the Greeks and was eagerly sought after by everyone, met him [Agesilaos] for the first time and spoke to him. Then he pompously thrust himself into his entourage and kept making himself

---

[12] Wilson (2000) 87 notes that this anecdote "has something of the air of an *ad hoc* moralising fabrication (how could a *khoregos* be expected to produce a crowd of extras on the spot in the theatre?)."

[13] For the Greek, see p. 73.

[14] Cf. Plut. *Mor.* 212f.

conspicuous, revealing that he thought that he [Agesilaos] would ini-
tiate some friendliness with him. Finally he asked, "Do you not recognize me, O King?" And he turned his attention to look at him and
said, "Aren't you Kallipides the clown?" This is what the Spartans call
mimes.[15]

Although this actor is not pretending to be anything but an actor, he
is laying claim to a "celebrity" status to which his profession, in some
peoples' eyes, does not entitle him. In this sense, he is acting offstage
like an *alazon*. In both the anecdote about the actor playing Phokion's
wife and the anecdote about Kallipides, the audience – whether it is a
real theatrical audience or simply the reader – gets to delight in seeing
self-important actors get put in their place. Whether we can trace this
delight to fourth-century BCE audiences, and not just to Plutarch's own
milieu, is a question we must take up by looking at attitudes toward actors
in other fourth-century sources.

PHILOSOPHICAL ATTITUDES
The philosophers of the fourth century were concerned with the *alazon*
as well, linking him to acting in subtle ways. Plato's depiction of Ion
the rhapsode in the *Ion* is a portrait of a fraud so effective that he has
deceived even himself; Ion thinks he has true knowledge of generalship
and navigation, simply because he recites passages of Homer describing
fighting and sailing. His performance as a rhapsode is similar to acting:
he modulates his voice to suit different characters' recitatives, emotes the
lines he reads, and wears a sumptuous costume. Thus Plato indicts all the
dramatic arts by showing that even the practitioner of a less fully mimetic
genre is a fraud, an impostor.

Aristotle discusses *alazoneia* in detail, considering it to be a fault of
excessive pretense.[16] He covers all incarnations of the *alazon*: the boaster,
the fraud, the pretentious person. In general, Plato tends to use the term
alazon in discussions of those who pretend to be philosophers but really

---

[15] Kallipides specialized in playing women of low character, according to Aristotle, who
also states that Aeschylus' actor Mynniskos called Kallipides an ape (*Poet.* 1461b26–
1462a14). Aristophanes makes fun of Kallipides' apparent tendency to play low characters and overact in a fragment from *Women Who Pitch the Tents* (*Skenas Katalambanousai*),
PCG F 490: "Like Kallipides I am sitting on the floor-sweepings." On Kallipides, see
Braund (2000).

[16] *Eth. Nic.* 1108a20; *Eth. Eud.* 1233b35.

are not,[17] while Aristotle uses *alazon* to describe boasters, such as those who pretend to be courageous but are really cowards.[18] In both authors, the defining feature of the *alazon* is the pretense of having certain qualities in order to gain something. It is also the job description of the actor. The opposite of the *alazon*, Aristotle declares, is the sincere man (ὁ φιλαλήθης) (*Nicomachean Ethics* 1127b1–20). As we have already seen, sincerity is the vexed question haunting actors.[19]

Xenophon takes up the issue of the *alazon* in both the *Cyropaidia* and the *Memorabilia*. In the *Cyropaidia*, he makes a distinction between those who tell fictional stories to amuse their friends and those who lie, pretending to be what they are not or have what they do not in order to gain some advantage; the former are entertaining, but the latter are *alazones* (2.2.12). The *Memorabilia* gives an example of Socrates teaching virtue by negative example:

Ἐνθυμώμεθα γάρ, ἔφη, εἴ τις μὴ ὢν ἀγαθὸς αὐλητὴς δοκεῖν βούλοιτο, τί ἂν αὐτῷ ποιητέον εἴη. ἆρ' οὐ τὰ ἔξω τῆς τέχνης μιμητέον τοὺς ἀγαθοὺς αὐλητάς; καὶ πρῶτον μέν, ὅτι ἐκεῖνοι σκεύη τε καλὰ κέκτηνται καὶ ἀκολούθους πολλοὺς περιάγονται, καὶ τούτῳ ταῦτα ποιητέον· ἔπειτα, ὅτι ἐκείνους πολλοὶ ἐπαινοῦσι, καὶ τούτῳ πολλοὺς ἐπαινέτας παρασκευαστέον. ἀλλὰ μὴν ἔργον γε οὐδαμοῦ ληπτέον, ἢ εὐθὺς ἐλεγχθήσεται γελοῖος ὢν καὶ οὐ μόνον αὐλητὴς κακός, ἀλλὰ καὶ ἄνθρωπος ἀλαζών. καίτοι πολλὰ μὲν δαπανῶν, μηδὲν δ' ὠφελούμενος, πρὸς δὲ τούτοις κακοδοξῶν, πῶς οὐκ ἐπιπόνως τε καὶ ἀλυσιτελῶς καὶ καταγελάστως βιώσεται;

(*Mem.* 1.7.2)

He said, if someone who isn't a good flute-player wants to seem one, let's consider what he should do. Shouldn't he imitate the good flute-players in the things external to the art? First, since they wear fine clothes and travel with many attendants, he should do these things. Then, since many people praise them, he should furnish himself with many people to praise him. But he should never take any work, of course, or he will reveal that he is laughable and not only a bad flute-player, but also an impostor (ἀλαζών). And so, having spent a lot of money and not

---

[17] Plato *Resp.* 6.486b, 6.490a; *Euthyd.* 2.83c. In *Phil.* 65c Socrates asks whether pleasure or mind is more akin to truth; Protarchos answers that mind is, and calls pleasure "the greatest of impostors."

[18] Arist. *Eth. Nic.* 1108a20, 1115b25, 1127a20, 1127b10.

[19] See chapter 2; Barish (1981) passim. Trilling (1972) 64–65 discusses Rousseau's view of "the characteristic disease of the actor, the attenuation of selfhood that results from impersonation," and compares it to Plato's equally negative view of actors.

gained anything, and being disgraced in front of many people, how will he not spend his life laboriously, unprofitably, and ridiculously?

This bad flute-player is not really a flute-player at all: he is an actor playing the role of a flute-player and hoping not to be discovered. He wears the right costume, surrounds himself with fellow actors, and even recruits an audience, but he cannot do the job. Xenophon's discussion of *alazoneia* makes the link between impostors and actors quite clear.[20]

Finally, rounding out the fourth century,[21] Theophrastos' *Characters* 23 concerns *alazoneia*, and it describes the *alazon* as someone who keeps up the pretense of being wealthy when he is actually poor. Over and over, the *alazon* tells lies and manipulates appearances in order to appear rich in front of people: he talks about his (nonexistent) shipping profits (2), his (imaginary) important connections in Macedon (3–4), his (fictional) assets (5–6). He makes a show of considering whether to buy an expensive horse (7). Although he rents a house, he pretends his family owns it, and pretends furthermore that he plans to sell it because it is too small for entertaining (9). As with Xenophon's bad flute-player, he knows what the discourse and external trappings of his desired identity should sound and look like, although he lacks the essential qualities.[22] Most tellingly, for our purposes, the *alazon* goes to the clothes-market and picks out a wardrobe that would cost two talents, and then scolds his slave publicly for not bringing any gold coins with him (8). This example highlights the theatrical nature of Theophrastos' character-type: he enlists his slave as a synagonist in his performance at the market. As with all the philosophical accounts of the *alazon*, what Theophrastos focuses on is the discrepancy between appearance and reality which the *alazon* exploits. It is this discrepancy that makes antitheatrical writers throughout the ages uncomfortable with theater.[23] In an interesting connection to the

---

[20] It also makes clear one conception of acting with a long history (going back at least to Plato's *Ion*). This view holds that acting is not a distinct activity with particular skills, like flute-playing; anyone can pretend to be a flute-player, but only flute-players can actually play the flute.

[21] See Lane Fox (1996) 134–8 for a discussion of the traditional dating of the *Characters* to 319 and his arguments for a compositional range for the collection from ca. 325 to 310/09 BCE.

[22] Lane Fox (1996) 142.

[23] On the antitheatrical tradition in general, see Barish (1981), especially ch. 1. On Theophrastos' *Characters* as a "handbook of characterization" for comic playwrights of the fourth century, see Ussher (1977); on the *Characters* as a combination of "philosophical classification and comic caricature" which provides an inverted

previous chapter, Lane Fox notes that some people have seen Theophrastos' *alazon* as supposed to represent Aeschines.

The philosophical writers of the fourth century, then, saw the *alazon* as a recognizable character-type: he is someone who pretends to be more or better than he is. While these writers imply that a discerning audience can see through the impostor, the *alazon* clearly knows enough about the status he desires to project so that he fools some people: "And he is clever at telling a fellow traveler on the road how he served under Alexander, and how Alexander felt about him, and how many jewel-studded drinking-cups he got as booty; and he argues that the craftsmen in Asia are better than those in Europe; and he says these things even though he's never traveled out of town" (*Char.* 23.3). He is the enemy of true philosophy in Plato, the enemy of sincerity in Aristotle, the enemy of virtue in Xenophon, the enemy of "men of quality" in Theophrastos. He is always opposed to their goals, a "blocking character" in real life as well as onstage.[24]

ALAZONES IN MIDDLE AND NEW COMEDY

The fragments of Menander reveal the presence of several *alazones*. Fr. 746 K–T gives three lines of a Menander play:

> σφάττει με, λεπτὸς γίνομ' εὐωχούμενος·
> τὰ σκώμμαθ' οἷα τὰ σοφὰ καὶ στρατηγικά·
> οἷος δ' ἀλαζών ἐστιν ἀλιτήριος.

> He slaughters me; I become thin in feasting.
> What jokes, what military intelligence!
> What an offensive phony (*alazon*) he is!

These lines sound like they are spoken by a *parasitos*, possibly in the parasite/braggart soldier pairing familiar from later plays (e.g., Terence's *Eunuch*, Plautus' *Miles Gloriosus*). Another "familiar" quality of these lines is the sense that they are spoken as an aside, like the asides of Plautine characters. If these lines are an aside, they only strengthen the idea that the *alazon* stands for the actor: the speaker metatheatrically calls attention to the *alazon*-character as someone who overacts. Brown wants to assign

---

"'discourse' in Alexander's Athens of how citizens should behave," see Lane Fox (1996) 139–42, 155.

[24] Given the ongoing concern of philosophy to legitimate itself, and later, of the different schools to differentiate themselves from their rivals, it is not surprising that the philosophical writers are at such pains to identify impostors. Cf. Plato, *Apology*.

this fragment to Menander's *Kolax*.[25] Fr. 520 K–T also seems to refer to an *alazon*:

πᾶς ὁ μὴ φρονῶν
ἀλαζονείᾳ καὶ ψόφοις ἁλίσκεται

> ... everyone who doesn't think
> Is found out by his false pretension (*alazoneia*) and empty noises

Some scholars want to assign this fragment to Menander's *Kolax* as well; Brown argues it could fit in any of several plays.[26]

Both fragments suggest that the *alazon* was already becoming more of a braggart than an impostor, a trend that becomes even more evident in Roman comedy. It is interesting to note, however, that Polemon in Menander's *Perikeiromene* is a soldier but not, as we might expect, an *alazon*: "far less the braggart warrior than a jealous, lovesick youth."[27] This could serve as further evidence of Menander's famous tendency to humanize and soften stock characters, or on the other hand as evidence that those stock characters are not altogether fixed by Menander's time – at least, not fixed as they appear later in Plautus.

THE *ALAZON* AT ROME: THE *MILES GLORIOSUS*

The *alazon* proper makes a few brief appearances on the Roman stage, most recognizably as the quack doctor in Plautus' *Menaechmi* who (mis)diagnoses Menaechmus I as insane. Another avatar of the *alazon* is the *advocatus*. There are three *advocati* in Terence's *Phormio* who give confusing legal advice to the old man Demipho; he says after they exit, "I'm much more confused than I was before" (459). The quack doctor and the *advocati*, like Xenophon's false flute-player, try to pass themselves off as experts without having any real knowledge. Even these vestigial *alazones* tend to look like actors. For example, the *advocati* in Plautus' *Poenulus* reply impatiently to a recapping of events:

> Omnia istaec scimus iam nos, si hi spectatores sciant;
> horunc hic nunc causa haec agitur spectatorum fabula:
> hos te satius est docere, ut, quando agas, quid agas sciant.
> nos tu ne curassis: scimus rem omnem, quippe omnes simul
> dedicimus tecum una, ut respondere possimus tibi.
>
> (*Poen.* 550–54)

---

[25] Brown (1992) 92–3.
[26] See the discussion in Brown (1992) 97 n. 18.
[27] Duckworth (1994) 28; see also Lape (2004) ch. 6; Zagagi (1995) 32–3.

> We know all that already, if these spectators know it;
> we're doing this play here now on their behalf:
> it's enough for you to instruct them, so they'll know what you're
>   doing when you do it.
> Don't worry about us: we know the whole thing, since we all
> learned our lines with you, so that we can reply to you.

These *advocati* also address the audience later on (597–9), explaining that they are using stage money but pretending (*adsimulabimus*) that it is real money.[28] Even in metatheatrical Plautus, the *alazon* characters tend to be extraordinarily self-conscious.

Most of the time, however, the *alazon* appears in his Roman costume as a mercenary soldier. This transformation makes some sense: the impostor and the soldier are both mercenaries, in a sense, and their reputations both precede and exceed them. When the Greek *alazon* becomes the Roman *miles*, all that is left of his identity as a fraud is a blustering braggadocio which covers up his cowardice, and, at times, a preposterous vanity. The *miles*, like the *alazon*, has a tendency to act with words instead of deeds. The most famous example is Plautus' *Miles Gloriosus*, which, we are informed in the prologue, is adapted from a Greek play (by an unspecified playwright) called *Alazon*. But there are also braggart soldiers in Plautus' *Bacchides, Curculio, Epidicus, Poenulus*, and *Truculentus*, as well as in Terence's *Eunuchus*.

In general, Plautus' braggart soldiers come onstage for brief scenes in which their boasting, and the other characters' skeptical reactions to it, makes them look foolish. Stratophanes in the *Truculentus* gives a metatheatrical description of his own stock character when he enters, pontificating on the tendency for soldiers to be braggarts (484).[29] He claims to be a doer, not a talker, but of course, he acts on none of his blustery threats during the course of the play. Pyrgopolynices in the *Miles Gloriosus* differs from other braggart soldiers in degree, not in kind. The plot of the play has him not only fooled, as usual, but humiliated, beaten, and threatened with castration. One of his slaves, the tricky Palaestrio, describes him as "dumber than a rock" (236), and his parasite Artotrogus undercuts the *miles*' hyperbolic claims of military and sexual prowess with asides (1–78). The *miles* is a sort of stock character among the stock characters, someone so predictable and so hollow that he is an easy mark for his fellow characters.

---

[28] On these *advocati*, see Moore (1998) 12–14.
[29] See Moore (1998) 148; Beacham (1991) 35–6.

Terence's *Eunuchus* has the fairly standard pairing of a braggart soldier, Thraso, and his parasite, Gnatho. The soldier is a buffoon whose own boastful stories ironically suggest the manner of his ultimate loss of face in the course of the play.[30] The parasite constantly undermines his fulsome praises of his master with asides to the audience describing his master's true nature (see 420–21, 782–3). When Gnatho betrays his master at the end and transfers his allegiance to the heroes of the play, he describes Thraso as "silly, tasteless, stupid; he snores night and day;/you shouldn't fear him and the woman shouldn't love him; you'll drive him out easily when you want" (1079–80). On the Roman stage, the *alazon* winds up a victim not only of the hero, but of his own servant as well; the *kolax*, or *parasitus*, always shows him up for what he really is.

The *alazon* was an object of great concern in the fourth century, when the actor emerged as a potentially powerful figure in Greek society and concerns about fraud ran high. As the Artists of Dionysus became a distinct and recognized organization in the Hellenistic period, stereotypes about actors as arrogant frauds proliferated even as the actual "threat" posed by the actor seemed to diminish because of his clearly demarcated status. In second-century Rome, the actor was just another Greek mercenary or shyster, someone to be cut down a notch or two and put in his place. But Roman attitudes toward actors were crystallized in another stock character, the parasite, or flatterer, which had its antecedents in Greek comedy but found its fullest expression in Roman comedy. The flatterer aroused anxieties in Roman society on a par with the anxieties aroused by the fraud in Athenian society.

THE *KOLAX/PARASITUS*: THE ACTOR AS FLATTERER

The fourth century saw the rise of various professions, and with them, the emergence of fraudulent professionals and professional frauds. The fourth century was also concerned about flatterers. The flatterer created resentment in Athenian society, which, despite real economic differences among citizens, was ideologically committed to *isonomia* (equality before the law) as part of the democracy.[31] But it was in the hierarchical, highly status-conscious society of Republican Rome that the flatterer was felt

---

[30] Frangoulidis (1994) 586–95.

[31] Ober (1989) 74–5, for example, connects the ideology of *isonomia* with the institution of ostracism as a means for the *demos* to check the power of the elite.

to be a distinct social threat. Accusations of flattery were another way in which anxiety about social mobility was expressed.

Plutarch's *Moralia* contains a treatise called "How to Know a Flatterer from a Friend." Although it was written centuries after the time period we are considering, it speaks to the ongoing concerns the ancients had about flatterers and parasites: that, far from being mere annoyances, they threaten the stability of the social order – and beyond that, the stability of the ontological order itself.

Τίνα οὖν δεῖ φυλάττεσθαι; τὸν μὴ δοκοῦντα μηδ' ὁμολογοῦντα κολακεύειν, ὃν οὐκ ἔστι λαβεῖν περὶ τοὐπτάνιον, οὐδ' ἁλίσκεται σκιὰν καταμετρῶν ἐπὶ δεῖπνον, οὐδ' ἔρριπται μεθυσθεὶς ὅπως ἔτυχεν, ἀλλὰ νήφει τὰ πολλὰ καὶ πολυπραγμονεῖ καὶ πράξεων μετέχειν οἴεται δεῖν καὶ λόγων ἀπορρήτων βούλεται κοινωνὸς εἶναι, καὶ ὅλως τραγικός ἐστιν οὐ σατυρικὸς φιλίας ὑποκριτὴς οὐδὲ κωμικός. ὡς γὰρ ὁ Πλάτων φησίν, ἑσχάτης ἀδικίας εἶναι δοκεῖν δίκαιον μὴ ὄντα,' καὶ κολακείαν ἡγητέον χαλεπὴν τὴν λανθάνουσαν οὐ τὴν ὁμολογοῦσαν, οὐδὲ τὴν παίζουσαν ἀλλὰ τὴν σπουδάζουσαν.   (*Mor.* 50e–f)

Against whom, then, must we be on our guard? Against the man who does not seem to flatter, nor admits it; whom you can't catch in the kitchen, nor is he caught measuring the shadows toward dinnertime, nor is he thrown out for being drunk when he meets you, but he will stay sober for the most part and he will meddle and think that he ought to be privy to your business and want to be in on your secret counsels; in a word, he who is a tragic actor of friendship, not a comic or a satiric actor. For, as Plato says, "It is the height of injustice to seem just while not being just," and so the flattery which must be considered difficult to deal with is that which is hidden, not that which is openly avowed, that which is serious, not that which is meant as a joke.

The flatterer (*kolax*) exploits the gap between appearance and reality to his advantage; he insinuates himself into the affairs of rich men and benefits from pretending to have a status he does not. Plutarch contrasts the real-life flatterer in this passage with his depiction onstage in comedy, the *kolax* or *parasitus* who is monomaniacally concerned with eating and drinking at someone else's expense. Yet the stock comic character of the flatterer is based on these "real life" anxieties about social climbers, as we shall see.

First, we will examine the *kolax* or *parasitos* in Old Comedy and philosophy, and then we will turn to the development of the *kolax/parasitos* of New Comedy into the *parasitus* of Roman comedy. The *kolax* of Old Comedy is sometimes depicted as a political creature connected to demagoguery, sometimes as an uninvited hanger-on at symposia. Fourth-century philosophical texts connect flattery to political misrule; it is the mark of a power imbalance. The anecdotal tradition associates actors with the reign of Alexander, reinforcing this linkage between absolute power and flattery. In Middle and New Comedy, the *kolax* begins to be called the *parasitos*, emphasizing his gluttony, but his association with acting and social mobility remains in evidence. In Roman comedy, the *parasitus* is a dissembling, servile creature; he lies to his superiors in order to make a living. He becomes a figure for the actor in the Roman world. To minimize the threat that the professional liar poses, Roman comic playwrights tend to have the parasite comment to the audience in asides that expose not only the absurd pretensions of his patron but his own meretricious, bad acting.

THE *KOLAX* IN OLD COMEDY

Like the *alazon*, the *kolax* became a stock comic character by the end of the fifth century.[32] In Aristophanes' extant comedies, references to the *kolax* occur in a political context – usually with reference to Kleon. In Aristophanes' *Knights*, Demosthenes calls Paphlagon (i.e., Kleon) a *kolax* (419, 683, 1033), and in his *Peace*, the Chorus describes itself doing battle with a monster in a tanning-pit (i.e., Kleon) whose face was licked by a hundred *kolakes* (756). It is interesting that Kleon is called a *kolax* in one play – implying that he acquired his political power through flattery of more powerful politicians – and in another, he himself is depicted as the target of flatterers. It seems a politician could be called a *kolax* at any point in his career. The title of Eupolis' *Kolakes* (fr.172 K-A) suggests that it featured a whole chorus of toadies, although the subject of the play is unclear.[33]

The *kolax* was also characterized as a freeloading glutton, an aspect of his character which remained constant for several hundred years. A *kolax* shows up in a mime by the fifth-century mime writer Epicharmus:

συνδειπνέων τῷ λῶντι, καλέσαι δεῖ μόνον,
καὶ τῷ γα μὴ λεῶντι, κοὐδὲν δεῖ καλεῖν·
τηνεὶ δὲ χαρίης τ' εἰμὶ καὶ ποιέω πολὺν
γέλωτα καὶ τὸν ἱστιῶντ' ἐπαινέω.
καἴ κά τις ἀντίον τι λῇ τήνῳ λέγειν,

---

[32] Damon (1997) 11–14 provides a concise overview of the history of the terms *kolax* and *parasitos*.

[33] See Tylawsky (2002) ch. 4.

τήνῳ κυδάζομαί τε κἀπ' ὦν ἠχθόμαν.
κἤπειτα πολλὰ καταφαγών, πόλλ' ἐμπιὼν
ἄπειμι....[34]

Feasting with him who wishes, he only has to summon [me],
And at any rate with the one who doesn't wish, and he doesn't have
    to summon:
I'm tasteful there and I create much
Laughter and I praise the man hosting the feast.
And if someone wants to say something against him,
I revile him and then I'm hated.
And after devouring a lot and guzzling a lot
I go away. . . .

The *kolax* here is already demonstrating a characteristic self-awareness in his discussion of the "role" he plays for his patron.[35] We see here a connection between dissembling, servility, gluttony, and metatheatrical asides to the audience that will characterize the flatterer through the period of Roman comedy.

Nick Fisher has argued that the evidence from Old Comedy points to a widespread anxiety in fifth-century Athens that some aspiring politicians were using *kolakeia*, flattery, as a means of upward social mobility and political advancement.[36] Fisher notes that the stereotype of the *kolax/parasitos* took on a life of its own as a fourth-century stock comic character: no longer explicitly connected with politics, the *kolax/parasitos* pursues food and drink to the exclusion of all other drives.[37] As with the *alazon*, the *kolax* on stage, I would argue, gradually came to represent the actor in society. The association between acting and flattery was already in the popular consciousness by the late fourth century: Aristotle (*Rhetoric* 1405a23) notes about actors that "Some call them 'Dionysus-toadies' (διονυσοκόλακας), but they call themselves 'artists' (τεχνίτας) (these are both metaphorical, the former disparaging, the latter the opposite)." In a later period, mime-actors, excluded from the Artists of Dionysus, would form their own union: the Parasites of Apollo.[38]

---

[34] Epicharmus *Hope or Wealth* fr.35–7 Kaibel; quoted in Athenaeus 6.235f–236b.

[35] On this role as requiring the parasite's acceptance of his diminished masculinity and independence, see Fisher (2000) 373.

[36] Fisher (2000).

[37] See Fisher (2000) 373–8.

[38] Csapo & Slater (1995) 241, 371, 375 give inscriptional evidence for the existence of the guild. Csapo & Slater estimate the origin of the guild, or of ones like it, to have occurred in the second c. BCE, but note that most of the attestation for the guild

THE PHILOSOPHICAL TRADITION

Plato, Aristotle, and Theophrastos all discuss the *kolax* as well as the *alazon*, often in the same passages on moral failings or character types. Plato deals with the *kolax* in several different passages of the *Republic*, usually in the context of tyranny.[39] The tyrant, he has Socrates assert, is paradoxically a miserable creature, "enslaved to cringings and servitudes beyond compare," who must flatter the worst people in order to retain power (9.579e). In the *Gorgias* (466a), Plato has Socrates call rhetoric a branch of flattery (κολακεία). The flatterer and the courtesan are examples of evils that give temporary pleasure in *Phaedrus* 240b. Plato associates flattery throughout his work with tyranny, enslavement, and performative artifice. The presence of the *kolax* among one's followers is a sign that one has wandered from the path of true philosophy to false goals, or, as Plato might put it, that one is an impostor pretending to be a true philosopher.

Aristotle discusses *kolakeia* as another fault of excess, like *alazoneia* (*Eud. Eth.* 1233b3). In his discussion of the "great-souled man" in the *Nicomachean Ethics*, he defines flattery and flatterers as inherently servile (*Eth, Nic.* 1125a). The great-souled man is immune to flattery, but "most men like flattery (κολακεία), for a flatterer (κόλαξ) is a friend who is your inferior, or pretends to be so, and to love you more than you love him" (*Eth. Nic.* 1159a15). Aristotle distinguishes between friendship and flattery thus (*Eth. Nic.* 1173b30): "And the fact that a friend is different from a flatterer (κόλακος) seems to make it clear that pleasure is not a good, or that there are different kinds of pleasures; for the friend is thought to associate with someone for their benefit, while the flatterer is thought to associate with someone for pleasure, and this is a reproach for the latter,

---

dates from the empire. On the exclusion of mime-actors from the Artists of Dionysus, see also Pickard-Cambridge (1988) 302; Bieber (1961) 84. Parry and Parry's study of the English medical profession in the eighteenth and nineteenth centuries provides an interesting comparandum with the hierarchy of prestige with the Artists and the Parasites. The three types of medical practitioners in England in the later eighteenth c. were, in descending order of prestige, physicians, surgeons, and pharmacists. Each had its own guild: the Royal College of Physicians, the Royal College of Surgeons, and the Worshipful Company of Pharmacists. The Royal College of Physicians controlled access to the profession, and to its own organization especially, quite successfully, fighting off significant Parliamentary reform for decades; they were even able to enlist the assistance of the Worshipful Company of Pharmacists in fighting reform by turning the pharmacists against their rivals from below, the druggists and chemists. See Parry and Parry (1976) pt.II. ch. 6, esp. 104–8.

[39] 9.575e, 9.579a, 9.579e; see 7.538a–b for an analogy in which flatterers and wealthy adoptive parents keep a boy from learning the truth.

but they praise the former because he associates with people for other purposes." As with the *alazon*, the *kolax* has an ulterior motive in his pretense. As he distinguishes among different men in the *Nicomachean Ethics*, so Aristotle distinguishes among different governments in the *Politics*; flatterers are pleasing to many in a democracy, but their presence is a sign of misrule. In the kind of democracy where demagogues hold sway, flatterers are honored and the mob controls the better classes; this situation is analogous to the power that tyrants and their toadies hold in a tyranny (*Pol.* 1292a15–20). Demagogues are the flatterers of the people (*Pol.* 1313b35–40). This definition calls Aristophanes' Kleon to mind strongly. The flatterer is a sham friend (*Pol.* 1371a20), that is, one who plays the role of a friend. The connection of flattery with demagogues and orators, who are themselves often compared to actors, highlights the performative nature of this false identity.

Theophrastos' *Characters* 2, which must have been written soon after Menander's *Kolax*, is concerned with *kolakeia*. The flatterer is the sort of man who tells his patron that everyone is praising his virtues (at the flatterer's suggestion), and asks, "Are you taking it to heart how people are looking at you?" (2) He picks lint off the patron's clothes and grey hairs out of his beard (3), reassuring him that his hair is still dark for his age. He shushes everyone for his patron's jokes and overreacts to the punchline, stuffing his cloak into his mouth "as if he can't contain his laughter" (4). He showers his own children with presents and affection in front of his patron (6). He showers compliments on his patron, saying that his foot is more symmetrical than the cobbler's shoes (7), his wine and food luxurious (10), his house well laid-out, his farm well cultivated, his portrait a perfect resemblance (12). The flatterer also waits on his patron obsequiously, halting everyone until he has walked by (5), announcing his visit to his friends (8), running his errands in the women's market (9), offering him a blanket at the dinner table (10), even snatching the cushions from the slave in the theater and placing them on the seat himself (11). The last sounds so much like Aeschines' denunciation of Demosthenes (3.76) that it might be directly alluding to that passage. All of this flattery is performed in front of other people as well as the patron, for added impact – and, I would suggest, because the *kolax* is acquiring a more and more theatricalized status. He is thought to ham it up in "real life" as well as on the stage.

It is no coincidence that Athenian writers in the later part of the fourth century are concerned with the flatterer. Athens came under Macedonian rule by the time Theophrastos wrote the *Characters*. The political context of very unequal power relations was thought to encourage flattery. Thus the philosophical writers take pains to identify and describe the flatterer, so that the undeserving might not receive more than their fair share in the new social order.[40] It is also not surprising, then, that with the Macedonian conquest of Athens and the rest of Greece, we find a cluster of anecdotes about actors flattering Alexander. First, there is the joke that began to circulate which played on the common nickname for actors, "Dionysus-toadies" (διονυσοκόλακας); Alexander enjoyed actors so much and surrounded himself with so many of them that people began to call them "Alexander-toadies."[41] (The joke is itself also a piece of flattery, since it compares Alexander with Dionysus.) Then there are the accounts of incidents such as the one in which a comic actor performing for Alexander inserted a line requesting ten talents into one of his speeches; Alexander supposedly laughed, and paid him.[42] This incident might seem at first to be the opposite of flattery, since it looks like a brazen demand for wealth. It is important to remember, however, that as early as Epicharmus, the *kolax* was a person who provided entertainment, usually at meals, and who expected in return some sort of material reward. A clever *kolax* would entertain Alexander by surprising him; a request for a huge sum of money is funnier than one for a modest amount of money, or for a free meal. But the request also manages to flatter: after all, it points to Alexander's singularly enormous fortune, and thus his unique – even godlike – potential for generosity. Alexander's favorable treatment of actors, or in other words, his rewarding of flattery, is depicted as the new mode for politics.[43]

THE *KOLAX/PARASITOS* IN MIDDLE AND NEW COMEDY

The *kolax*, as he became common on the Middle and then the New Comic stage, slowly acquired a somewhat different identity and a new name: the παράσιτος, or parasite, who flatters his social superiors in return for free meals.[44] Alexis fr.262 K-A calls the same character *kolax*

---

[40] For an interesting recent account of some of the ways in which Athens attempted to maintain its democratic ideology (in the fictional world of the comic stage, at least) in the face of Macedonian occupation, see Lape (2004).

[41] Athenaeus 12.539.

[42] Plut. *Vit. Alex.* 29.3.

[43] See Lape (2004) 58, 64 on flattery as a mode of political survival for Hellenistic Athens under Macedonian control.

[44] For a more detailed analysis of the evolution of the *kolax/parasitos*, see Wilkins (2000) 71–86.

and *parasitos* in consecutive lines, indicating that the terminology is not entirely fixed in the fourth century.[45] Many Middle Comic plays use the term *kolax*. Diphilos fr.23 K-A describes a *kolax* upsetting everyone with his malicious talk. Menander wrote a play titled *Kolax*, and his *Eunouchos* and *Theophoroumene* contain *kolakes*.[46]

In Menander's *Theophoroumene*, someone (apparently an old man, possibly named Kraton) talks about how bad modern times are:

> ἄνθρωπος ἂν δ' ᾖ χρηστός, εὐγενής, σφόδρα
> γενναῖος, οὐδὲν ὄφελος ἐν τῷ νῦν γένει.
> πράττει δ' ὁ κόλαξ ἄριστα πάντων, δεύτερα
> ὁ συκοφάντης, ὁ κακοήθης τρίτα λέγει.
> ὄνον γενέσθαι κρεῖττον ἢ τούς χείρονας
> ὁρᾶν ἑαυτοῦ ζῶντας ἐπιφανέστερον.
>
> (fr.1 Körte/223 Kock, ll.14–19)

> But a man who is good, well-born, and very
> Noble, is no use in this current age.
> The flatterer (*kolax*) does best of all, the informer
> Is next, and the malicious man is third.
> Better to be an ass than to see inferior people
> Living more notably than me.

The anxiety about social mobility is clear in this passage: the powers that be apparently reward flatterers and informers, while nobody takes any notice of the *kaloi kagathoi* anymore. If we consider that this passage comes from approximately the same time period as Theophrastos' *Characters*, then we see that the stock character of the flatterer gained added resonance in a time when the political power structure had been radically altered and when real actors were amassing huge fortunes.

Menander's *Dyskolos* and *Sikyonios* have characters called *parasitoi*, rather than *kolakes*, and some of these *parasitoi* resemble their Roman descendants in the way they "coach" other characters in deception. The fragments of the *Sikyonios* contain a scene in which a parasite, Theron, is

---

[45] Some scholars have argued that this fragment is evidence of the moment of transition between the two terms, while others disagree: see the discussion of this controversy in Brown (1992) 99 n. 25; see also Wilkins (2000) 74, Lane Fox (1996) 140. Others, like Fisher (2000) 372–3, see this as evidence that the two terms (and others) were both in use throughout Old, Middle, and New Comedy. Tylawsky (2002) provides a detailed history of the Greek background of the parasite/flatterer, beginning with Homer.

[46] On Menander's *Kolax*, see Tylawsky (2002) 96–100.

bribing an old man to act as if he is Kichesias, and to claim that the girl Philoumene is his daughter. Apparently, the irony of the scene is that the old man really *is* Kichesias and that he really *is* the father of the girl, and that the parasite is unaware of it.

ΚΙΧΗΣΙΑΣ· οὐκ εἰς τὸν ὄλεθρον.
ΘΗΡΩΝ·   χαλεπὸς ἦσθα.
ΚΙ·   ἀποφθερεῖ
    ἀπ᾽ ἐμοῦ; Κιχησίαν σὺ τοιοῦθ᾽ ὑπέλαβες
    ἔργον ποήσειν ἢ λαβεῖν ἂν παρά τινος
    ἀργύριον. ἀδίκου πράγματος. Κιχησίαν;
ΘΗ·   Σκαμβωνίδην γε τὸ γένος· εὖ γ᾽· ἆρ᾽ ὑπέλαβες;
    τούτου με πρᾶξαι μισθὸν αὐτοῦ, μηκέτι
    ὧν ἔλεγον ἄρτι.
ΚΙ·   τοῦ τίνος;
ΘΗ·   Κιχησίας
    Σκαμβωνίδης γε· πολὺ σὺ βέλτιον λέγεις.
    νοεῖν τι φαίνει τὸν τύπον τοῦ πράγματος.
    οὗτος γενοῦ· καὶ σιμὸς εἶ γὰρ ἀπὸ τύχης
    καὶ μικρός, οἷον ἔλεγεν ὁ θεράπων τότε.
ΚΙ·   γέρων ὅς εἰμι γέγονα.
ΘΗ·   πρόσθες θυγάτριον
    Ἁλῆθεν ἀπολέσας ἑαυτοῦ τετραετές
    Δρόμωνά τ᾽ οἰκέτην.
ΚΙ·   ἀπολέσας.
ΘΗ·   εὖ πάνυ.
ΚΙ·   ἁρπασθέν ὑπὸ λῃστῶν· ἀνέμνησας πάθους
    τὸν ἄθλιόν με καί †θυρας† οἰκτρᾶς ἐμοί.
ΘΗ·   ἄριστα. τοῦτον διαφύλαττε τὸν τρόπον
    τό τ᾽ ἐπιδακρύειν. ἀγαθὸς ἄνθρωπος σφόδρα.
                                   (*Sik.* 343–60)

KICHESIAS: Go to hell!
THERON: You're being difficult.
    KI: Won't you leave me
        And be damned? Did you actually think that Kichesias
           would do
        This sort of thing, or take a bribe from someone?
        This evil deed? Kichesias?
    TH: Yeah, you of the race of Skambonides. All right then;
           you follow me?
        Take your pay from me for this, and not
        For that which I mentioned earlier.
    KI: For what?

TH: For being Kichesias Skambonides. You say it much
    better.
    You seem to understand this kind of matter.
    You become *him*; you're snub-nosed, fortunately,
    And short, just like the servant described him.
KI: I have become the old man that I am.
TH: Add that you lost
    Your daughter from Halai when she was four years old,
    Along with Dromon, a servant.
KI: I lost her.
TH: Excellent!
KI: She was stolen by pirates; you have reminded me
    Of my wretched suffering and of my pitiable child.
TH: Great! Keep up that sort of thing
    And weep over it. [*Aside*] He's a great guy!

This scene reveals the histrionic quality of the *parasitos*, who "directs" his "actor" just like one of Plautus' later metatheatrical slaves. It also portrays the *parasitos* as a scheming, lying scoundrel, someone so well versed in dissembling that he is willing to coach and bribe others to lie in support of his stories.[47] He is, in a certain sense, a professional actor.

THE PARASITUS AT ROME

The *kolax/parasitos* of Greek New Comedy made a few appearances in his Greek name: Naevius wrote a *Colax*, and plays titled *Colax* were also attributed to Plautus and Laberius. Naevius's *Colax* was probably modeled on Menander's play by that name; fr.1 "seems to show that the soldier there compared himself with Hercules in dialogue with the parasite."[48] The character became standardized, however, as the *parasitus* of Roman comedy (see Plautus' *Bacchides, Captivi, Curculio, Epidicus, Menaechmi, Miles Gloriosus, Persa, Stichus*; Terence's *Eunuchus, Phormio*). The parasite's standard attribute was his desire for a free meal; he often appeared alongside a patron (sometimes a braggart, *miles gloriosus* type[49];

---

[47] See Lape (2004) 236–7 on the metatheatrical quality of this scene.
[48] Brown (1992) 97, n. 19.
[49] *Pace* Segal (1996) xxiii and others who, following Aristotle's categories and not stage usage, see the εἴρων as the opposite – and therefore the fitting "partner" – of the *alazon*. The *eiron*, the "ironic man," makes himself out to be less than he is, just as the *alazon* claims to be more than he is (Ar. *Eth. Nic.* 1108a20; see Theophrastos 1), and could thus serve to deflate the *alazon's* boasting. But understatement is not as common a comic strategy in ancient comedy as overstatement, for fairly obvious reasons, and the deflation usually occurs in asides to the audience by the parasite, who continues

see *Bacchides, Miles Gloriosus, Eunuchus*) who would provide that meal in exchange for flattery or useful services. The prologue of Terence's *Eunuchus* defends the poet from the charge of lifting the braggart soldier and parasite pair from Naevius' and Plautus' *Colax*, saying he borrowed them from Menander's *Kolax* instead (19–34). Whatever the source, it is clear that they were a fairly standard pair.

Plautus' parasites are a richly metatheatrical lot. In arguing her thesis that "in Plautine comedy we are constantly invited to see a play about a play," Frances Muecke notes that "if all dramatic characters are to a certain extent actors-as-characters, Plautus privileges characters who are primarily actors. In general these are cunning slaves or parasites...."[50] A quick survey of Plautus' parasites will reveal the great extent to which they serve as figures for the actor.[51] One interesting aspect of this stock character is the extent to which he is depicted not just as an actor, but as a *bad* actor; where the Greek solution to the problem of the impostor was to emphasize the gap between the *alazon*'s appearance and reality, the Roman solution to the problem of the parasite was to emphasize his overacting.[52] In each case, this approach served to reassure the audience

---

to feign admiration for his master. The parasite, that is, may reveal the *miles* to be an empty braggart, but he himself continues to engage in theatrically overblown flattery and declarations of hunger. The *eiron* is not a figure for the actor in society in the way that the *alazon* and the *kolax/parasitus* are; if he even occurs onstage, he might be rather a mouthpiece for society's criticism of actors. For an especially schematic pairing of the *alazon* and the *eiron*, see Fishelov (1993) 98–117, which contends that the two are essential to the functioning of comedy, although the only ancient play he discusses is the *Miles Gloriosus*, and he does not identify an *eiron* figure in it.

[50] Muecke (1986) 224.

[51] Muecke (1986) 224–5 argues that the actor thematized here is not "the real Roman actor...but the fictitious actor whom Plautus has written into the play...representing the element *actor* in the complex notion of *actor-as-character*." I would argue that while references to actors and acting in a play always fictionalize the actor to some extent (just as no reference to "the poet" in an Aristophanic parabasis is purely and transparently autobiographical), the parasite in Roman comedy does have something to say about real Roman actors.

[52] McCarthy (2000) 202 describes Plautus' parasites as "so similar as to almost to merge into a single character," a character that is defined by his "willingness to say anything or praise anyone for a meal," his "flexibility," and his "opportunism." McCarthy reads the parasite as "a useful figure through which naturalistic comedy can poke fun at the weaknesses of farce" and as a figure for the comic playwright (202–03); it is also possible to read her description of his essential nature as a useful figure for Plautine comedy to poke fun at actors.

that they could detect the social climber, rather than being taken in by him.

The parasite in the fragments of the *Bacchides* is unamed. At one point, he calls himself his patron's "bodily covering" (illius sum integumentum corporis, 601). Damon discusses this line as evidence that there exists an unusually good "fit" between parasite and patron in this play,[53] but I would argue that this unnamed parasite represents the norm, not the exception. For the parasite to describe himself as a "covering" suggests both a literally parasitic relationship and the sense that the parasite is in essence a covering, a costume, a role. He may or may not "really" agree with his patron's motives and opinions, but he always acts as if he does.

Ergasilus is the parasite of Plautus' *Captivi*. In the first lines of his opening monologue, he tells the audience that "the youths have given me the nickname Whore [Scorto],/because I'm usually present at their banquets unbidden" (1–2).[54] The equation of the parasite with a whore suggests another register for Roman views of actors: not only are they parasites, but they are whores as well.[55] In a later monologue, the parasite "auctions" himself off to the lowest bidder (179–81). His asking price: one dinner.[56] He gets no takers, however, and complains later that everyone is conspiring not to laugh at his stories or feed him anymore (460ff.). When he enters with good news for his master, he says he will never have to *supplicare* another man again (770) and then announces he will do the running-slave routine to deliver the news.[57] He revels in the thought of never having to do his act for anyone again – except, of course, his master.

In *Curculio*, the parasite Curculio is the hero, working as the tricky slave instead of serving the *miles* or another patron. As the metatheatrical tricky slave, he "directs" the *adulescens* in a plot to fool the *miles* and get the girl. His first appearance onstage is a melodramatic, over-the-top

---

[53] Damon (1995) 79, citing Peniculus as a Plautine parasite who "refused" to fit himself to his patron's desires.

[54] On the pun on *invocatus* in these lines, see McCarthy (2000) 174; Moore (1998) 28–9; Damon (1997) 74. On parasites' nicknames in comedy, see Wilkins (2000) 80–2; Damon (1997) 30; see also Tylawsky (2002) 61.

[55] On the prostitute as another figure for the actor in Greek and Roman comedy, as well as in Roman society, see ch. 4. On Ergasilus as a whore, see McCarthy (2000) 182–3.

[56] See Moore (1998) 192.

[57] McCarthy (2000) 195–8; Damon (1997) 79. On the "running slave" routine in general, see Hunter (1985) 80–81.

rendition of the "running slave" set-piece, in which he announces he'll faint if he goes without food any longer (309).[58] Later on, he denounces pimps and bankers in general (494–511), almost as if he is talking about the stock characters of "pimp" and "banker." When he comes onstage by himself after stealing the girl, he begins his speech with "An old dramatist, so I've heard, once wrote in a tragedy that two women are worse than one..." (591).[59] Curculio's metatheatricality even extends to the level of dissembling that he is the parasite of one man in order to get money for his real patron to use: "the parasite plays the role of a parasite."[60] Most curiously in this play, a character called "choragus" ("producer" or "stage manager") comes onstage between "acts" and delivers a substantial metatheatrical monologue on the characters in the play and "bad characters" in contemporary Rome.[61] In a fascinating conflation of "real life" and dramatic character, the *choragus* notes Curculio's trickery and assumes that he has already stolen the company's costumes (463). This *parasitus* is a rogue onstage and off, he tells the audience – as if the actor playing the *parasitus* is a rogue himself, or more precisely, as if the *parasitus is* the actor.

In Plautus' *Menaechmi*, the parasite Peniculus also works on a metatheatrical level, orchestrating two eavesdropping scenes (465–86, 570–602), revealing other characters' pretenses in asides (193, 608), and commenting on his own role as an actor. When he enters the stage at one point, his patron Menaechmus says, "You couldn't have come at a better time for me"; Peniculus replies, "Yeah, it's my habit; I know every convenient turning point" (139–40). He might as well say, "I like to enter on cue." At another point in the play, Menaechmus asks Peniculus, "What do you say?" Peniculus's quick-witted response is "Whatever you want – that's what I say and unsay" (160). Peniculus makes clear the performative and dissembling nature of the parasite's role.[62]

The braggart soldier Pyrgopolynices in *Miles Gloriosus* employs a parasite named Artotrogus. This parasite appears only in the opening scene, in which he plays the flatterer to his patron while exposing his empty lies and preposterous vanity in asides to the audience. When the soldier asks the parasite to help him remember a particularly worthy deed, the

---

[58] See Moore (1998) 14, 128–9.

[59] See Hunter (1985) 119.

[60] Damon (1997) 46–8.

[61] On this speech, see Moore (1998) 131–9, who notes that the Roman types the *choragus* describes are made into comic stock characters.

[62] See McCarthy (2000) 62–3 on Peniculus.

parasite "recalls" that he blew away legions with a single breath. The soldier modestly notes,

PYRGOPOLYNEICES: istuc quidem edepol nihil est.
ARTOTROGUS: nihil hercle hoc quidemst
                praeut alia dicam – quae tu numquam feceris.
                peiiuriorem hoc hominem si quis viderit
                aut gloriarum pleniorem quam illic est,
                me sibi habeto, ego me mancupio dabo;
                nisi unum, epityra estur insanum bene.
                                                    (*MG* 19–24)

PYRGOPOLYNEICES: By Pollux, that was nothing.
ARTOTROGUS: By Hercules, it was indeed nothing
            Compared to other deeds I could mention (*aside*) which
                you never did.
(*to audience*) If anyone knows a man who's more of a liar
            Or fuller of boasts than this guy is,
            He can have me, I'll give myself to him for sale,
            Except for one thing: I eat this guy's olive spread like crazy.

A moment later, the parasite is again betraying his master's vanity, and his own exaggerations, when he claims the soldier smashed an elephant's leg to bits:

PY.:   nolo istaec hic nunc.
AR.:   ne hercle operae pretium quidemst
         mihi te narrare tuas qui virtutes sciam.
         venter creat omnis hasce aerumnas: auribus
         peraudienda sunt, ne dentes dentiant,
                 et adsentandumst quidquid hic mentibitur.
                                                    (*MG* 31–35)

PY: I don't want this story now.
AR.:   Indeed, by Hercules, it isn't worth the effort
         For you to recount your excellences to me who knows
            them.

(*to audience*) My stomach creates all these troubles: these things must
            be heard
         To the bitter end by my ears, so that my teeth get some
            grinding,
         And so I have to agree with whatever this guy lies about.

Artotrogus makes it quite clear that his relationship with Pyrgopolyneices is mercenary; he would "sell himself" to anyone else who could offer him a meal. He aids and abets the soldier's lies in order to eat. He is the original starving actor. After this scene, Pyrgopolynices' tricky slave Palaestrio is the one who appears on stage with the *miles*, flattering his vanity while leading him into the trap he has schemed. It is interesting to note the difference in the way that they each interact with the soldier: Artotrogus speaks to the audience much more, while Palaestrio simply plays along with the soldier's false idea of the situation, with only an occasional aside to another character. The parasite works to establish the outrageousness of the soldier's self-image at the beginning of the play, creating a sense of amused condescension in the audience which other characters can later exploit.

The aptly named Saturio is the parasite of *Persa*. He enters, as the parasite usually does in Plautus, to give an opening monologue about his profession alone on stage (53–80).[63] Unlike many Plautine comedies, however, the parasite has an active role in the plot: he dresses his daughter up as a Persian captive in order to help the heroes foil the pimp – and in order to get himself a meal, of course. Typically, though, he is an expert in coaching others in dissembling. When he reenters with his daughter in costume, he makes sure she is prepared:

> SATURIO: scis nam tibi quae praecepi?
> VIRGO: omnia.
> SA.:   et ut vi surrupta fueris?
> VI.:   docte calleo.
> SA.:   et qui parentes fuerint?
> VI.:   habeo in memoria.
>
> *(Persa* 379–81)

> SATURIO: Do you remember what I've taught you?
> GIRL: Everything.
> SA.:   And how you were stolen?
> GI.:   I understand perfectly.
> SA.:   And who your parents were?
> GI.:   I've got it memorized.

---

[63] As is also the case in Terence and writers of New Comedy, as noted by Damon (1995) 183; see *Captivi, Persa, Stichus; Eunuchus.* This habit suggests the metatheatrical tendencies of this character, as well as his extreme predictability as a stock character; his features are very clearly established. It also suggests that Plautus was confident that the parasite character could "hold" an audience all by himself on stage; the stock speech, full of hyperbole about the misery of hunger and complaints about making a living by wheedling meals out of other men, must have been thought extremely funny.

His daughter, ironically, is a paragon of virtue and does not wish to play a part in this deception (uerum insimulari nolo, "I don't want to dissemble the truth" (358)) because she fears it will ruin her marriage prospects.[64] Saturio reassures her that all men care about is her dowry and that she will have one: a "hamper full of books" (392) that are full of Attic witticisms. It is a laughably unimpressive dowry, and an appropriate one; Saturio will have his daughter read up to play her wifely role, just as he rehearses witty remarks for his patrons. He, of course, performs the role of the outraged Persian father beautifully.

The parasite in the *Stichus* is named Gelasimus, and in his opening monologue he says, "if anyone's looking for a laughable man/I am for sale along with my entire costume" (171–2). He explains the origin of his name and his identity:

Gelasimo nomen mi indidit parvo pater,
(propter pauperiem hoc adeo nomen repperi)
quia ind' iam a pusillo puero ridiculus fui,
eo quia paupertas fecit ridiculus forem;
nam illa artis omnis perdocet, ubi quem attigit.
(*Stich.* 174–8)

My father gave me the name Gelasimus when I was little
(Because poverty made me be laughable),
Because ever since I was little, I've been laughable.
I got this name because of poverty,
For poverty teaches all the arts to him whom she takes hold of.

Poverty has made Gelasimus a professional humorist, or in other words, a comic actor. Like Ergasilus in the *Captivi*, he announces jokingly that he is auctioning himself off for a meal (195–233). He is understandably distressed when he is told that his long-absent master has returned home with fabulous wealth – including a whole crew of witty parasites (388).

[64] Interestingly, the girl manages to avoid lying during much of her conversation with the pimp, using dramatic irony to mislead him with ambiguous statements. She does give a false name (Lucris), though, and she reassures Toxilus in an aside, "Be quiet, I'll take care of it as you wish" (taceas, curabo ut voles, 610). Rei (1998) 95 links the girl's reluctance to dissemble to the tendency for free women in Roman comedy not to engage in any "tricky slave"-like behavior; they are kept from being associated with actors. McCarthy (2000) 146–52, however, argues that the girl as well as the parasite is play-acting in this scene, although the girl exhibits ambivalence about participating in theatrical deception. See also Hunter (1985) 126.

This lie about rival parasites spurs him to go home and prepare his wittiest remarks for his patron's homecoming (464–7). He does end up providing entertainment for his patron, but as the worried butt of the patron's teasing threats not to feed him anymore.[65]

While Terence has a reputation for tweaking stock characters counter to type, in order to surprise his audience,[66] Terence's parasites share most of the standard attributes of comic parasites: a propensity for metatheatrical "coaching" of other characters in deception, a desire to expose the lies of their patrons. Terence's *Eunuchus* presents a parasite, Gnatho, who is so adept at flattering that he says he has offered lessons to a less fortunate parasite that he met earlier that day (232–53). Just like Theron in Menander's *Sikyonios*, the "coaching" ability of the parasite reveals how much of an act he regularly puts on. As Gnatho continues his self-praise, he thinks of opening a school for parasites, much like the schools that philosophers found (261–4). This sounds like an allusion to the philosophical tradition's writings on *kolakeia, alazoneia*, and other character faults, though of course we cannot be sure. Gnatho's description of his own flattery sounds, in fact, very much like Theophrastos 2.2 and 2.4. Speaking of patrons in general, he says,

> quidquid dicunt laudo; id rursum si negant, laudo id quoque;
> negat quis: nego; ait: aio; postremo imperavi egomet mihi
> omnia adsentari. is quaestu' nunc est multo uberrimus.
>
> (*Eun.* 251–3)

> Whatever they say, I praise; if they go back and deny it, I praise that too;
> if someone says no, I say no; if he says yes, I say yes; in short, I've ordered myself
> to agree with everything. This occupation is the most lucrative by far, these days.

While he may think of himself as an excellent actor, the audience sees that he is a consummate faker.

Phormio is the parasite in Terence's *Phormio*. As is often the case with Terence, he has drawn his characters in this play somewhat counter to type. Phormio is not as hungry and wheedling as the parasite in a Plautine play, but works more as the tricky slave, conceiving a scheme to help the

---

[65] Moore (1998) 13 notes that Gelasimus' overexplanation of the plot to the audience also marks him as an actor-figure.

[66] See Duckworth (1994) 174.

young man in love fool his father. Even when acting out of character, so to speak, he makes clear his theatrical nature in an aside: "Now I need to change my bearing and my facial expression" (890). Damon notes Phormio's "parasitical talent for pretense" and the success of his "sycophant act," but does not link this talent to acting as such.[67] Yet this metatheatrical aptitude for dissembling makes Phormio, like the rest of his parasitical brethren, a figure for the actor.

THE FRAUD AND THE FLATTERER: IMAGES OF ACTORS

The *alazon* crystallizes negative stereotypes about actors in the Greek world, while the *kolax/parasitus* represents the actor in the Roman world. The *alazon* is a pompous, pretentious official of some sort, someone with some authority who is at base a fraud. This makes sense in a culture that nominated famous actors to serve on prominent embassies.[68] Athens, moreover, was for at least a time a radical democracy; every citizen was eligible to hold many of the city's positions of power and importance on the basis of an annual lottery, and this must have meant that some officials were seen as unqualified for their positions, at least by some people. The *parasitus*, on the other hand, has no authority at all; he is a scheming mooch who is tolerated for his entertainment value, which derives in part from his declarations of misery. This makes sense in a highly hierarchical culture in which actors were socially despised and, by the early Empire at the latest, legally *infames*,[69] a culture that empowered magistrates to strike actors with impunity, off or on stage.[70] Both the *alazon* and the *parasitus*, then, embody anxieties about social mobility, but for very different societies: the *alazon* tries to rise from the middle toward the top in a nominally equal society, while the *parasitus* tries to rise from the bottom toward the respectability of the middle in a strongly stratified society.

The philosophical writers' snobbery hints at anxiety about social mobility as one source of the hostility toward the figure of the *alazon*. Despite the democratic institutions of Athens, there was a lingering sense

---

[67] Damon (1997) 92.

[68] See Demosthenes 18, 19; Aeschines 1, 2, 3; Pickard-Cambridge (1988) 279.

[69] Cornelius Nepos *Preface* 5; Ulp. *Digest* 3.2.2.5.

[70] Suet. *Aug.* 45.3 states that Augustus limited magistrates to striking actors during the *ludi* and within the theater, as opposed to the earlier law which did not limit this power. See Plaut. *Cist.* 785.

of what we are tempted to call class distinctions, revealed in the use of expressions like καλός κ᾽ ἀγαθός to describe wealthy, educated men.[71] Actors were one group of men who were able to move up the economic ladder because of the tremendous fees the stars could demand.[72] Since most actors in Greece were freeborn men[73], this entailed a rise in social status as well, despite lingering attitudes that valued only landed wealth.[74] The anecdote recounted earlier about Agesilaos and Kallipides, despite its Spartan setting, demonstrates this kind of old aristocratic snobbery quite clearly. The *alazon* is the perfect target for this kind of snobbery and anxiety, for he always tries to pass himself off as higher in status than he really is.[75]

The *parasitus*, on the other hand, represents the changed status of the actor at Rome: he is a shabby, poor, fawning creature who makes his living off the rich by his quick-witted dissembling. Although he is constantly acting, he fools no one. He feeds on Rome's indulgence of him. Thus Plautus' parasites overact, hamming up their hunger; they are signaling their status as dependents, as social inferiors, both to their patrons onstage and to the audience. The *alazon* and the *parasitus* serve as vehicles for Greek and Roman anxieties about social mobility, but the *parasitus* plays an additional role in the Roman cultural unconscious: he embodies Roman anxiety about drama.

---

[71] Ober (1996) 5–6, 18, 21, 25–6, 127–8, takes pains to uncover the assumptions of most historians of Classical Athens that the aristocratic elite "really ruled" the demos, but he does not dispute the existence of such an elite. On καλός κ᾽ ἀγαθός, see Dover (1976) 41–5 for cautionary notes on a simplistic search for the term in Attic writers in order to ascertain their "class consciousness"; after all, as he points out, no one at Athens would have willingly admitted to not being καλός κ᾽ ἀγαθός.

[72] The fourth century BCE witnessed an explosion in top actors' incomes: see Plut. *Alex.* 29, [Plut.] *X Orat.* 848b, Aulus Gellius *NA* 11.9; *FD* III 5.3.67. As already noted, top actors could become political players by serving on embassies.

[73] The Artists of Dionysus did not admit slaves; see Garton (1972) 171.

[74] The status of bankers in fourth-century Athens provides an interesting comparandum to the status of actors. Many bankers started out as slaves to other bankers, then inherited the business, and were manumitted when the master died. Often these ex-slaves amassed astronomical fortunes and served as major benefactors to the city, as in the case of Phormion – yet Apollodorus, in Demosthenes 45.71–2, still sneers at Phormion's servile background. Wealth alone, it seems, could not make someone καλός κ᾽ ἀγαθός. See Cohen (1992) 82–90.

[75] Baker (1992) finds that Shakespeare's plays avoid having characters plan or desire to disguise themselves up the class ladder. This to her suggests the existence of a taboo, which Shakespeare observed by self-censorship.

As a Greek import, drama was often seen as another enervating luxury product.[76] Drama was an immensely popular entertainment put on by the aristocratic elite to bolster their prestige, but it came with several costs. There was the financial cost of producing *ludi*. There was also felt to be a social and possibly even political cost in watching drama. Since many actors at Rome were slaves or foreigners (or both),[77] drama in general and the *parasitus'* slavish dependence on his patron (and his belly) in particular could serve to foreground Roman anxieties about slavery and empire. Romans feared becoming slaves to the pleasures of Greek art and culture, as attested in anecdotes the Romans told about the dangerous power of the theater. When the Roman fleet entered the Greek port of Tarentum in 282 BCE, so the story goes, they met with no initial resistance, because all the inhabitants were in the theater watching the *hilarotragoidia*. A Tarentine citizen took the opportunity to address the assembled populace in the theater and urged them to destroy the Roman fleet.[78] This anecdote displaces Roman anxieties about theater buildings as places where spectators wasted time, at best, or plotted against the Roman state, at worst, onto the convenient target of the theater-mad Greeks. But the Romans told stories about their own military history in which they juxtaposed the duty of battle with the lure of theatrical entertainment. One story relates that the first mime dancer at Rome, Pompilius, kept dancing at the Ludi Apollinares in 212 BCE when the Carthaginian army was encamped right outside the Porta Capena.[79] The immediate danger to Rome's interests is averted in

---

[76] This is not to deny the existence of native Italic dramatic forms, such as the Atellan farce, nor their influence on Plautus at least; Lowe (1989) posits that the Atellan character of the glutton Dossenus had a major influence on Plautus' depictions of parasites. I think it is safe to say, however, that despite the existence of Atellan farce and other "subliterary" native dramatic forms, the *fabula palliata* in the period of Plautus and Terence was presented as a Greek import brought to Rome: Greek characters, Greek settings, and in Terence's case, explicit discussion of Greek plays as sources. The issue is much more complicated, of course, but the fact that drama was divided into "Roman" (*togata*) and "Greek" (*palliata*) genres, and the degree to which playwrights played self-consciously with "Romanizing" the *palliata*, is significant.

[77] See Bieber (1961) 161; Duckworth (1994) 65–6. Donatus *ad Eunuchum* 57 states that it was forbidden to depict Roman slaves as cleverer than their masters, which would not only help "explain" the settings of Roman comedies in Greece but would also speak clearly to Roman anxieties about their own slaveholding society.

[78] Dion. Hal. *Ant. Rom.* 19.4; cf. Cass. Dio. fr.39.5; see Bieber (1961) 137.

[79] Macrob. *Sat.* 2.7.2; cf. Livy 25.12.12–15; see Gruen (1992)186 n. 12.

this story, but the hint lingers that drama is a seductive distraction from duty. These anecdotes betray a concern that drama does not give anything back to those who pay to produce or watch it, or worse, that watching it takes away something: one's military power, one's sense of duty, one's dignity, one's very *Romanitas*. If the *parasitus* is the actor, then from a certain perspective, the actor is a parasite.

Drama was not only seen as a potentially corrupting luxury product; it had the added problem that it was not a tangible "product" at all. From a literal-minded point of view, one does not leave the theater with anything more than one had when one entered; in fact, if tickets were not subsidized, then one left the theater literally poorer for the experience. Symbolically, the *parasitus* eats his host's dinner and gives him nothing in exchange but words. The *parasitus* is almost always the butt of humor in order to allay these anxieties, and when he is not, as in *Phormio*, he is performing the selfless service of tricking one master in order to serve another. The *parasitus* also performs the function of exposing liars, especially the *miles gloriosus* but also himself, as a means of allaying anxiety about the way theater deceives the audience. Even Terence's parasites give themselves away in asides. The parasite's job, in a sense, is to betray: he betrays the *miles* to the audience, revealing him to be a blustering fool; he betrays him to the other characters; but he also betrays himself to the audience with his metatheatrical asides and monologues. With these betrayals, he reassures the Roman audience that they can see through any con job, any acting.

Ghiron-Bistagne suggests that in the Classical period in Greece at least, the actor was always a "stranger" or "foreigner" (*étranger*) because of the extensive travel required by the profession.[80] During the Hellenistic era, members of the Artists of Dionysus were granted safe passage to any city and personal immunity from hostile action, and they may have enjoyed freedom from military service in their home states.[81] It is interesting to consider the fact that

> ...the guild, from its inception, could and did behave like a state, appointing not only administrative (*prytaneis*) and financial officers

---

[80] Ghiron-Bistagne (1976) 191.

[81] Pickard-Cambridge (1988) 279. Csapo & Slater (1995) 240 note that the Artists also repeatedly demand freedom from taxation and the right to wear crowns, purple robes, and gold. The Artists of Dionysus seems to have been formed after the death of Alexander; see Ghiron-Bistagne (1976) 164, Csapo & Slater (1995) 239. Pickard-Cambridge (1988) 281–2 dates its foundation to between 294 and 279 BCE.

(*oikonomoi*) but even ambassadors – thus emphasising its supra- and international status – and official delegates (*theoroi*) to the major festivals. The artists therefore enjoyed a unique and indeed anomalous constitutional and legal status. On the other hand, its was still formally a religious organization, with priests acting as executives, dedicated to the worship of Dionysus. The guild celebrated Dionysia as their main feast day, with the usual procession, feasting, drinking, and sacrifice. The guild itself had its own laws and protocols (*diagraphai*); officers were appointed usually annually by the *technitai*, though the actual executive positions varied greatly with place and time. In the world organization, the chief officers were the archon, secretary, and legal expert, and a chief priest, who was priest of Dionysus and of the emperors at the same time.[82]

In a sense, actors really were "diplomats" in the Greek world, sent on missions by their extra-national union. The actor as *alazon* makes sense in terms of international politics as well as within the dynamics of a play.

In the Roman world, actors, like parasites, were entertainers hired by rich men. One of their tasks was to defuse Roman anxieties about the deceptive nature of theater, in particular anxiety that the socially inferior actor would be able to put one over on his socially superior audience. By betraying his ridiculous master and his ridiculous self to the audience, the parasite does a reassuringly bad job of dissembling. In the next chapter, we will see how another stock comic character – the *hetaira*, or *meretrix*, or prostitute – serves as a figure for the actor in a different way: the actor as an object of desire. And in chapter 5, we will see how one Republican Roman actor was able to rise above his theatrical role as a parasite and his parasitical role as an actor to become a member of the equestrian class.

---

[82] Csapo & Slater (1995) 240. On the Artists of Dionysus as a semiautonomous nation, see also Pickard-Cambridge (1988) 287.

CHAPTER FOUR

INFAMOUS PERFORMERS: COMIC ACTORS AND FEMALE PROSTITUTES IN ROME

T HE ROMANS MADE PERSISTENT CONNECTIONS BETWEEN PROSTITUTES and actors in law, in literature, and in clothing conventions. These connections suggest an association in the Roman cultural imagination between sexuality, public life, and performance. Essentially, both prostitutes and actors were thought to be people who "faked it" for a living. Conventionally, both female prostitutes and male actors cross-dressed. The stigmatization of both groups by the upper classes as "low-Other" worked to constitute both prostitutes and actors as objects of desire. This chapter will trace out the ways in which these connections were made: in Roman law, by making both professions *infamis*; in Roman comedy, by the stock character of the duplicitous, self-serving prostitute (*meretrix*); and in Roman clothing conventions, by the customary cross-dressing of both female prostitutes and male actors. We will spend the most time on Roman comedy, because of its status as a genuinely popular entertainment. In each of these three arenas, we will see that the very traits that were used to marginalize prostitutes and actors in terms of their social status also worked to establish them as central to the Roman cultural imagination, and that the qualities imputed to them that were used to justify viewing them as objects of suspicion also served, not coincidentally, to make them objects of desire.

PRELIMINARIES: STALLYBRASS AND WHITE, AND ROMAN SUBJECT FORMATION

In their influential 1986 study, *The Politics and Poetics of Transgression*, Peter Stallybrass and Allon White set forth a more nuanced, historically sensitive version of Bakhtin's theory of carnival and the grotesque. Their refinement of Bakhtin is indebted to Foucault's insight that the most peripheral institutions of the state – prisons, madhouses – are central to the state's imagination. Stallybrass and White describe the ways in which English subject-formation from the seventeenth to the nineteenth centuries was developed by constructing a series of "low-Others," which were contrasted with the normative bourgeois subject. These low-Others were always changing, as the discourses of medicine, science, technology, and the law informed emerging bourgeois notions of respectability, but they were always tied to carnival, to the grotesque body, to the "lower bodily stratum," and to sites seen as analogous to the lower bodily stratum: the working classes, the sewer, the slum, the Unconscious. Over and over again, Stallybrass and White find that "what is socially peripheral is symbolically central"; the more areas of human experience that are marked off as beyond the bounds of bourgeois taste and respectability, the more they loom large in the images, thoughts, and writings of the bourgeois. Transgression, in Stallybrass and White's reading, is a way of designating boundaries; even as the transgressive agent (whether it be a "low" animal like the pig or the rat, a "low" person like a house maid, or a "low" location like the sewer) cuts across boundaries of class, geography, gender, or taste, the horror that the transgressive agent arouses reassures the bourgeois subject that he[1] is on the "right" side of the boundary, and the agent is on the "wrong" side.

Paradoxically, this very horror works not only to arouse disgust and thus reassurance, but also to arouse desire; as the bourgeois subject increasingly cordons himself off from the various low-Others who help define him, he finds them increasingly, and disturbingly, desirable. "A fundamental rule seems to be that what is excluded at the overt level of identity-formation is productive of new objects of desire."[2] This mechanism, in which rejection of identification leads to desire for the Other, means that politics and *eros* are at odds with each other: "Repugnance and fascination are the twin poles of the process in which a *political* imperative to reject and eliminate the debasing 'low' conflicts powerfully and unpredictably with a desire for this Other."[3] Stallybrass and White present several accounts of the desire of a higher-class man for a woman of low social status: the case of a bourgeois Englishman who secretly married his housemaid,[4]

---

[1] The normative subject described by Stallybrass and White's sources and by their project is male; the same will hold true when I discuss Roman subject formation below.

[2] Stallybrass & White (1986) 25; see also 77.

[3] Ibid., 4–5, original italics; see farther down on 5.

[4] Ibid., 154–6.

Freud's analyses of the "Rat-man" and the "Wolf-man" (who both recall desiring their governesses when they were young boys[5]), and Freud's own boyhood fascination with his governess.[6] As society, and the city in which society is based, becomes more stratified, more subdivided, more segregated, the bourgeois subject experiences a greater desire to transgress the boundaries of his station, culminating in the extreme polarities of nineteenth-century London, with its prostitutes' quarter, slums, sewers, and herds of wild pigs, extensively visited, photo-documented, analyzed, legislated about, and reported on by bourgeois journalists, doctors, government commissions, and – in the case of the prostitutes – customers.[7]

Like London, Rome was a city of extreme disparities in wealth,[8] a city intersected and divided by aqueducts and sewers,[9] a city with its market center, slums, graveyards, mansions, prostitutes' quarter,[10] theaters, and shops. And like London, Rome was the center of a number of discourses – legal, scientific, literary, rhetorical, philosophical – that worked to establish a normative Roman subject by contrasting him with undesirable alternatives: women, foreigners (especially Greeks), slaves, and all those who were seen as not masters of themselves. Obviously, Republican Rome and Early Modern or Victorian England are literally and figuratively worlds apart, and I do not mean to use Stallybrass and White's theories of English subject-formation as simply and unproblematically appropriate to Roman subject-formation. But there are some significant correspondences between the two cultures, and there are ways in which what we see emerging at Rome in the last two centuries BCE is the construction of an ideal Roman subject: the *vir bonus dicendi peritus*, as made famous in Cato's phrase (fr. 14 J) – the man of "good" family with

---

[5] Ibid., 152–3.

[6] Ibid., 156–70. Through a detailed examination of Freud's correspondence, Stallybrass & White reveal the process by which Freud revised and sublimated his own recollections of a desire for his governess into a desire for his mother. Apparently, incestuous desire was more tolerable, acceptable, or conceivable than cross-class desire.

[7] Ibid., see ch. 3, especially 126.

[8] See MacMullen (1974) ch. 4, especially his discussion of "verticality" as the defining feature of the Roman socioeconomic system.

[9] See Gowers (1995).

[10] The Subura: see Juv. 11.51, 141; Mart. 2.17, 5.22.5–9, 6.66.1–3, 7.31, 10.94.5–6, 12.18.2; Pers. 5.32. See also Plaut. *Curc.* 465–83, on both male and female prostitutes in different parts of the Forum; *Truc.* 64–73 on prostitutes sitting near the bankers' tables (in the Forum); *Cist.* 562, and Williams (1999) 39, on the Vicus Tuscus section of the Forum.

political aspirations, connections, and some money. That is, I am arguing that what Stallybrass and White claim for the bourgeois subject in Early Modern and later England is applicable to the senatorial class, the aristocracy (and those aspiring to move into the ranks of the aristocracy – the knights, or *equites*, and the "self-made men," or *novi homines*).[11]

The ideal Roman subject was created through a number of discourses and practices: through the emergence of a popular Roman theater culture, financed by the elite, in the second century BCE;[12] through the sumptuary legislation enacted to curb, or at least regulate, ostentation based on strict class demarcations;[13] through the expansion of the boundaries of the Roman empire, especially with regard to Greece and the self-conscious appropriation of Greek culture;[14] through the development of the patronage system;[15] through the publication and circulation of (supposedly) nonfictional, autobiographical prose narratives;[16] and through the proliferation of didactic handbooks, whether rhetorical, agricultural, philosophical, or literary,[17] all of which claimed to teach the elite man what to think, how to live, and just as importantly, how to present himself. All this combined to produce the image of an ideal Roman subject, in the last two centuries BCE, who was wealthy, an effective manager of his estates, cultured but not too effete,[18] politically engaged but not "a slave to the mob," an excellent public speaker (without seeming too histrionic), virtuous, brave, and self-controlled. (This image, it must be said, was informed by a great deal of nostalgia; it seems to be a distinguishing feature of Roman ideology that it constantly located its

---

[11] On the inclusion of the *equites* among the aristocracy, see Scullard (1984) 177; MacMullen (1974) ch. 4, esp. 89.

[12] See, e.g., McCarthy (2000) ch.1; Gruen (1992) ch. 5.

[13] The *Lex Oppia* limited the amount of gold women could carry and the kind of garments they could wear, and prohibited them from riding in carriages within Rome except in the performance of religious rites. The law was passed in 215 BCE and repealed in 195 BCE; see Culham (1982) and Plaut. *Aul.* 474–536. Although this law targeted women, and thus might seem out of place in a discussion of masculine subject formation, Culham (1982) 792 makes the point that the true object of female ostentation is to reflect on the status of the man. There were similar sumptuary laws in Early Modern England: see Garber (1992) 25–32, 35–7; Howard (1994) 33, 96–7.

[14] See Gruen (1992) chs. 2, 6.

[15] See Wallace-Hadrill (1989).

[16] Most notably Cicero's letters and Caesar's commentaries on the Gallic War.

[17] Rhetorical: the *Rhetorica ad Haerennium*, Cicero's *De oratore, Brutus, Orator*. Agricultural: Cato's *De agricultura*, Varro's *De re rustica*. Philosophical: Varro's (lost) *Disciplinae*, Cicero's *De republica, Consolatio*. Literary: Horace's *Ars Poetica*.

[18] See Edwards (1993) 22–4.

ideals in the past, as if gloomily acknowledging that they could never be fulfilled.[19])

The creation of this ideal was aided by the creation of a number of low-Others as well. The list of ideal qualities above, with its string of counterexamples, suggests a beginning: among the low-Others were slaves, the poor, women, eunuchs, foreigners, gladiators, pimps, actors, and prostitutes.[20] Yet, as Stallybrass and White note about the low-Others of English bourgeois sensibility, "difference is productive of desire"; what is despised can also come to be intensely desired, as the maid and the prostitute were in Victorian London. It is the connections between the last two groups of Roman low-Others listed above, actors and prostitutes, and their place in the "desiring economy" of Roman thought, that the rest of this chapter will take up and explore.[21]

INFAMOUS PERFORMERS: PROSTITUTES, ACTORS, AND THE LAW

The Romans consistently placed actors and prostitutes[22] at the bottom of the ladder in terms of their legal status. Numerous early Imperial statutes ascribe to both professions the status of *infamis* (as well as to a number of other despised occupations, such as gladiator, gladiator-trainer, and pimp).[23] During the Republican period, prostitutes could marry

[19] See Edwards (1993) 1, 30–31.
[20] Eunuchs: Catullus 63. Foreigners: Plautus' *Poenulus*. Gladiators: see Barton (1993) ch. 1.
[21] I should emphasize early on that the bodies of the actor and the prostitute were (for the most part) not *literally* grotesque; the strength of Stallybrass and White's methodology is that it enables them to draw connections between the old, carnival grotesque, and the later, somewhat sublimated, socially-despised-but-not-grotesque body. It is this body that the prostitute and the actor share.
[22] I address only female prostitutes in this study; there are no male prostitute characters in extant Roman comedy (Paegnium in *Persa* is a slave at the sexual service of his master, but not explicitly a prostitute). Some "real" male prostitutes may be referred to as sitting on the edge of the stage in Plautus' *Poenulus* 17–18, but this is a metatheatrical prologue. Male prostitutes did not cross-dress, as far as we know. Depending on whether we identify the *cinaedi* of satire and epigram as "male prostitutes," and to what degree we think of the *cinaedi* in satire and epigram as based on historical persons, they may have worn flamboyant and effeminate clothing; see Richlin (1993) and Taylor (1997). All this is not to say that male prostitutes are wholly cut off from the discourse of duplicity and theatricality that I outline in this chapter, but the issues around them are different. On male prostitutes and theatricality, see Williams (1999) 24, 221.
[23] Flemming (1999) 50–51; Parker (1999) 164–6; McGinn (1998) 33, 41–2, 59, 65–9; Edwards (1997) *passim*, esp. 70, 72–3; see also Dupont (1985) 95–102.

freeborn men, although the man would then share his wife's *infamia*; after Augustus' marriage legislation, even retired prostitutes were forbidden to marry freeborn citizen men.[24] Under Augustan marriage law, a Roman husband was allowed to kill an adulterer caught in the act with the man's wife only if the adulterer was of low status – a convicted criminal, a freedman belonging to the family, a pimp, a slave, or an actor.[25] As one sign of actors' low status, a law existed during the Republic that empowered magistrates to beat actors at any time, onstage or off, for any reason; it was restricted by Augustus around 10 BCE to allow beatings only at the time and place of performances.[26] Cicero reports that his fellow citizens felt actors should even be removed from their tribes by the censors.[27]

Yet the legal infamy in which actors and prostitutes lived and worked did not function entirely unproblematically as a social stigma. A number of statutes were passed (suggesting their ineffectiveness) by the time of Augustus' marriage legislation, the *lex Julia et Papia*, in 18 BCE, prohibiting marriage between members of the higher social ranks (equestrian and up) and actors.[28] Conversely, under the *lex Julia*, the daughter of a senator who had been a prostitute or an actress could legally marry a freedman, because she gave up her honor when she pursued those professions.[29] A law was also passed prohibiting women of the senatorial classes from registering themselves as prostitutes in order to evade prosecution for adultery,[30] and statutes were passed repeatedly (suggesting their ineffectiveness) prohibiting men and women of senatorial rank from degrading themselves to appear onstage (or in the arena).[31] All of these laws suggest the paradoxical allure of social stigma and cross-class desire. That laws were repeatedly passed in an attempt to prohibit the aristocracy from

---

[24] Gardner (1986) 133. Edwards (1993) ch. 1 has a fascinating discussion of Augustan marriage law as a kind of moralizing discourse that aimed to address anxieties about political chaos during the transition from Republic to Empire.

[25] Scafuro (1997) 220 and n. 94 for the testimonia; see also Edwards (1993) 38.

[26] Suet. *Aug.* 45.3.

[27] Cic. *Rep.* 4.10.

[28] French (1998) 298–9; Gardner (1986) 32: "Actors and actresses were regarded [in terms of the marriage legislation] as no better than prostitutes," 129; McGinn (1998) 72, 103.

[29] French (1998) 295 n. 9.

[30] During the reign of Tiberius, after a woman attempted to do this very thing; "she was apparently not the first to do so," Gardner (1986) 130; see also Flemming (1999) 53–4.

[31] French (1998) 297; Bradley (1989) 85; Gardner (1986) 247–8.

marrying *infames* or adopting *infamis* occupations is powerful testimony to the illicit appeal of the low-Other in this time period.[32]

Catharine Edwards has discussed the ways in which the Romans viewed actors, prostitutes, and gladiators as low, shameful, yet desirable performers; she argues that the Romans associated public performance of any kind with immorality, especially if women were involved.[33] Her findings are supported by Dorothea French's study of the status of mime-actresses in the Christian era of the Roman Empire.[34] Both articles make the case for a Roman tendency to view women who "performed" in public as whores, both figuratively and insistently literally.[35] I will argue not only that the Romans punished public performers (male and female) for their occupations, but that the Romans' repeated attempts to isolate and stigmatize these groups of people also worked to make these people objects of desire.

Creating an Other to help construct the Self often creates a desire for that Other. Legally, creating a low-Other as a means of demarcating the boundaries of the juridical Self can cause subjects to desire to transgress those boundaries, to explore life and love on the other side of the law.[36] Some aristocratic Roman men kept actors as boyfriends,[37] and a few aristocratic women took the bold step of registering as prostitutes in order to avoid the financial penalties of adultery (and, perhaps, to increase

[32] For connections between prostitutes and actors continuing into the Imperial period, see Flemming (1999); French (1998); Edwards (1997). Dupont (1985) 95 describes certain Romans under the Empire who defied the laws and degraded themselves to appear in the arena or onstage: "ils montent sur scène, s'exhibent en chanteurs comme ils descendent combattre dans l'arène pour y verser leur sang sur le sable safrané, *prostituant* un corps et une voix dus à la République, pour le plus grand plaisir de la foule romaine," (italics mine).

[33] Edwards (1997). The bulk of her evidence comes from the early Empire.

[34] French (1998).

[35] Ibid., 296. See also Dupont (1985) 98–9: "La star." On the connections between actresses and prostitutes in Roman law, see French (1998) 296–7; Gardner (1986) 246–7.

[36] Stallybrass and White present something of a "case study" in the way class barriers worked to increase desire in the Victorian era: see 154–6 on the bourgeois gentleman who fell in love with and secretly married his maid; he was especially aroused by her dirtiness, and the fact that she was physically stronger than he was. As Stallybrass and White repeat, "difference is productive of desire."

[37] Sulla kept Metrobius, a type of "female impersonator," as his boyfriend (Plutarch, *Sulla* 3.3; Garton (1972) 148); the first-c. BCE Roman actor Roscius was in his youth the boyfriend of Catulus (Cic., *Nat. D.* 1.79; Weber (1996)); the actor Bathyllus was loved by Maecenas (Tac. *Ann.* 1.54).

their sex appeal). Actors and prostitutes were both *infames*; they were both versions of the Roman masculine subject's low-Other. But a crucial distinction separated them from citizen women, eunuchs, foreigners, slaves, or even gladiators: actors and prostitutes operated under the sign of the fictional, the feigned, the fake.[38] Actors and prostitutes could thus be seen as standing in for each other: the actor is a prostitute, the prostitute is an actor. The fact that the *meretrix* in Roman comedy is so often accused of lying is another sign of the interrelatedness of prostitutes and actors; the sincerity of her affections is never above question.

PROSTITUTES IN GREEK NEW COMEDY AND ROMAN COMEDY

Much productive work has been done on metatheater in Roman comedy, especially in terms of the *servus callidus* as poet/director/lead actor in the plays of Plautus.[39] I have been arguing that we can see other stock characters in Roman comedy as actor figures: the *alazon* (and his different incarnations in Roman comedy as the *miles gloriosus*, the *advocatus*, the doctor, and the quack official in general) and the parasite. Now I will argue that there is another character we can add to this list: the *meretrix*, or prostitute. *Meretrices* appear in both Plautus and Terence, and they have a strong antecedent in the *hetaira*, or courtesan, of Greek New Comedy. I will briefly address the *hetaira* in Menander's extant play and fragments before moving on to discuss the *meretrix* in the comedies of Plautus and Terence.[40]

MENANDER

As opposed to their minimal presence in Old Comedy, *hetairai* begin to appear more frequently in Middle Comedy, and become significant characters with extended monologues in New Comedy.[41] Even as our

---

[38] Edwards (1997) 79: "actors were explicitly in the business of trickery and illusion." I would argue that prostitutes were seen to be as well, but that gladiators, Edwards' other subject, were not to the same extent – although see the discussion in ch. 6.

[39] McCarthy (2000); Moore (1998); Muecke (1986); Slater (1985) 16, 28, 32–3, 47–53, and passim.

[40] McCarthy (2000) 15–16 discusses the need for reading "'horizontally' across the corpus" of Plautus in order to ascertain the significance of "a particular plot situation, character type, or speech pattern."

[41] Henry (1985).

only extant representative playwright of Greek New Comedy, Menander presents us with a number of *hetairai* among his characters: Habrotonon in *Epitrepontes*, another Habrotonon in *Perikeiromene*, Chrysis in the *Samia*, Malthake in *Sikyonios* (who does not speak in the extant fragments), the two sisters in *Dis Exapaton* (whose lines do not survive in the single fragment of the play; we infer them from Plautus' *Bacchides*, on which see below), and a girl whose name we do not know in *Kolax* (who is referred to in the extant fragments but has no lines; two men are fighting over her). Several of Menander's comedies that have not survived, such as *Glykera* and *Thais*, are named after prostitutes.[42] Furthermore, some critics have seen elements of the *hetaira* in some of Menander's female characters who are not technically *hetairai*. David Konstan reads Glykera, the concubine of a solider in the *Perikeiromene*, as having an ambiguous status: she is spoken of as the soldier's "wife," yet she has the independence (and consequent lack of legal protection) of a *pallake*.[43] She will turn out to be a citizen girl who can legally marry her lover, in the tradition of the *pseudo-hetaira*, like Krateia in Menander's *Misoumenos*. I will focus on the "true" *hetaira* in this section (and on the "true" *meretrix* in the discussion of Roman comedy below), but I include a brief discussion of one *pseudo-hetaira*, Glykera in the *Perikeiromene*, as an illustration of the essential theatrical difference between this stock character and the stock character of the prostitute.

The *Epitrepontes* concerns a newlywed couple who are estranged because the wife has given birth just five months into the marriage. She was raped at a women's all-night religious festival, by a drunken, unidentified man; her only clue to his identity is his signet ring, which she wrenched from his finger. The *adulescens* who is her new husband, furious at his apparent cuckolding, has chosen to drown his sorrows in wine and the companionship of Habrotonon, a *hetaira*. Slowly, the

---

[42] Henry (1985) 44–5 lists titles of New Comedies by Philemon and Diphilus which may refer to *hetairai*; she also provides an Appendix of Menander's plays which may have contained *hetaira* characters. See also Brown (1990) 245.

[43] Konstan (1987). A *pallake* is a "courtesan" or "mistress," as distinguished from a *hetaira*, "companion," and a *porne*, "whore" – as in the famous statement "But we have *hetairas* for pleasure, and *pallakes* for the daily service of our bodies, but wives for the production of legitimate offspring" ([Dem.]59.122) – although along with many scholars, I find this distinction exceedingly hard to draw in practice, and most scholars admit that the Ps.-Demosthenes passage purposely gives a misleading impression of a tidy schematic distinction. On the interchangeability of these terms in New Comedy, see Brown (1990) 247–9 – although he thinks that a distinction can be drawn between the *hetaira* and the *pallake*.

characters in the play begin to figure out that the man who raped the
new bride is none other than her new husband – which, in the logic of
New Comedy, constitutes a "happy ending."[44] But instrumental to the
revelation of this information is Habrotonon, who undertakes to get the
truth out of her lover, the young husband, by pretending that *she* was
the girl he raped. She tells a colleague:

ΑΒΡΟΤΟΝΟΝ: θέασ', Ὀνήσιμε,
 ἂν συναρέσῃ σοι τοὐμὸν ἐνθύμημ' ἄρα.
 ἐμὸν πόήσομαι τὸ πρᾶ[γ]μα τοῦτ' ἐγώ,
 τὸν δακτύλιον λαβοῦ[σ]ά τ' εἴσω τουτονὶ
 εἴσειμι πρὸς ἐκεῖνον.
ΟΝΗΣΙΜΟΣ: λέγ' ὃ λέγεις: ἄρτι γὰρ
 νοῶ.
ΑΒΡ·   κατιδών μ' ἔχουσαν ἀνακρινεῖ πόθεν
  εἴληφα. φήσω 'Ταυροπολίοις, παρθένος
  ἔτ' οὖσα,' τά τ' ἐκείνῃ γενόμενα πάντ' ἐμὰ
  ποουμένη: τὰ πλεῖστα δ' αὐτῶν οἶδ' ἐγώ.

HABROTONON: Onesimos, see
  if my idea pleases you.
  I'll pretend that this happened to me,
  and, taking the ring inside
  I'll go in to him.
ONESIMOS: Say what you're saying; I'm just now
  understanding you.
HAB: When he sees me wearing it, he'll ask me where
    I got it. I'll say, "At the Tauropolia, when I was still
    a virgin," pretending everything that happened to her
    happened to me; I know most of it.
                                      (*Epit.* 510–20)

As she continues to explain her scheme to Onesimos, she says,

  τὰ κοινὰ ταυτὶ δ' ἀκκιοῦμαι τῷ λόγῳ
  τοῦ μὴ διαμαρτεῖν· 'ὡς ἀναιδὴς ἦσθα καὶ
  ἰταμός τις.'

---

[44] Lape (2004) 24–8 has a brilliant reading of the "rapist marries his impregnated victim"
   plot of New Comedy: it is a plot mechanism that solves the problem of the inequality
   of wealth between the prospective groom (who is usually rich) and the prospective
   bride (who is usually poor). Once the girl has been raped, the bride's family no longer
   has to provide a ruinous dowry to the groom's family, because the groom has devalued
   her in the marriage economy; rape, therefore, has a "leveling effect."

> In order not to fail, I'll dissemble in words
> clichés like these: 'How shameless you were,
> and how rushed!'"

(*Epit.* 526–8)

In response to hearing her plan, Onesimos says in admiration, "Craftily and wickedly done, Habrotonon" (πανούργως καὶ κακοήθως, Ἀβρότονον, 535).

It is convenient for the plot that Habrotonon claims to have actually witnessed the crime, and to have actually been a virgin herself at the time of the festival – but these elements also contribute to the interest in the present impersonation: a prostitute will pretend to be a virgin, citizen girl, someone who ought to be off-limits to the lust of young men. She will play the role of her opposite.[45] And she succeeds, judging from the fragments of the play which suggest the revelation of the baby's father, the reconciliation of the couple, and the revelation of the truth to everyone concerned. Some critics read Habrotonon as a "good" prostitute with a sincere interest in helping others.[46] Even in the service of the "noblest" possible cause, however – the reunion of an estranged husband and wife, with the immediate consequence of a lost customer for her – this prostitute shows her ability to impersonate, to deceive. Scafuro notes that "her preparatory session has the veneer of an actor's rehearsal."[47] Even the most golden-hearted hooker can lie like a professional.

The *Samia* is named for a Samian *hetaira*, Chrysis, who at first glance seems to be utterly self-sacrificing, contrary to expectations for her stock role. She is the *hetaira* of a wealthy man, Demeas, who has been away on a business trip during her pregnancy with his neighbor Nikeratos; he left her with orders to expose the child if it lived, since he had no desire to raise an illegitimate child, but the child (conveniently) died. While Demeas was away, his son Moschion raped Nikeratos' daughter at a women's religious festival held in Demeas' house; she, too, became pregnant and gave birth. Moschion agreed to marry the girl, but is afraid to ask his father's consent for fear of exposing his own wrongdoing to the criticism of both fathers. Chrysis agrees to wet-nurse the baby until Moschion is safely married. When Demeas returns at the beginning of the play, he thinks Chrysis has disobeyed his orders and kept their

---

[45] See Lape (2004) 167.

[46] Zagagi (1995) 33; Henry (1985) 51–60.

[47] Scafuro (1997) 29. Lape (2004) 247 and n. 9, Henry (1985) 54, and Goldberg (1980) 64 also describe Habrotonon in this scene as engaging in play-acting.

child; later, when he overhears Moschion's old nurse refer to the baby Chrysis is nursing as Moschion's child, Demeas becomes enraged, thinking Chrysis has had an affair with his son in his absence. He throws her out of his house with a particularly nasty tirade, reminding her of her economic and social vulnerabilty as a prostitute without his patronage (369–98)[48] – and despite this, Chrysis refuses to reveal the truth. At last, when Nikeratos sees his daugher breastfeeding the baby, Moschion confesses the truth about the baby's parentage to his father, and the wedding proceeds. Chrysis' perseverance in providing a cover story for Moschion has been seen as noble, self-sacrificing behavior; she refuses to reveal the truth of his rape to his father even when threatened with dire consequences.[49] But Chrysis gives her own explanation at the beginning of the play for her ability to persevere in deceiving Demeas: he is madly in love with her, and she is confident that he will eventually forgive her (80–83). Chrysis has calculated exactly how far she can push her lover when she undertakes a deception of him; moreover, she coaches the other women in Nikeratos' household not to admit to anything (559–60). In helping Moschion, she does not stand to profit directly – but she does not stand to lose anything either, at least not permanently. And the way she helps Moschion is by playing a role: she pretends to be the baby's mother in front of her audience, the other male characters in the play.[50] She may act in the service of a noble goal, but she acts all the same.

The *Perikeiromene* concerns fraternal twins, a boy and a girl, who were exposed at birth, were taken up and raised separately, and wind up living next door to each other as young adults. The boy, Moschion, has been raised within respectable society and does not know he has a sister; the girl, Glykera, is the *hetaira* of a mercenary soldier and knows her brother's identity. The soldier sees them kissing each other one day and, in a jealous rage, crops Glykera's hair. The tension here is between the apparently shameless – and typical – behavior of a courtesan, who will receive the

---

[48] Lape (2004) 141, 159–67 notes that Demeas' tirade draws on stock expectations of the prostitute character, rather than acknowledging Chrysis' real personality, and argues that Chrysis' characterization makes her indistinguishable from a respectable citizen wife and mother. While I agree with her reading of Demeas' speech as a stereotyped attack on a stereotyped prostitute, I believe Chrysis is marked out as different from a respectable wife/mother precisely by her calculating deception of Demeas.

[49] See Henry (1985) 61–73.

[50] Henry (1985) 62, 71 notes that Chrysis remains onstage to eavesdrop on Moschion and Parmenon (lines 59–60); eavesdropping is characteristic of tricky slaves and other scheming characters.

advances of any man that approaches her, and the truth of the situation, which is that Glykera is faithful to the soldier and knows that the young man is her brother. (There is, of course, another tension: the brother desires Glykera because he does not know that she is his sister.) This is just one example of the stock character of the *pseudo-hetaira*, the girl in the position of a prostitute whose unusual nobility of character (and state of virginity) is explained by the fact that she is originally of free, and usually noble, citizen birth, which will be revealed in the course of the play. "She's not come here like a call-girl, or a common street-walker" (340), says the slave to the *adulescens* in admiration and surprise. Glykera appears to the soldier and the other male characters to be a standard-issue, opportunistic call girl, but the audience is aware that she is actually behaving with utter fidelity and sincerity; she allows Moschion to kiss her because she knows it is not improper, given their secret, true relationship. And sure enough, she is revealed to be a free girl of citizen birth by the end of the play, rewarding her sincerity, her "true" nature. By contrast, jokes at the expense of the minor character of Habrotonon the flute-girl leave no questions about her trustworthiness; in discussing stratagems to enter a house, the soldier's slave Sosias says that he expects she will be able to help them, since she knows many "siege-tactics" (482–5). As in *Epitrepontes*, the tricky slave expects help from his usual ally in scheming, the crafty prostitute, with the usual double entendres referring to her trade. The *Perikeiromene* thus demonstrates the fundamental distinction between the stock characters of the *hetaira* and the *pseudo-hetaira*: it is precisely the difference between an insincere and a sincere nature, a difference that is equated with both sexual experience and theatrical instincts.

The connection between prostitutes and actors shows up in a fragment of Menander as well. Menander fr. 185 K–T begins in mock-epic style, but quickly devolves into the standard litany of complaints against mercenary prostitutes:

ἐμοὶ μὲν οὖν ἄειδε τοιαύτην, θεά,
θρασεῖαν, ὡραίαν δὲ καὶ πιθανὴν ἅμα,
ἀδικοῦσαν, ἀποκλήουσαν, αἰτοῦσαν πυκνά,
μηδενὸς ἐρῶσαν, προποουμένην δ' ἀεί.

Sing to me, then, Muse, such a one,
a bold woman, but blooming and persuasive,
who wrongs men, shuts them out, makes demands fast and thick,
loving no one, but always faking it.

The association of the prostitute with acting (προσποουμένην) is explicit; she "acts," rather than truly loving. The anecdotal tradition complements New Comedy's interest in *hetaira* characters. Menander, Philemon, and Diphilus all supposedly had *hetairai*; legend has it that Menander's beloved courtesan, Glykera, used to help him select the masks that he famously used to assemble his plots before writing his plays.[51] There are several artistic representations of this legend, in bas-reliefs and mosaics, suggesting it was widely dispersed.[52] The logic of the anecdote, I would suggest, is that the *hetaira* is as suited to selecting the masks that will be used to compose a plot as the poet is – in other words, that prostitutes know something about acting, or about throwing different character types into conflict with each other, or perhaps about constructing plots (in both the dramatic and the scheming sense of the word).

Within Menander's fragments, then, the *hetaira* is commonly joked about as a cunning strategist and expert dissembler, and she is differentiated sharply from the *pseudo-hetaira*, the woman who appears to be a *hetaira* but in fact is a respectable, free – and sincere – girl. The same stereotypes and the same distinctions will hold true for the *meretrix* in Roman comedy. And within the tradition of biographical anecdotes about Menander and his rivals, playwrighting is associated with prostitution.

PLAUTUS

Meretrices in Roman comedy sort themselves into two basic types: the "sincere" or "good faith" ones, those who truly love the *adulescens* (even if they occasionally "have to" feign affection towards another lover for money), and the "bad faith" ones, those who do not truly love anyone, but play everyone for money. The "bad faith" *meretrix* lies about her feelings and intentions to everyone in order to get what she wants; she occasionally even impersonates someone else, whether a respectable *matrona* (as in *Miles Gloriosus*) or a new mother (as in *Truculentus*). But even the "good," "sincere" *meretrix* feigns affection for her less appealing clients in order to wring more money and gifts out of them. Sometimes, as in the *Cistellaria*, the "good faith" *meretrix* is really a *pseudo-hetaira*, a freeborn girl who has been brought up as a *meretrix* but is revealed to

---

[51] Menander and Glykera: Alciphron 4.9.5. Philemon: Athenaeus 13.594d. Diphilus: Athenaeus 12.583. See Brown (1990) 253 and Henry (1985) 43–4.
[52] Bieber (1961) 88–9, figs. 317, 321.

be of citizen birth and therefore eligible to marry the *adulescens* (which then "explains" her nicer-than-usual character while she was living as a *meretrix*[53]). Significantly, the "bad faith" *meretrices* are always real prostitutes. But whether she is a good, sincere courtesan who is truly in love with her young man – the proverbial "hooker with a heart of gold" – or a bad, self-serving, conniving whore, all *meretrices* in Roman comedy display an ability to seduce, charm, and deceive, and all of them display an awareness that they have to take certain measures to ensure their own financial security (something that the old *lena*, or madam, one of the most consistently vilified characters in Roman comedy, is always urging her to do; see n. 65). And regardless of whether she is "really" good or bad, most *meretrices* are accused of being bad (that is, faithless, self-interested, and mercenary) at some point during a given play, whether by the *adulescens* who supposedly loves her, his slave, or both.[54]

The *adulescens*, or "young man in love," typically complains about the two-facedness of the *meretrix*: when he has money, she is sweet and welcoming, but when his money runs out, she shuts him out of the house. But this complaint reveals the two-facedness of the *meretrix's* client: he values the *meretrix* because she will love him because of his money – that is, he values her availability – but he wants her to love only him – that is, he devalues her availability. He wants to be able to buy an exclusive relationship, but he does not want to have to keep paying for it, and he does not want anyone else to be able to buy it. As the exasperated slave says to the *adulescens* in Terence's *Heauton Timoroumenos*,

---

[53] Gilula (1980) 147; Fantham (1975) 57–8.

[54] The "good"/"bad" distinction among comic prostitutes goes back to remarks by Donatus, *ad Hecyra* 774, and Plutarch, *Quaestiones Conviviales* 7.8.712c. Modern scholars often dispute the utility of these categories, noting that they are ideologically loaded. For example, Gilula (1980) argues that all of Terence's prostitutes are "bad." Brown (1990) argues that the whole good/bad distinction is not very useful. Knorr (1995) argues that this is not a moral category, but rather good/bad from the customer's economic point of view, which is not useful (but then he argues that Bacchis in *Heauton Timoroumenos* is "good-hearted," not "a ruthless gold-digger" which sounds as if he is using the same moral categories: 222). Goldberg (1986) uses the term *mala*, although he urges critics not to insist on using this classification system (117 and n. 30). I am in agreement with these scholars that the terms "good" and "bad" are not morally transparent or free of Roman ideology, which is why I am using the terms "good faith" and "bad faith" (again, from the customer's point of view) to describe Roman comic *meretrices*. One scholar who does not fundamentally dispute the categories is Anderson (1984): he argues that Plautus makes the *meretrix* a comic heroine, but he assigns each Roman comic *meretrix* a "good" or "bad" label.

vis amare, vis potiri, vis quod des illi effici;
tuom esse in potiundo periclum non vis; haud stulte sapis,
siquidem id saperest velle te id quod non potest contingere.
aut haec cum illis sunt habenda aut illa cum his mittenda sunt.

(*HT* 322–5)

You want to love her, you want to have her, you want money to be
   got to give her;
You don't want to risk yourself in having her; you're hardly stupid in
   your wisdom,
If, indeed, it's wisdom for you to want what can't happen.
You must either take the risks with your desires or let go of your
   desires along with the risks.

And in comedy at least, the *adulescens* keeps bringing love into the picture.[55] He loves the appearance that the *meretrix* presents when all is going
well: that they are in love, that she loves only him, that her beauty and
her hospitality and her costly upkeep and her attentions are all for his
sake (and not for his money). But he hates the moments when he feels
he has glimpsed the truth behind the appearance: that the *meretrix* loves
only money, that she has been putting on a show for him, in order to
get his money, and that she will put on that show for anyone who has
money – and not for anyone who doesn't.[56]

   In this way, the *meretrix* in Roman comedy functions as a figure for the
actor; she feigns for a living. And therefore, the *adulescens*, who oscillates
between rapturous delight and desire for his beloved special girl, and
bitter, disillusioned contempt for his mercenary whore, functions as a
figure for the Roman theatrical audience, oscillating between delight in
theatrical pretense and suspicion of the performance and the performers
that they are watching. Neither view is "the" Roman view of prostitutes,
or actors – both were available in Roman culture, and audiences could
tap into either one at any given moment. But the more the *adulescens*
desires the *meretrix*, the more bitterly he feels he has been duped when
she shuts him out of the house – and the more the audience enjoys the

---

[55] See Adams (1983) 325–6.
[56] The anecdotal tradition emphasizes the connection between actors and prostitutes
   through the motif of the appearance/reality gap: Athenaeus 13.587b mentions a prostitute (in Antiphanes' *On Courtesans*) who was nicknamed "Proscenium" because,
   although she had a pretty face and expensive clothing and jewelry, she was revealed to
   be exceptionally ugly when naked.

actor, the more anxious they feel about their desire for empty spectacle and literally infamous performers.

PLAUTUS' PROSTITUTES: TRICKY *MERETRICES* AND SWEET YOUNG THINGS

The *meretrix* appears in a number of Plautine plays (*Asinaria, Bacchides, Cistellaria, Menaechmi, Miles Gloriosus, Mostellaria, Persa*, and especially *Truculentus*[57]) and whenever she has any kind of speaking role, she functions as a figure for the actor. The *meretrix* is an expert dissembler, sometimes compared explicitly to an actor, who typically tells her "director" (usually the tricky slave) that she needs no coaching in deception. The paradigmatic example is Phronesium in Plautus' *Truculentus*, which will occupy the majority of our discussion; we will work up to her character by examining the smaller roles in other plays first. We will find that the "good faith" prostitute is a bad actor, because her "goodness" consists of her antitheatrical sincerity, while the "bad faith" prostitute is a good actor. The "good faith" prostitute reassures the spectators that they will not be fooled by theater's seductive lies, while the "bad faith" prostitute keeps the spectators pleasurably unsettled.

Asinaria contains a "good faith" *meretrix* named Philaenium. The *adulescens*, Argyrippus, has run out of money to continue paying her mother/*lena* for her company. The *lena* shuts him out of their house, and he bitterly chastises her for her unfairness and hard-heartedness; she responds with a series of coolly logical statements that this is business, and that he is welcome back when he gets more money. Argyrippus then proposes to raise enough money to pay to have Philaenium exclusively for himself for one whole year – as long-term a relationship with a "real"

---

[57] There are two other comedies of Plautus with characters who could arguably be described as *meretrices*: *Curculio* and *Mercator*. I am not including them in my discussion, however, because in each case, a character may be thought to be a *meretrix* or called a *meretrix* by certain characters, or she may be in the position of a *meretrix* (owned by a pimp, etc.), but she turns out to be a freeborn girl *before* her first sexual encounter. This distinguishes her from characters like Selenium in *Cistellaria*, who is a *pseudo-hetaira*; Selenium, who will turn out to be freeborn and will marry the *adulescens*, is not a virgo – but she has only had sex with the man she sincerely loves. This may seem like pointless quibbling over terminology, but the distinction highlights a crucial aspect of my argument. The *virgo* rarely if ever exhibits any theatrical guile (the exception would be someone like the parasite's daughter in *Persa*, on which see McCarthy (2000) 149–50 n. 77), while both the "bad faith" *and* the "good faith" *meretrix* demonstrate a propensity toward acting. This ability or propensity is apparently connected with their sexual experience.

prostitute (as opposed to a *pseudo-hetaira*) as Roman comedy ever imagines, and the first appearance of the motif of the desire for exclusivity that we will see recur over and over again.[58] With his father's blessing Argyrippus' tricky slave steals money to continue paying for the young man's good time. In return, the father asks for a night with the girl, which the son grudgingly grants, but the threatened paternal intrusion is thwarted by the intervention of the shrewish wife.

As a "good faith" *meretrix* who truly loves the *adulescens*, Philaenium meekly protests against her *lena's* advice to string multiple men along at once. But she also plays along when the tricky slaves demand that she sweet-talk them to get the money they've obtained for the lovers (664–92), quoting a proverb, "Whatever poverty demands" (quidvis egestas imperat, 671), and saying what would sound like a "bad faith" statement in another context, "Please, I'll do what you want, just give us that money" (amabo, faciam quod voles, da istuc argentum nobis, 692). She plays the attentive dinner companion at the banquet with Argyrippus' father – until his wife arrives and Philaenium, relieved of her duty, can confess that she was bored by him (920–21). Even the "good faith" *meretrix* has to make nice to anyone who has any kind of hold over her; even the sweetest sincere prostitute has to play-act in some situations.[59]

Bacchides features identical twin sister *meretrices* with the same name, Bacchis. The opposite of the sincere Philaenium in *Asinaria*, they are "bad faith" prostitutes who ensnare two *adulescentes* with their charms and then, when the young men's fathers object, they ensnare them as well. Although the *meretrices* are onstage only in acts I and V, in both they showcase their seductive techniques, complete with asides to each other about their performances. Bacchis I, in the earliest preserved scene in the play, urges her *adulescens* to "pretend you love me" (simulato me amare, 75) in order to make the *miles* jealous (this exhortation combines her interest in prostitution and acting concisely and elegantly). Despite his fears that she is ensnaring him like a bird in birdlime to do her bidding, he capitulates.[60] In the last scene in the play, Bacchis II confesses in an aside

---

[58] The *lena* sums up the *adulescens'* dilemma in this play and every play when she says, "You alone lead her away, as long as you alone always give me what I demand" (Solus ductato, si semper solus quae poscam dabis, 165): she's exclusively yours, as long as you keep paying for it. See below on *Eunuchus*.

[59] Anderson (1996) 83: "We have seen Philaenium of the *Asinaria* play the naïve affectionate girl, at the start of the play, until she gets caught up in the tricks of the libidinous slaves and old father."

[60] On hunting and bird-catching imagery in *Bacchides*, see George (2001).

to her sister that she will do her part in seducing one of the *senes*, even though it will be like embracing a death's head (1152); she then proceeds to wheedle and flatter him. The audience is treated to seeing two consummate professionals at work.

Cistellaria contains two *meretrices*, Selenium and Gymnasium. Selenium is a "good faith" prostitute who truly loves the *adulescens* Alcesimarchus; in fact, she has never had sex with any other man but him. Given these two facts, it is unsurprising that she is a *pseudo-hetaira* who will be revealed to be of legitimate citizen birth at the end of the play, when she and her lover can get married. She is accordingly the least deceptive or theatrical of Plautus' *meretrices*; significantly, her one deception consists in pretending not to be a prostitute (83–5). The other prostitute, Gymnasium, has a much smaller role; she is a weak advocate of the stereotypical "bad faith" prostitute's lifestyle, agreeing to do whatever her mother/*lena* wishes and counseling Selenium against having any genuine feelings for any customer (46–75).

Menaechmi concerns long-lost identical (and identically named) twin brothers, one of whom keeps getting mistaken for the other through the course of the play. Menaechmus in Epidamnus, who is married, has been carrying on a relationship with a *meretrix*, Erotium; the arrival of the other Menaechmus in Epidamnus throws the first Menaechmus' lifestyle into chaos, as wife and mistress both become enraged at real and perceived deceptions and thefts by "Menaechmus." Erotium is initially flattering to Menaechmus, telling him that her house is always open to him (351–68), but when she believes she has been swindled by him (in fact, she has interacted with two different Menaechmuses), she turns nasty and shuts him out (688–95), saying, "Unless you bring money, you won't be able to take me home for nothing" (nisi feres argentum, frustra me ductare non potes, 694). As the parasite remarks, "A prostitute is always flattering, while she sees something she can take" (meretrix tantisper blanditur, dum illud quod rapiat videt, 193). While not very developed, her character is the stereotypical "bad faith" prostitute: mercenary, greedy, and two-faced. It is perhaps significant that, at the end of this play, Menaechmus I takes leave of both wife and *meretrix* to sail away with his long-lost twin; both women have become unappealing.[61]

Miles Gloriosus contains two *meretrices*, the love object Philocomasium, and the helpful client Acroteleutium of the helpful *senex* Periplectomenus. Both prostitutes are consummate actresses, but Philocomasium is a "good

---

[61] See McCarthy (2000) 40, 63–6, who argues that Erotium mimics and is ultimately conflated with the wife in this play.

faith" *meretrix* in that she truly loves the *adulescens* and uses her deceptive abilities on the *miles* in order to escape his clutches, while Acroteleutium is a "bad faith" *meretrix* in that she seems simply to enjoy lying. The plot of the play hinges on two scenes in which the *meretrices* must play other characters in order to fool the *miles gloriosus* or his slaves. Philocomasium has to play identical twins in order to fool the slave who is set as a guard over her; by convincing him that he glimpsed her twin sister kissing a strange young man, she prevents the slave from reporting her infidelity with the *adulescens*. Acroteleutium is costumed as a *matrona* by the tricky slave Palaistrio and set to play the role of the *senex*'s estranged wife, who supposedly lusts after the *miles*; her acting ability is essential to the final deception of the *miles*.

> PERI.: habeo eccillam meam clientam, meretricem adulescentulam.
>   sed quid ea usus est?
> PAL.:   ut ad te eam iam deducas domum
>   itaque eam huc ornatam adducas, ex matronarum modo,
>   capite compto, crinis vittasque habeat adsimuletque se
>   tuam esse uxorem: ita praeciplundum est.
>   (*MG* 789–93)

> PERI: See, I have my client right here, a young little prostitute.
>   But what use is she?
> PAL: See to it that you lead her away to your home at once
>   And then lead her back here costumed like a married woman,
>   With her head arranged, let her have plaits and headbands
>   And let her pretend that she is your wife: she has to be instructed
>   thus.

Note the use of the term *ornata*, "adorned" but more precisely "costumed," and note the attention paid to the markers of *matrona* identity: hairstyle and hair ribbons. The verb *adsimulare* completes the theatrical context. We could say that she is dressing as the stock *matrona* character, since she adopts all the simple markers of the *matrona*'s identity onstage: hairstyle (mask) and deportment (walk). "How appropriately she walks in costume, not like a prostitute at all!" (quam digne ornata incedit, hau meretricie! 872) exclaims Palaestrio as Acroteleutium approaches him in her *matrona* costume.[62]

---

[62] On *ornata*, see below on *Truculentus*. That the prostitute could "pass" as a *matrona* is obviously a subject of some anxiety as well as of much comedy in a society as class-conscious as Rome. After all, if clothing is used to indicate status (on which see the section on "Transvestite Trades," above), then a simple change of costume could potentially undermine the social order. See also French (1998) 296.

The tricky slave coaches the *senex* and the *adulescens* about their roles in this fake marriage; both of them express nervousness about learning their parts. But when any character attempts to coach either of the *meretrices*, both women reply that they need no coaching; they are expert actors. To Philocomasium, as she prepares to play her "twin sister," the tricky slave Palaestrio says,

> PAL: praecepta facito ut memineris.
> PHIL: totiens monere mirumst.
> PAL: at metuo ut sati' sis subdola.
> PHIL: cedo vel decem, edocebo
>   minime malas ut sint malae, mihi solae quod superfit.
> (MG 354–6)

> PAL: See to it that you remember what you've been taught.
> PHIL: It's a wonder you warn me so often.
> PAL: But I'm afraid that you won't be deceitful enough.
> PHIL: If you like, give me ten girls; I'll teach the least bad ones
>   To be bad with what I alone have left over.

When the *senex* Periplectomenus tries to coach his client prostitute Acroteleutium in playing her role as the *matrona*, she responds,

> ACRO: stultitia atque insipientia mea istaec sit, <mi patrone,>
>   me ire in opus alienum aut [t]ibi meam operam pollicitari,
>   si ea in opificina nesciam aut mala esse aut fraudulenta.
> PERI: at meliust <com>monerier.
> ACRO: meretricem commoneri
>   quam sane magni referat, nihil clam est. quin egomet ultro,
>   postquam adbibere auris meae tuae oram orationis,
>   tibi dixi, miles quem ad modum potisset deasciarei.
> (MG 878–84)

> ACRO: I'd be stupid or foolish, my dear patron,
>   To undertake someone else's work or promise to help him there,
>   If I didn't know how to be bad or deceitful in the workshop.
> PERI: But it's better to warn you.
> ACRO: Of *course*, it's no secret that it's *very* important
>   To warn a prostitute. In fact, moreover, after my ears
>   Drank in just the coastline of your ocean of oratory,
>   I personally described to you how the soldier could best be cheated.

Acroteleutim goes on to say that women are naturally good at being bad. Despite the standard comic misogyny of this sort of line in Plautus, it is not all women who are good at being bad, but *meretrices*; their actor-like occupation brings out the liar in them. Even Acroteleutium's maid, Milphidippa, is a skilled actress, feigning admiration for the *miles* in her role as go-between while exchanging asides with the tricky slave. In fact, Palaestrio is so impressed with Milphidippa's acting abilities that when she later salutes him as "architectus" of the plot, he replies that compared with her, he is nothing (1140).[63] *Miles Gloriosus* reveals two prostitutes enthusiastically and skillfully playing roles and engaging in theatrical deception: the "good faith" one out of a desire to escape with her true love, the "bad faith" one out of a simple love of deceit and mockery.

The *Mostellaria* contains two *meretrices*, Philematium and Delphium.[64] Philematium, the beloved of the *adulescens*, is the ideal of the "good faith" *meretrix* – or the antitype of the scheming prostitute, who is represented by Scapha, Philematium's slave and a retired prostitute herself. Scapha and Philematium engage in an argument over Philematium's unprofessional and surprisingly selfless devotion to the *adulescens* Philolaches, which Scapha warns her is imprudent (157–290). This is a stock scene in plays with a "good faith" *meretrix*.[65] The "good faith" *meretrix* presents the surprising (and, to the eavesdropping *adulescens*, pleasing) news that she sincerely loves Philolaches, even against her own professional interest; Scapha presents the stereotypical, "bad faith" side of the argument, urging her to think of her retirement. This scene typically occurs either with the *adulescens* or his slave eavesdropping unobserved, as here in *Mostellaria*, or with only the audience as "eavesdroppers" – in other words, its function is to establish the "good faith" *meretrix*'s sincerity by making her unaware she has an audience (other than her slave) for her speech.[66] We could say it makes her less metatheatrical, that it increases her sincerity by deliberately detheatricalizing her character. If the *adulescens* is eavesdropping, as in the *Mostellaria*, he exhibits both reactions to prostitutes that have been outlined above, but split into responses to the two characters: in

---

[63] Both in this play and in *Truculentus*, the *meretrix* is paired with an equally deceptive and theatrically gifted maidservant. In both plays, the *ancilla* makes a pair with the slave character, while the *meretrix* herself uses her skills on the higher-class characters.

[64] The other *meretrix*, Delphium, has very few lines, in which she tends to her drunk master/boyfriend.

[65] Cf. *Asin.* 504–44, *Cist.* 78–81, *Mostell.* 184–247, *Hec.* 58–75. Scapha here is the mother/*lena* figure.

[66] See Moore (1998) ch. 2.

reaction to the "good faith" *meretrix*'s statements, he swoons and swears that losing his fortune to buy her is worth it; in reaction to the "bad faith" prostitute Scapha, he threatens violence and expresses outrage at her callous manipulation of lovers.[67] Philematium repeatedly asserts her sense of obligation and fidelity to Philolaches and disavows any stereotypical prostitute's ploys, saying, "I love truth, I want truth to be spoken to me; I hate a liar" (ego verum amo, verum volo dici mihi; mendacem odi, 181). It is no coincidence that this conversation takes place during the *meretrix*'s "toilet scene" – that is, she and her slave have a conversation over whether sincerity or manipulation is the best policy with the *adulescens* while she applies makeup and adorns herself. It is one degree removed from a costuming scene, such as we have examined in *Miles Gloriosus* – and it may add an ominous note to Philematium's repeated protestations of sincerity that she is the one who keeps putting on more makeup, while Scapha, the cynical old slave, assures her that her real self is pretty enough.

Persa is an unusual play in that it represents something of an authorial experiment with stock characters: the young man in love and the tricky slave are one and the same character, Toxilus. The play also contains a "good faith" *meretrix*, Lemniselenis, who has a very small role onstage. The plot of the play involves the ruse that Toxilus uses to hoodwink the pimp Dordalus into both freeing Lemniselenis, whom Toxilus loves, and giving Toxilus a large sum of money. Lemniselenis has so few lines (she is only onstage in Act V) that it is not clear whether she is a "good faith" or "bad faith" *meretrix*, although she seems to belong to the former category. Of her few lines, one contains a hint of deception: when Toxilus and the assembled company start gloating at their drinking party over how they tricked the pimp, the pimp says to her,

> DOR: at, bona liberta, haec scivisti et me celavisti?
> LEMN: stultitiast,
>   quoi bene esse licet, eum praevorti
>   litibu'. posterius istaec te
>   magi' par agerest.
>
>   (*Persa* 798–801)

> DOR: But you, good freedwoman, you knew these things and hid
>   them from me?

---

[67] Asides praising the "good faith" *meretrix*: 206–07, 222–3, 227–8, 233–4, 241–4. Asides threatening the "bad faith" *meretrix*: 191–3, 203, 212–13, 218–19, 237–8.

LEMN: It's stupid for a man to turn to quarreling when he could be enjoying himself. Deal with this matter later, that's more fair.

This may be the evasiveness of good manners, or it may be the evasiveness of a trained professional; her character is so minor that it is impossible to tell.

In contrast, the last Plautine play we will examine makes the character of its *meretrix* very clear. By far the baddest of the "bad faith" *meretrices* in Plautus' extant corpus is the aptly named Phronesium in *Truculentus*. Like *Persa*, *Truculentus* is an authorial experiment with combining stock characters: the *meretrix* Phronesium is the *servus callidus*, the "tricky slave."[68] She proves to be a master of clever intrigue as she plays three lovers off against each other, using each one in turn to leverage gifts and cash out of the other two.

Of Phronesium's three lovers – an *adulescens* from the city, a rustic youth, and a *miles* – the *adulescens*, Diniarchus, is clearly supposed to be the most sympathetic,[69] and Diniarchus is bitter over his fall from favor as his money has run out. In his monologue opening the play (21–94), he reiterates many of the standard complaints against *meretrices*: that a lover is only welcomed by a *meretrix* so long as he has money; that a *meretrix* ensnaring lovers is like a fisherman hauling in his catch; that the *meretrix* constantly demands more gifts and more money; and that he, and the rest of Rome's youth, cannot resist throwing away their inheritances on *meretrices*. Despite this litany of complaints against prostitutes in general, and his prostitute in particular, Diniarchus presents himself as more than willing to continue seeing Phronesium (and wasting his money), if only she will consent to see him. Thus the peculiar tone of the Roman discourse on prostitutes is set early on in this play: the *adulescens* knows he is being gulled out of his money, taken for a ride, snared in birdlime,

---

[68] Dessen (1977) 160. McCarthy (2000) 179 notes that Plautus' female characters do not undertake deception schemes on their own behalf – with the significant exception of Phronesium in *Truculentus* – and concludes that "Plautine comedy find the deceptiveness and agency required for a good disguise scheme difficult to reconcile with the passivity common to all love objects in the corpus, whether *pseudo-meretrices* or genuine *meretrices*." The deceptiveness and agency are reserved for prostitutes, I would argue, thus both signaling and averting Roman anxiety about prostitutes as selfish actors.

[69] Diniarchus gets the most lines and audience addresses of the three lovers; see Moore (1998) 144–7, on Diniarchus' sympathy with the audience, and on the way his character in particular works as a stand-in for the audience. Anderson (1996) 85 finds him to be a "scoundrel," however.

fleeced (the metaphors used in comedy are numerous), but he can't resist her charms – even though he knows her "charms" are all an act.

In this opening monologue, Diniarchus also reveals Phronesium's most outrageous plot to date, which involves passing off a "borrowed" baby as her own by another one of her lovers, the *miles*, in order to extort child support out of him (this baby turns out to be Diniarchus' with the respectable girl to whom he is engaged – and whom, it turns out, he raped nine months ago while drunk at a festival). Phronesium is deliberately and self-consciously impersonating a mother, as the *adulescens* bitterly describes:

> peperisse simulat sese, ut me extrudat foras;
> eum esse simulat militem puero patrem;
> atque ut cum solo pergraecetur militi . . .
> *(Truc. 86–8)*

> She pretends to have given birth, so that she can force me out of
> doors;
> she pretends that this soldier is the father of the baby,
> so that she can "greek it up" with only the soldier.

The use of the verb *simulat* twice in three lines suggests the feigning, theatrical quality of this deception.[70] Phronesium herself discusses her scam in some detail with the audience (450–80),[71] complete with a reference to her maternity clothes, which is to say, her costume as a new mother:

> vosmet iam videtis, ut ornata incedo;
> puerperio ego nunc med esse aegram adsimulo.
> *(Truc. 463–4)*

> You see me now, how I'm going out in costume;
> I'm feigning that I'm sick from childbirth just now.

She, too, uses a compound of *simulare* to describe her act. *Ornata*, "costumed," is the word used in Plautus when a character disguises him- or herself;[72] by using this word here to describe herself dressed in maternity

---

[70] See Muecke (1986) 224 n. 44; cf. Plaut. *Amph.* 200, *Bacch.* 75, *Curc.* 391, *Epid.* 373, *MG* 909, *Persa* 677, *Rud.* 1399, *Truc.* 86; Ter. *Adel.* 734, *Heaut.* 782–3, 888, 901, *Hec.* 188.

[71] See Slater (1985) ch. 8 on the creation of rapport between the principal tricky character and the audience through different forms of audience address, especially 155–8 on monologue.

[72] Muecke (1986) 219–20 and n. 14; Duckworth (1994) 74.

clothes, Phronesium is calling attention to her outfit as a theatrical costume. She presents herself as an actor playing a role.[73]

If Phronesium is likened to an actor, then the *adulescens* especially, but all her lovers in general, are stand-ins for the spectators. All are captivated by her charming performance. And yet they fret about their expenditures on something so essentially wasteful.[74] This oscillation between enchantment and unease, especially unease about a leisure activity, is the same dynamic at work in Roman culture at large in terms of theater. We see it in this play in Diniarchus' oscillation between suspicion of Phronesium and rapturous belief that he is the only man in on her con, that he is the one who is special to her.[75]

But the split is perhaps most vividly illuminated in the character of Truculentus himself, who at first upbraids Phronesium's maid Astaphium for helping her mistress send Truculentus' rustic young master Strabax on the road to ruin, and then slowly comes to find himself irresistibly captivated by Astaphium's charms. The slave of the prostitute and the slave of the rustic youth duplicate the relationship of their social superiors, and Truculentus eventually hands over his wallet to Astaphium – though not without some grumbling:

> . . . in tabernam ducor devorsoriam,
> ubi male accipiar mea mihi pecunia.
> (*Truc.* 697–8)

> . . . I'm being put up in an inn
> where I'll be entertained badly for my money.

Truculentus is the living embodiment of Roman nostalgia: he is the rustic Roman yeoman of yore, who is satisfied with the simple country life and distrusts "painted" and loose women and would never, ever, give them his hard-earned cash. But Truculentus is really more of a caricature than a character, a stereotype of a certain idea about the good old days, and thus he serves, not exactly as a character that the audience

---

[73] See Williams (1999) 40–42; see Slater (1985) 24 and n. 8, 27 n. 10, 162 on Phronesium as "assuming a role" in this scene. Connors (2004) 190–91 argues that the name of Phronesium's slave girl, Pithecium, suggests "monkey-like" deception is the order of business in this scene.

[74] See the comments of the soldier, 893–5; of the rustic, 645–62; of the *adulescens*, 21–94, 341–9; see the argument between the rustic and the soldier at the end of the play, when each recounts his gifts to Phronesium in a competition for her favors.

[75] On Diniarchus' unusual position as both customer and confidante, with the willing self-deception that goes along with his split role, see Dessen (1977) 152–6.

identifies with (he is a slave, after all, and not a tricky one either), but as a foil to the audience; they can feel superior but akin to him, as he falls prey to Astaphium's charms and hands her his wallet.[76] In Truculentus' downfall to the charms of the *meretrices*, we see the downfall of Rome (or Roman men) to luxuries in general: wine, prostitutes, loose living, wasteful extravagance – and theater.

The *adulescens* Diniarchus sums up this fear of Rome's decline when he says,

> postremo id magno in populo multis hominibus,
> re placida atque otiose, victis hostibus:
> amare oportet omnis qui quod dent habent.
>
> (*Truc.* 74–6)

In short, this is what a great and populous people does
when the state is peaceful and leisure-full, after the enemies have
    been defeated:
everyone who has some cash to give must have love.

Here we see the standard accusation of the old against the young in Roman comedy: that the young squander their money (that is, their fathers' money) on high living, instead of practicing traditional Roman thrift.[77] But this statement, in the context of this play, makes particularly clear what is at stake: instead of conserving their paternal estates, young men are squandering their patrimony on *meretrices*. Young men pay lavish sums to be entertained by a *meretrix* for a while, or, put more negatively, they waste money on an actor who temporarily flatters them. And Phronesium confirms this association between going to the theater and going to a prostitute, between prostitutes and actors, when Stratophanes the *miles* asks her incredulously,

> STRA: qui, malum, bella aut faceta es, quae ames hominem isti
>   modi?
> PHRO: venitne in mentem tibi quod verbum in cavea dixit histrio:
>   omnes homines ad suom quaestum callent et fastidiunt.
>
> (*Truc.* 930–32)

---

[76] See Dessen (1977) 152–3; Moore (1998) 150.

[77] See Dessen (1977) 152; Moore (1998) 142 argues that "Conspicuous allusions to Rome and Italy are arranged so as to encourage the spectators to recognize that the play's profligate lovers are Roman as much as Greek phenomena" in this play; see also 144.

STRA: How, dammit, can you be pretty or clever, if you love a
    man of that sort?
PHRO: Don't you remember what the actor said in the theater?
    "All men are eager or squeamish, as their own profit
    calls for."

How can you love that other man, asks the *miles*, when he is a poor
rustic, and I, a fine soldier, am a much better match for you? The soldier's
question implies that Phronesium is wasting her charms, her beauty and
cleverness, on an unworthy customer. Phronesium replies that there is
no such thing as an unworthy customer: she "loves" the other man, the
rustic Strabax, because it profits her to do so. The quotation from the
actor claims that all men act as they need to in order to protect their
own interests, but it takes an actor to articulate the prostitute's principle
of conduct.

Phronesium is no "hooker with a heart of gold" – she is a hooker
whose heart is set on gold, and she is a consummate actress. At the end
of the play, she has lost one customer, Diniarchus, to marriage (perhaps),
but she is still successfully stringing along the other two men; in fact, she
compels them to compete with each other in giving her cash. In the last
lines of the play, Phronesium ties together the themes of prostitution and
acting by making a direct appeal to the audience – not only for the usual
applause, but also for business:

> lepide ecastor aucupavi atque ex mea sententia,
> meamque ut rem video bene gestam, vostram rursum bene geram:
> rem bonam si quis animatust facere, faciat ut sciam.
> Veneris causa adplaudite: eius haec in tutelast fabula.
> spectatores, bene valete, plaudite atque exsurgite.
>
> (Truc. 964–8)

> By Castor, how cleverly I've gone bird-catching to my satisfaction,
> And since I see my own affairs well-arranged, I'll arrange yours too:
> If anyone has a mind to make his affairs pleasant, please let me know.
> For Venus' sake applaud: this play is in her care.
> Spectators, fare well; applaud, and arise.

Usually, the character speaking the last words to the audience steps at
least somewhat out of character and asks for applause; here, Phronesium
is both out of character (in that she addresses the audience directly) and
fully in character (in that she solicits new customers boldly). As the star of

Truculentus, she seduces the entire Roman audience with her enchanting performances.[78] Even though everyone knows her character, they find her irresistible.

TERENCE'S PROSTITUTES: THESE *MERETRICES* ARE NOT WHAT THEY SEEM

Meretrices in Terence's comedies are often seen as the exception to the rule. Terence himself implies, in the prologue to the *Eunuch*, that the audience will find no "bad prostitutes" (meretrices malas, 37) in this play, with the implied contrast to the plays of his rivals.[79] And in general, Terence shows a great deal of interest in unsettling audience expectations, whether through "rewriting" stock characters to play opposite to type (such as the altruistic parasite in *Phormio*, the kindly mother-in-law in *Hecyra*, or the indulgent father in *Adelphoe*), or through stretching generic conventions to the breaking point by, for example, sending the tricky slave offstage for most of the plot (*Hecyra* again).[80] Yet Terence's *meretrices*, upon close examination, fall into the same dichotomy of "good faith" and "bad faith" that we have seen in Plautus, and they are just as bound up in issues of theatricality and sincerity.

The *Eunuch* presents us with a *meretrix*, Thais, who appears to be the standard mercenary prostitute, but in fact is sincere and "good faith."[81] In the opening scene of the play, the *adulescens*, Phaedria, laments the fact that she has shut him out of the house and attempts to berate her for doing so, but he is thwarted by her protestations of sincere affection and her revelation that her behavior is part of a plan to save her foster sister from the clutches of a *miles*. The prostitute's sincerity is proven by her addresses to the audience when she is alone (or believes herself to be alone).[82] Despite her sincerity, she engages in quite a bit of theatrical manipulation and play-acting in order to achieve her laudable objective; in other words, even this sincere *meretrix* acts very much like a "bad

---

[78] Dessen (1977) 147, 164, notes that Phronesium's last lines force the audience to applaud her deeds, and possibly to become her next victims; see also Moore (1998) 157.

[79] See above, n. 54.

[80] Goldberg (1986) 16, 152–8, 211.

[81] Ibid. 22, 117–19 notes that Thais in *Eunuch* is being set up by Terence as opposite of the stock prostitute. See also Gilula (1980) 149.

[82] *Eunuchus* 81–3, 197–206; see Knorr (1995) 226–7, Anderson (1984) 131.

faith" *meretrix*. The line is hard to draw,[83] and the *adulescens'* anxiety over whether he is being duped is understandable:

> utinam istuc verbum ex animo ac vere diceres
> "potius quam te inimicum habeam"! si istuc crederem
> sincere dici, quidvis possem perpeti.
> (*Eun.* 175–77)

> If only you were speaking that word from the heart and truthfully,
> "Rather than have you as an enemy"! If I could believe
> You said that sincerely, I could endure anything.

He grudgingly agrees to leave town for a few days while she plays up to the soldier, even though he fears that Thais is simply shutting him out and leaving him for a wealthier customer. His final request to her before leaving sums up every comic *adulescens'* wish of his *meretrix*, in fact the wish of every customer who hires a prostitute in Roman comedy, and thus it sums up the problem with all comic prostitutes:

> egone quid velim?
> cum milite istoc praesens absens ut sies;
> dies noctesque me ames, me desideres,
> me somnies, me expectes, de me cogites,
> me speres, me te oblectes, mecum tota sis:
> meu' fac sis postremo animu' quando ego sum tuos. –
> (*Eun.* 191–6)

> Is there something I'd like?
> When you're with that soldier, be absent;
> Night and day love me, desire me,
> Dream of me, wait for me, think of me,
> Hope for me, enjoy yourself with me, be with me wholly:
> Please make your heart mine, in short, since I am yours.

He desires her to desire only him, to think only of him, to be faithful (in spirit, if not in body) to him. Act with *him*, Phaedria is urging, because you're being sincere with *me*. But that, of course, is the one thing that a customer cannot ask of a prostitute – that is, unless he pays her for the privilege of exclusivity, and that is no reassurance of sincerity at all.

---

[83] For the other characters, for the audience, and for the critics: Gilula (1980) 161–4, for example, argues that Thais is as "bad" as all of Terence's other prostitutes, even though she has to admit that Thais' soliloquy proves the sincerity of her affections (162).

The *Heauton Timoroumenos* contains a *meretrix*, Bacchis, the girlfriend of one *adulescens* who impersonates the girlfriend of another *adulescens* in order to fool both men's fathers. She is described by the *senex* Chremes who hosts her as ruinously expensive to provide for, with all the standard accusations of excessively luxurious living and demanding behavior we have come to expect of prostitutes in comedy by now.[84] In a twist on the usual *meretrix-lena* conversation, Bacchis has a conversation with the other love interest in the play, a poor *virgo* who truly loves her *adulescens* (381–95). Bacchis compliments the other girl, the significantly named Antiphila ("Loving in Return"), on having her character match her beauty. This is exactly what does not happen in the case of *meretrices*, whose surface beauty does not match their mercenary natures, and it is the job description of actors; this is another instance in which the *meretrix* figures the actor onstage. Bacchis makes the standard defense in her own behalf that she doesn't enjoy fleecing men of their wealth, but her customers clearly value only her beauty, and she has to think about her retirement. Usually it is the *lena* who counsels the *pseudo-hetaira* to think of her retirement; here it is a *meretrix* who admits to a *pseudo-hetaira* that that is her motivation.[85] Not surprisingly, Bacchis is also adept at pretending to be somebody else's girlfriend; she is a competent actor. In fact, when she believes that her *adulescens* is going to abandon her, she pretends to prepare to seek the affection of a *miles* nearby.[86] The tricky slave makes the usual reassurance about her acting abilities: "she's been thoroughly taught" (perdoctast probe, 361). Bacchis, then, is a typical "bad faith" *meretrix* who has chosen her duplicitous profession with open eyes, yet looks with momentary longing at the life of the *virgo*.[87]

The *Hecyra* contains three *meretrices*, Philotis, Syra, and Bacchis. Syra is an old retired prostitute, Philotis is a minor "good faith" *meretrix* character, and together they have the standard conversation about taking care of one's retirement (58–75).[88] Although she only appears onstage in Act V,

---

[84] Knorr (1995) 229 argues that the audience comes to realize that "her fastidiousness and extravagant behavior at Chremes' dinner party were nothing but an act, deliberately performed in order to distress him," emphasizing the theatrical nature of the *meretrix* character in this play even as he insists that Bacchis is a much nicer character than critics have heretofore acknowledged.

[85] Ibid. 225–6.

[86] On this scene as a bit of play-acting, see Ibid. 229–30.

[87] Duckworth (1994) 259 sees her as "Terence's only mercenary [i.e., bad faith] courtesan"; Gilula (1980) 152–3 sees her as the worst of Terence's *meretrices malas*.

[88] See n. 65 above. See also Gilula (1980) 150–51; McGarrity (1980–81) 150–51.

Bacchis is a more major character, for she is the hinge upon which the plot turns. She is the former lover of the *adulescens*, Pamphilus, who grudgingly gave her up at his father's insistence to marry his wife. As Pamphilus' slave Parmeno tells it, after initially refusing all conjugal duties with his new wife, the *adulescens* found himself gradually coming to love her, because of her meek, submissive, properly wifely behavior, and coming to despise Bacchis, because she became more mercenary. Pamphilus left on a business trip and when he returned, found that she had given birth to a child in his absence. Furious at his apparent betrayal, he prepares to divorce his wife. It is Bacchis who figures out that the child is his – he raped his future wife at a festival in the dark – and selflessly effects the reunion of husband and wife, at the expense of a good customer for herself. Her sterling character is highlighted by statements such as

> haec tot propter me gaudia illi contigisse laetor:
> etsi hoc meretrices aliae nolunt; neque enim est in rem nostram
> ut quisquam amator nuptiis laetetur. verum ecastor
> numquam animum quaesti gratia ad malas adducam partis.
> (Hec. 833–6)

> I rejoice that because of me all this joy befalls them,
> Even if other prostitutes don't want it, for it is not in our interest
> That any lover should rejoice in marriage. Truly, by Castor,
> I will never lead my mind toward bad parts for the sake of profit.

Yet even this remarkably selfless *meretrix* engages in deceit; she lies to the *senex* about having been the one to end the relationship with the *adulescens* as soon as he got married (750–52), when in fact, as the slave earlier revealed to the audience, he was the one who gradually ended relations with her after his marriage (167–70).[89] Bacchis is perhaps the most ambivalent prostitute we have encountered in this survey: she is reported to exhibit all of the typical mercenary behaviors of "bad faith" prostitutes in the first four acts of the play, yet she resolves the problem of the plot at her own expense; she seems to conduct herself in "good faith," yet she lies.

---

[89] Noted by Gilula (1980) 157, and see 158–61; Gilula reads Bacchis, like all of Terence's *meretrices*, as "bad." Both Goldberg (1986) 157–8 and McGarrity (1980–81) 154–5 argue that Bacchis does not lie, but is misrepresented by the overly hostile slave in the earlier scene. Knorr (1995) 224 n. 11: "slaves are notorious for being even more biased against hetaerae than the other characters of comedy."

SUMMARY

Plautus's prostitutes tend to be rather clear-cut, with the major *meretrix* characters fairly evenly distributed between "good faith" and "bad faith" types. Terence's prostitutes admit of slightly more ambiguity, in keeping with Terence's general interest in unsettling audience expectations of stock chraracters. But every major *meretrix* character displays an ability to lie, flatter, and feign when it suits her purposes, and no *adulescens* rests completely secure in his relationship.

The prostitute's dangerous allure for the *adulescens* in Roman comedy demonstrates the mechanism by which a society's low-Other becomes the object of desire. Prostitutes in Plautus and Terence all display a knack for acting, and all are accused, to some extent rightly, of being insincere performers. What seems especially marked is the *adulescens'* use of the language of love and trust, rather than that of commercial sex; the ideology of Roman comedy makes the *meretrix emotionally* important. The *adulescens'* desire for the "good faith" *meretrix* is based on the idea of mutual devotion, but he expects her to help him in his money-swindling schemes; while the *adulescens'* desire for the "bad faith" *meretrix* is whipped to a froth by her teasing and flirting, her inconstancy, her elaborate jewelry, clothing, and makeup, her demands for money. In both cases, what ultimately arouses the *adulescens* and, at the same time, makes him anxious, is the markers of her despised status. The prostitute is *infamis*; the prostitute is a hired actor.[90] And the *adulescens* frets about the prostitute's trustworthiness in the same way that Roman intellectuals fret about theater's value.[91]

The insistent connections between prostitutes and actors made by the prostitute characters themselves, by the other characters onstage, and by structural features in the comedies reveal that the *meretrix* is as much a figure for the actor as the *servus callidus*. The split of the character into "good faith" and "bad faith" *meretrices* suggests a desire on the part of the audience to have the character's essential duplicity clarified, to have some level of control, through audience expectation, over the *meretrix's* mendaciousness.[92] In a culture that both denigrated and desired theatrical

---

[90] See Richlin (1993) 568 on the Roman actor as a sex object.

[91] The most obvious, and often-cited, example of Roman elite ambivalence toward theater was the delayed construction of a permanent stone amphitheater, which did not happen until 55 BCE; until then, temporary wooden structures were built for performances and immediately torn down, at significant cost. See also Cic. *Rep.* 4.9–10; Cornelius Nepos, *De excellentibus ducibus exterarum gentium, prologus*.

[92] McCarthy (2000) 179 n. 24 traces out an important distinction between *meretrices* under someone else's power and those (*Bacchides, Menaechmi, Truculentus*) who are

entertainment, such a reaction is not surprising.[93] But it is "bad" qualities of prostitutes – their accessibility to anyone who can pay, their lack of commitment or loyalty, their social infamy – that make them, as low-Others, so useful and so desirable to the Roman cultural imaginary.[94]

TRANSVESTITE TRADES

The third component of the actor-prostitute correspondence at Rome is the shared custom of cross-dressing. Both female prostitutes and male actors (which is to say, all actors, except for mime-actresses – who were commonly assumed to be whores as well[95]) cross-dressed as part of their professional presentation: female prostitutes wore the *toga*,[96] and actors regularly costumed themselves as women to play female roles.

The assumption of the *toga* is a complex cultural signifier. To contemporary Westerners, cross-dressing signifies gender deviance, perhaps gender defiance.[97] But a woman dressing as a man (in a "transvestite trade") can also signify within a culture what Marjorie Garber calls the "progress narrative" – that is, she "has" to cross-dress because it allows her access to opportunities or resources that she could not gain access to as a woman.[98] And to the Romans, the woman wearing a *toga* signified that

their own bosses: the *meretrix* under someone else's power tends to be a "good faith" character and often turns out to be a *pseudo-hetaira*, because the blocking function is being performed by the *leno/lena/miles/*etc. Independent *meretrices*, on the other hand, combine both alluring and blocking functions within themselves. I agree with McCarthy's findings, but I would add that even the sweet, innocent, "good faith" *meretrix* under someone else's power still engages in play-acting and deception, which suggests a fundamental ambivalence in the Roman audience about prostitution and theatricality.

93 See Barish (1981) ch. 2; Beacham (1991) 65–7.
94 This trend continues into late antiquity: see French (1998) 310–12.
95 French (1998); Gardner (1986) 246–7.
96 Cicero *Phil.* 2.44–5, [Tib.] 3.16.3–5, Non. 635L, [Acro] schol. Hor. 1.2.63, possibly Mart. 6.64.4, possibly Hor. *Serm.* 1.2.63; see Adams (1983) 340, Dyck (2001) 127, Edwards (1997) 81, Richlin (1993) 545. Gardner (1986) 251–2 disputes the often-repeated scholarly assertion that prostitutes (and adulteresses) were *legally* required to wear the *toga*; she sees the practice as a socially enforced custom (and one that makes sense as "advertising" for prostitutes, if not for adulteresses).
97 Thus, e.g., Butler (1990).
98 For example, women who cross-dressed as soldiers, in order to fight alongside their husbands; women who cross-dressed as (male) pirates, in order to work as sailors; women who cross-dressed as (male) musicians, in order to pursue their love of music; or any woman who cross-dresses as a man to work outside the home in cultures where women are forbidden to do so. Disney's "Mulan" is an example of the "progress

her sexual appetites exceeded the womanly norm/ideal; she had "masculine" levels of lust.[99] We must be careful to "read" the cross-dressed female prostitute as the Romans did, not as we are tempted to by our own cultural predilections. It is instructive to note that female prostitutes in Elizabethan England and sixteenth-century Venice cross-dressed as well; they wore men's breeches.[100] And they were similarly regarded as having unwomanly sexual appetites, lust beyond what a "good" woman should feel – lust more like that of a man. So to the Romans (and to the Elizabethans), the cross-dressed female prostitute makes a statement about sexuality, whereas to us, she makes a statement about gender.[101]

But why the *toga*, of all garments? It was not only because it signified that the prostitute had lusts more appropriate to a man. Wearing the *toga*, the ultimate signifier of Roman citizen manhood, marked out the female prostitute as a public figure, while working both to naturalize and to privilege the customary garment of respectable Roman women, the *palla*. Respectable citizen women (that is, women with any social aspirations) wear the *palla*; citizen men, would-be ideal Roman masculine subjects, wear the *toga*; prostitutes (and convicted adulteresses), those women of insatiable appetite and no honor, wear the *toga* too.[102] Respectable Roman women, while apparently not as secluded as women were (at least ideally) in Classical Athens, did not go out in public unattended, and they did not conduct business in the public eye alone. The female prostitute, on the other hand, made her living in the streets, or sitting in front of a brothel, or, if she was very unfortunate, in places like graveyards; she worked in public, in the public eye, and she worked alone. She acted, in this way, more like a citizen man, out on business in the Forum, than like a woman, tending to stay at home, or to go out accompanied by servants and/or male guardians.

And this brings us to the final significance of the *toga* for the Roman prostitute: it signified that she acted. It was her costume. The prostitute's

---

narrative," as is "Tootsie" (with the genders uncharacteristically switched: the out-of-work actor "has" to apply for the only role available, that of a female character in a soap opera). Garber argues that the "progress narrative" often serves as a "cover story," that it often is not a sufficient explanation for a person's (or character's) cross-dressing. Garber (1992) 67–92.

[99] Parker (1997) 58–9: "the active (phallic) woman is denoted by male dress, marked out as one who crosses boundaries, as a violation of the norm."

[100] Garber (1992) 86.

[101] McGinn (1998) 159, 164, 202, and n. 499 discusses the prostitute's *toga* as "symbolic transvestism."

[102] See Vout (1996) 215–16; Edwards (1993) 40.

toga worked like any actor's costume: it called attention to the appearance-reality gap (that is, to the fact that she was a woman, but not one wearing a *palla*, not a "good" woman), even as it worked to assimilate the woman wearing it to her known role. It both revealed and concealed.

CONCLUSION

Prostitutes and actors were seen as analogous or equivalent low-Others from the point of view of the ideal Roman subject. The *meretrix* in Roman comedy could be seen as a figure for the actor in society – and conversely, the actor could be seen as just another kind of prostitute: they both displayed themselves in costume for the enjoyment of an audience. It was *because* the prostitute's appearance did not match her reality in many ways (in her cross-dressing, in her feigned affection, in her affluent appearance yet constant demands for more money) that she was low-Other, like the actor. Neither the prostitute nor the actor had any place in the high-stakes aristocratic game of politics and power, where it was of the utmost concern that a man's appearance as a public speaker should match his gestures, his words, and his conduct.[103] It is the rhetoric of sincerity, ultimately, that defines the prostitute and the actor as *infamis*, and therefore as low-Other, as useful ideological opposites of the ideal Roman subject. And it was because prostitutes and actors flaunted their insincerity that they were terribly appealing to the upper orders as objects of lust or identification. Their status as low-Other and their work as performers eroticized a status boundary, and in the process, revealed the dynamics of Roman subject formation.

---

[103] Aulus Gellius, *NA* 1.5 (referring to ca. 69 BCE), relates that the second most famous orator of the first century BCE, Hortensius, was ridiculed for his fancy clothes and his histrionic hand gestures; he was nicknamed "Dionysia" after the famous mime-actress of the time.

CHAPTER FIVE

THE ACTOR'S FREEDOM: ROSCIUS AND THE SLAVE ACTOR AT ROME

I N BOOK 2 OF VERGIL'S *AENEID*, THE TROJANS ARE PERSUADED TO BRING the wooden Horse inside the walls of Troy because they believe the lies of Sinon. Sinon, a Greek agent of Ulysses posing as a deserter, tells the Trojans that the Greeks created the Horse as an offering to the gods for their safe passage home; he assures the Trojans that they will win divine favor – and thwart the Greeks' attempts to do the same – if they bring the Horse inside their city walls. That the Trojans do so to their ultimate ruin is, as they say, history. One of the interesting aspects of this passage is the narrator's "editorial comment" in lines 105–6: he notes that Sinon was able to fool the Trojans because they had no experience of theater.[1] In other words, the Trojans – ancestors of the Romans – could not differentiate lies from truth, because they had not institutionalized (yet) a form of lying. The Trojans were simple, honest – sincere. The Vergilian narrator draws an obvious contrast with Greece; despite the existence of native Italian dramatic traditions, the Romans were fond of regarding drama as a corrupting Greek import.[2] Vergil here inserts a bit of Roman antitheatrical sentiment into his epic "history" of the rise of Rome from the ashes of Troy. The dissembling of one Greek actor was responsible for the fall of Troy.

Whereas the Greek world sent its actors on important diplomatic missions, the Romans passed a law allowing magistrates to beat actors publicly

---

[1] Vergil refers to theater in this passage as the "Pelasgian art"; see also *Aeneid* 2.152, 2.195. Thanks to Taylor Corse for pointing this out to me.

[2] On this view, see Edwards (1993) 98–103; Gruen (1992) ch. 5, esp. 207. On native Italian dramatic traditions from the third to the first c. BCE, see Rawson (1991) "Theatrical Life in Republican Rome and Italy."

at any time, onstage or off.[3] This contrast is often cited as the difference between Greek and Roman attitudes toward theater in a nutshell. Roman attitudes toward actors and acting, however, were more complicated, conflicted, and – in certain ways – respectful than this contrast would suggest. The life and career of Roscius, probably the most famous actor of the first century BCE, provides an illuminating case study of Roman attitudes toward actors and acting. Whereas most actors at Rome were foreigners and were either slaves or freedmen, Roscius was a free Roman; whereas most actors performed in only one genre, Roscius acted in both tragedies and comedies. He was knighted by Sulla and thus had to stop charging fees for his performances. Roscius' anomalous status as the only actor of his generation to transcend genre boundaries, as one of the few native Roman actors, and as the first superstar actor at Rome threw Roman anxieties about actors and acting into sharp relief.

In this chapter, we will look at the evidence for Roscius' life and career, as expressed mostly in anecdotes. We will also examine three texts, ranging from the second century BCE to the first century CE, that play out Roman attitudes toward actors in more or less explicit ways: Plautus' *Captivi*, Cicero's *Pro Quinto Roscio Comoedo*, and Quintilian's *Institutio Oratoria*. Plautus' *Captivi* provides a glimpse of Roman anxieties by dealing with issues of slavery and innate nobility. When the slave character "passes" as a free man, we can read concerns about the power of acting to override class and status, concerns that Roscius' being knighted also raised. Cicero's *Pro Roscio*, a speech in defense of Roscius, attributes all of the stereotypical qualities of actors to Roscius' opponent in order to clear Roscius of a charge of fraud. Quintilian's rhetorical handbook raises the specter of the actor as the orator's evil twin; if the elite man is to become an orator, he must take great care not to seem like a servile actor. These texts, together with the anecdotes about Roscius, suggest a deep Roman anxiety about acting as enabling a threatening social mobility, or even as exposing the fundamental arbitrariness of Roman social organization. The rhetorical texts in particular reveal what was at stake in defining the actor as the inverse of the ideal man. In conclusion, I will compare the

---

[3] On Greek actors serving as diplomats, see Pickard-Cambridge (1988) 279. On the Roman law about actors, see Suet., *Aug.* 45.3; Csapo & Slater (1995) 276; Edwards (1993) 124–5. Suetonius states that Augustus narrowed the law to allow actors to be beaten only at the time and place of their performances; the law was changed around 10 BCE.

anecdotes about Roscius with anecdotes about his contemporary and rival, the tragic actor Clodius Aesopus, arguing that they express two ongoing, competing theories of acting, which we first discussed in the Introduction: acting as a technical skill akin to oratory, and acting as possession. Each theory has its dark side: if acting is a skill, then anyone can learn it – and misuse it; if acting is possession, then the actor is dangerously unstable. Each conception of acting implies a threat to the stable identity of Roman citizens and Roman society itself.

HISTORICAL BACKGROUND: THE STATUS OF SLAVES AND ACTORS

By no means all or even most actors in Republican Rome were slaves, but many were, and so we must take issues surrounding slavery as an institution into account when we attempt to get at Roman attitudes toward actors.[4] The history of slavery at Rome is beyond the scope of this project, but a few points as they relate to actors can be made quickly. One interesting feature of slavery at Rome, in contrast to slavery in the New World, is that at Rome, most people became slaves through being captured by pirates or in war.[5] This means that while there could be ethnic differences between slaves and masters, in theory anyone could become a slave. Conversely, many captives were ransomed, and slaves could buy their freedom or be manumitted by their owners. Once freed, ex-slaves could even become citizens. The situation in general was more fluid and shifting than in slave-holding societies where one racial or ethnic group makes up the master class and another a permanent slave class. At Rome, the dependence on slave labor, combined with the fact that some slaves were unaccustomed to thinking of themselves as such, made for an uneasy state of existence. Slaves at Rome were not dressed markedly differently (i.e., more poorly) than free men, supposedly because the masters wanted to keep the urban slave population from realizing how greatly they outnumbered their masters.[6] Rebellion was always a distant possibility, and while there were relatively few slave uprisings over

---

[4] The scholarly consensus has swung from a somewhat uncritical belief that all actors were slaves, relying on evidence like Plaut. *Cist.* 785, to a perhaps overly skeptical emphasis on the fact that many actors were not slaves. For a brief survey of some recent studies, see Slater (1994a) 365; Parker (1989) 238 n. 35.

[5] Bradley (1989) 19–21 (slaves taken in war), 22, 69–71 (slaves taken by pirates).

[6] Seneca. *Clem.* 1.24. MacMullen (1974) 92 estimates the slave population in Italy during the period he considers (50 BCE – 284 CE) as one-quarter of the entire population.

the course of Roman history, there were slave revolts in 217 BCE (in Rome), 198 (Sestia), 196 (Etruria), 185 (Apulia), 137–3 (Sicily), and 104–1 (Sicily), and Spartacus led his famous revolt across the Italian peninsula in 73 BCE.[7] It should be noted that several of these revolts occurred during Plautus' lifetime; as we shall see, the *Captivi* makes interesting reading in light of these facts.

The status of slaves must be in the background in any discussion of acting at Rome. It is important to keep in mind the low social status of actors, whether slaves or freedmen. During the Republic, actors tended to be foreigners who were either slaves or freedmen. Actors seem to have come mostly from Greece and other eastern lands, although many were apparently from Italy.[8] By the time of the early Empire, acting as a profession carried certain legal penalties that point to a desire on the part of the ruling class to keep actors in their place. Regardless of his status before he entered the profession, once a man became an actor he became legally *infamis*.[9] It is unclear whether actors were legally *infamis* in the last two centuries of the Republican era,[10] but it is clear that acting was marked out as a profession that Roman citizens should not pursue. In the late Republican era, actors could not hold office or vote;[11] Cicero claims that his fellow citizens felt actors should even be removed from their tribes by the censors.[12] In a sense, they were all treated like slaves. The very visibility of actors made them greater targets for disciplinary action; hence the beatings by the magistrates at any time, onstage or off.[13]

When the Romans of the Republican era watched plays, then, they watched actors, many of whom were slaves and/or foreigners, playing a variety of roles on stage. A performance of a Roman tragedy might have featured a Greek slave actor playing a king or a heroine from Greek

---

[7] See Bradley (1989) 41–4 and chs. 2–5; Dumont (1987) ch. 3; Parker (1989) 237–8; Hopkins (1978) ch. 2.

[8] Slater (1994) 365.

[9] Ulpian, *Digest* 3.2.2.5, commenting on a Hadrianic edict and quoting an Augustan jurist; see ch. 4.

[10] See Cornelius Nepos, *Preface* 5, who suggests that acting was regarded as bringing *infamia* in the late Republic.

[11] *Lex Iulia Municipalis* 123 (= *FIRA* 1.18), which applies to small towns at least and dates to ca. 45 BCE; see Csapo & Slater (1995) 276.

[12] Cic. *Rep.* 4.10.

[13] On the metatheatrical comments on the servile status of actors as a theme in Plautus' plays, see Moore (1998) 10–11; on the "vulnerability" of actors to their audiences, see his ch. 1.

mythology. A performance of a *fabula palliata*, or Roman comedy "in Greek dress," might have featured a Greek slave actor playing a *servus callidus*, or tricky slave, in a story set in Greece but performed in Latin. Or the *fabula palliata* might have featured a slave actor playing an *adulescens*, or free youth. Or it might have featured a free Roman actor playing a Greek slave character. There was ample opportunity, in other words, for the spectators to see a large status mismatch between the character's appearance and the actor's identity. Roman society, hierarchically organized and status-obsessed, only occasionally acknowledged the anxieties and resentments surrounding the institution of slavery in controlled rituals such as the Saturnalia, where slaves and masters traded places for one day. In the theater, however, this sort of role reversal was common.[14] The anxieties that were inevitably aroused by role reversal and social mobility had to be managed in various ways, as we will see in our examination of Plautus' *Captivi*.

Before turning to the *Captivi*, however, we should briefly examine the issue of social mobility in the Roman Republic. Upward social mobility is well attested in the Roman Empire, particularly the phenomenon of powerful Imperial slaves such as Pallas and Narcissus (under Claudius) becoming wealthy, and influential, freedmen. The phenomenon also appears in literature, as exemplified by Trimalchio in Petronius' *Satyricon*. The extension of Roman citizenship to almost all provincials in 212 CE might be seen as another example of social mobility for those at the lower end of the social spectrum. And on the higher end of the social spectrum, the wealth requirements for the senatorial class were so high that families were constantly moving in and out of the senatorial census category.[15] But upward social mobility was already a phenomenon – and

---

[14] McCarthy (2000) 19–20 argues that the tricky slave in Plautine comedy functions to relieve the anxieties of the Roman theater audience, who were all implicated in relationships of both domination *and* submission with respect to others higher up and lower down on the status ladder, and who all, therefore, could identify with the *servus callidus* through their own experience of subordination. She sees the audience's identification with the tricky slave as a release from the anxious pressures of mastery; my argument is complementary in that I believe comedy raises the audience's anxieties in order to allay them, by marginalizing the stock characters other than the tricky slave (the braggart soldier, the parasite, the prostitute), who represent socially mobile actors.

[15] On upward social mobility for freedmen and slaves, see De Quiroga (1995); Weaver (1974); see also Edwards (1993) 24, 180. MacMullen (1974) 101 argues that the portrait of freedman social mobility in the Empire is greatly exaggerated, but see his 109, 126. On social mobility (in both directions) for aristocrats, see Edwards (1993) 161–3, 183–6; Hopkins (1974). See also Hopkins (1978) 90 on Imperial-era aristocrats paying

an issue – in later Republican Rome. The very category of the *novus homo*, or "new man," well established by Cicero's time, suggests that the Roman elite was no longer (if it had ever been) exclusively an aristocracy of birth. Horace's father was a freedman, yet he could afford to give his son the best education money could buy; Horace himself became quite wealthy by the end of his life, thanks to Maecenas' patronage. Plautus and Terence both supposedly had servile origins – in Terence's case, servile and foreign origins. All of these men rose above the station of their birth in one or several categories (legal status, prestige, wealth, connections) through the exercise of a profession that the elite valued.[16] And yet three of the four men evince considerable sensitivity about their status in their writings,[17] suggesting that social mobility was hardly unproblematic in Republican Rome. It is in this context of social mobility through professional achievement that we should consider Plautus' *Captivi*, which attempts to portray an idealized aristocracy of birth but, to do so, must depict a slave acting his way up the social ladder.

PLAUTUS' *CAPTIVI*: WHO IS THE "REAL" SLAVE?

The *Captivi* is often singled out from the rest of Plautus' plays, often for its "nobility" of tone, occasionally for its complete lack of female characters.[18] While it does have a more serious mood than most of Plautus' comedies, it makes use of most of the standard plot elements of the *fabula palliata* subgenre of Roman comedy: the tricky slave, the bamboozled father, the hungry parasite, mistaken identities, the insanity ruse, the "running slave" routine.[19] What differentiates the play, I would suggest, is its flirtation with tragedy, its sustained examination of the

---

professionals (rhetoricians, doctors, architects, and actors) huge fees as part of elite status competition.

[16] Hopkins (1974) 109: "So long as an aristocracy depends upon birth alone it can remain exclusive; when it admits complementary criteria of achievement, whether money or professional skill, it opens the way to *arrivistes*. If aristocrats want to be literateurs, literateurs have a credit which helps to disguise them as aristocrats. If aristocrats want to be generals, generals who are not aristocrats have a fulcrum by which they can lever themselves into respectability."

[17] E.g., *Cic. Ad Att.* 16.10; Hor. *Sat.* 2.6.40–42; Ter. *Haut.* 23–7. See Edwards (1993) 17, 152–7.

[18] On its "nobility": Thalmann (1996) 112 n. 1, Leach (1969) 271–2, 275. On the lack of female characters: Thalmann (1996) 137; Duckworth (1994) 144; Leach (1969) 264 n. 3.

[19] Segal (1987) 191–214; Konstan (1986) 59.

institution of slavery, and its strange "happy" ending, which "requires that the moral values of the community be upheld rather than subverted."[20] For our purposes, we are most concerned with the play's treatment of slavery.

Briefly, the plot of the *Captivi* is as follows: Hegio, an Aetolian, had two young sons, Tyndarus and Philopolemus. Tyndarus was kidnapped at age four by a family slave, who sold him into slavery to pirates. Tyndarus was bought by an Elean man who raised him up with his own son, Philocrates. When Philocrates and Tyndarus became men, they went to war against Aetolia and were captured. Hegio's remaining son Philopolemus was also captured by Eleans in the war. In his desire to ransom his remaining son back, Hegio buys a number of Elean captives, including Tyndarus and Philocrates. Tyndarus and Philocrates come up with the scheme of switching identities in order to enable Philocrates' escape; they persuade Hegio to let "Tyndarus" (really Philocrates) return home to Elea to deliver the message to the father that his son is being held for ransom, while "Philocrates" (really Tyndarus) remains as surety with Hegio. The old man falls for the trick and releases Philocrates. A friend of Philocrates recognizes Tyndarus and inadvertently reveals to Hegio that he has been duped. Enraged, Hegio sends Tyndarus to the mines. Fortunately, Philocrates returns with Philopolemus and the slave who originally kidnapped Tyndarus, and Tyndarus is recognized as Hegio's long-lost son.

The play is rich in dramatic irony, as the spectators are aware not only of the identity-switching scheme, but of Tyndarus' real identity as a free man. Much of the fun – and the anxiety – comes from Tyndarus' uncertainty about whether Philocrates will prove as loyal to him as he has been to Philocrates. Their speeches of fidelity to each other, loaded with dramatic irony, have inspired the term "noble" which has been so often applied to this play.

William Thalmann has offered a penetrating critique of the traditional view of the play as "noble." Thalmann argues that the play is unusual in that it directly confronts the issue of slavery as an institution and that it solves "the contradiction at the heart of slavery itself: the need to view the slave simultaneously as human and as thing" by offering up

---

[20] The quotation is from Franko (1995) 167 n. 16. McCarthy (2000) ch. 5 suggests another reason for the uniqueness of *Captivi*: it puts the two modes of Plautine comedy, naturalism and farce, into a unique relationship in which naturalism appropriates the structure of farce for its own moralizing, essentialist message about "true" nobility.

two different models of slavery: the "suspicious" and the "benevolent" models.[21] The suspicious model justifies the slave's position in society by invoking innate nature; slaves are naturally inferior and thus fit to be owned. (We could say that the suspicious model of slavery is akin to the antitheatrical prejudice: both view the subject in question (the slave or actor) as a base creature, prone to deceit.[22]) The benevolent model assimilates the master–slave relationship to kinship and offers the image of the obedient, loyal slave as a way of encouraging the slave to accept his or her position. (We could say that the benevolent model of slavery is motivated by a fear of upward social mobility.) Both models, significantly, naturalize slavery: the suspicious model through theories of difference in natural worth, the benevolent model through a mystifying analogy to kinship.[23] Thus, for a critic to call Tyndarus' loyalty and self-sacrifice to his master "noble" is to accept the ideology of slavery implicit in the play, to accede to the benevolent model.[24]

When we remember that some of the actors performing the *Captivi* might have been slaves, the play takes on an added significance. There is an extra layer of dramatic irony if we consider the actors as slaves and the slaves as actors. In this light, Tyndarus' identity-switching ruse and its resolution speak volumes about Roman anxieties – not only about slaves, but also about actors, and about the arbitrary foundation of Roman society itself. Tyndarus, the slave who "passes" as a free man, suggests that acting can facilitate illegitimate upward social mobility; the play defuses this threat by having Tyndarus turn out to "really" have been free all along.

While they are alone in Hegio's house, Tyndarus and Philocrates take pains to ask each other, and to reassure each other, that they will remain faithful to their bond of loyalty and mutual dependence while performing their identity switch.[25] The manner in which each asks the other not to betray him is indicative of the anxieties of their respective statuses: Philocrates asks Tyndarus "do not honor me otherwise than when you were my slave,/and remember both who you were and who you are now" (247–8), while Tyndarus begs Philocrates not to abandon him, "to turn from the best to the worst," once he has gotten the favor he needs (235–6). Philocrates, trying to minimize his dependence on his (former)

---

[21] Thalmann (1996) 113, 117. McCarthy (2000) 21–5 also analyzes the contradiction implicit in Varro's definition of a slave as a "speaking tool" (instrumentum vocale).

[22] See Moore (1998) 182 on Roman stereotypes of servile inferiority.

[23] Thalmann (1996) 115–17, basing his discussion on Bradley (1987) 26–31, 33–9.

[24] Ibid., 112 and *passim*; it also causes us to miss the humor, observes Segal (1987) 206.

[25] On the issue of *fides* in this play, see Thalmann (1996) 114–15; Franko (1995).

slave, speaks in the mystified language of the benevolent model, while Tyndarus, from his position as both slave and primary risk-taker, speaks in the language of the suspicious model. Both entreaties, interestingly enough, have a metatheatrical quality.[26] "Remember our upbringings, and do not forget your *true* identity while you play my master," is the gist of what Philocrates says, and Tyndarus in effect pleads, "Do not lie to me." Acting is thus revealed as dangerous to the social order: "both captives are aware that the temporary relinquishment of true identity that comes with acting a role may weaken the position that a man holds in reality."[27]

Hegio is persuaded by the "honesty" of "Tyndarus" and "Philocrates," and he agrees to send "Tyndarus" back to Elea to collect the ransom – allowing the free Philocrates to escape, while leaving his slave behind. This arrangement occasions another loaded exchange between Tyndarus and Philocrates, this time in front of Hegio. Tyndarus exhorts Philocrates to carry his message and return swiftly, to honor the agreement they have made, and to remember his kindnesses toward him. He even adds that he is certain Tyndarus will be rewarded with freedom for his service (378–413)! Philocrates assures him that he will carry out his task faithfully, but adds a disconcerting vow: "I swear by Jupiter almighty, Hegio,/I will never be unfaithful to Philocrates" (426–7). While Hegio praises the nobility of master and servant, Tyndarus and the spectators are left wondering whether Philocrates will ever return. The vow is a punchline as well, of course, and we should not underestimate the comedy in this scene, or in the play as a whole. In fact, the humor is quite significant: it emphasizes Philocrates' current role as the tricky slave. This means the audience is aware of Tyndarus' predicament, but may be laughing at it, instead of (or as well as) feeling nervous with him. Somehow, the power dynamic has reshifted; even though Tyndarus has the power to reveal that Philocrates is the real master, because of Tyndarus' devotion (that is, his acceptance of the benevolent model of slavery with regard to Philocrates), Philocrates has the power to escape and abandon Tyndarus.[28] This is one way the play defuses audience anxieties about Tyndarus getting the upper hand through his successful impersonation of a free man: it shows Philocrates

---

[26] Muecke (1986) 222 argues that disguise is inherently metatheatrical and that disguise in comedy "can be unveiled as an image of acting."

[27] Leach (1969) 277.

[28] *Contra* Thalmann (1996) 126.

reinstating the power differential between them *by playing the tricky slave.*[29] Tyndarus displays his own anxiety about Philocrates' acting ability when he says, "It is these words [of yours] that I wish you to prove by works and deeds" (429). He is becoming suspicious. It is Hegio's turn to become suspicious next.

After Philocrates leaves Tyndarus alone onstage, Hegio and Aristophontes enter. Aristophontes is an old friend of Philocrates', and as soon as Tyndarus sees him, he realizes that his identity-switching ruse is in trouble; Aristophontes will recognize him. He is unable to come up with a truly clever scheme and settles on the old chestnut of the insanity ruse.[30] The scene that ensues, with Tyndarus trying to persuade Hegio that Aristophontes is mad for thinking he is Tyndarus and not Philocrates, while trying to signal to Aristophontes behind Hegio's back, is one of the more standard comic scenes in the play;[31] it is in fact self-consciously standard, deliberately an old chestnut, because it reveals that Tyndarus is not very good at acting like a tricky slave.[32] The insanity ruse also invokes theater and theatricality, for Tyndarus compares the frustrated and uncomprehending Aristophontes to Alcumenus, Orestes, and Lycurgus (562), and then later to Ajax (615), all famous madmen from mythology – and from the stage.[33] The comparison to Ajax is especially interesting: Tyndarus tells Hegio, "When you look at this man, you're looking at Ajax himself, minus the costume (*ornamenta*)."[34] Tyndarus' allusion to the *Ajax* calls attention to his own (ineffective) play-acting even as he tries to persuade Hegio of the reality of his interpretation. Aristophontes fails to grasp the situation, however, and insists on the truth of Tyndarus' identity. The scene ends with Hegio realizing he has been duped and

---

[29] See Moore (1998) 191–2; Frangoulidis (1996) 148.

[30] Hunter (1985) 128 discusses this stock scene. McCarthy (2000) 194–5 argues that Tyndarus first makes use of the stock scene and then drops it because he functions in this scene both as a free character (who tends, in Plautine comedy, to use the insanity ruse to get out of trouble) and as a tricky slave (who tends to simply admit the trick).

[31] Segal (1987) 204.

[32] Leach (1969) 280 comments on the "awkwardness and incompetence" (and humor) of "Tyndarus' actions as a tricky slave" in the scene with Aristophontes.

[33] On the first three characters in tragedy, see Frangoulidis (1996) 149–50.

[34] See Frangoulidis (1996) 152 and Muecke (1986) 219 and (1985) 176–7 on *ornamenta* as a metatheatrical term in Plautus. Muecke (1986) 229 comments on Tyndarus' use of metaphor in this line: "That is, he's not *acting* mad, he is mad. In this type of scene the idea of acting is never entirely absent, yet it is significant that it is referred to negatively."

ordering Tyndarus sent to the mines.[35] It is an especially dour end to a stock comic scene.

Before Tyndarus is taken away, he and Hegio have an exchange that is significant in terms of our discussion of ideologies of slavery and attitudes toward acting. Hegio is enraged because Tyndarus has betrayed him by allowing Philocrates to escape. Tyndarus claims not to be able to understand Hegio's rage; after all, he has not betrayed his *true* master. Furthermore, he says, Hegio would be pleased if one of his slaves performed the same trick to save Hegio's son. Hegio agrees to this logic, but does not relent in his anger and threats of torture (659–750). Tyndarus' "logic" is, on the one hand, the usual cheekiness of the tricky slave who continues to defy the *senex* after he is caught.[36] On the other hand, his logic is difficult for Hegio to contradict, even though Hegio continues to feel betrayed. How could he expect instant loyalty from a recently purchased slave comparable to the loyalty built up over a lifetime? Tyndarus thus uses the logic of the benevolent model of slavery against itself. His admission of guilt calls attention to the impossible contradiction in Hegio's expectations: that his slaves will act in his best interest, regardless of other claims on their loyalty. Tyndarus reveals that the benevolent model of slavery would require a slave to betray later masters in order to serve his first master; his loyalty, in a perverse way, demystifies the benevolent model even as it seems to uphold it. Thalmann's reading of this scene is that from Hegio's point of view, Tyndarus is acting according to the suspicious model, while from Philocrates' and the audience's points of view, Tyndarus is acting according to the benevolent

---

[35] Parker (1989) 240 argues that crucifixion jokes in Roman comedy "confirm the Roman audience in its sense of superiority and power. They serve to remind the audience of the servile nature of the characters as well as the actors who perform them, and of the absolute and everyday nature of the power that the audience wields over them." At the same time, he seems to suggest that only "blocking characters" – "good (i.e., cowardly or stupid) slaves, and the pimps and braggarts" are ever actually physically punished onstage, while the "uppity slaves" get off scot-free (240–41). Tyndarus' being sent to the mines partially contradicts this claim; while he is not punished onstage, his return in chains, groaning (and joking) about the hellish misery of the mines, is a unique instance of the protagonist slave actually being punished during the course of the play; see Moore (1998) 190; Thalmann (1996) 113. The fact that Tyndarus is "really" free makes his suffering all the more anomalous, although it also provides a partial explanation for the anomaly: the punishment of a "heroically bad" slave (the term is William Anderson's; see Anderson (1996)) is a serious matter only when the slave is really a free man.

[36] Segal (1987) 105–6.

model.[37] Thus the audience's anxiety about the tricky slave is assuaged – as, indeed, it always is; the tricky slave never betrays the *adulescens* on whose behalf he intrigues.[38] But Tyndarus' disquisition on loyalty also reveals the problem inherent in the benevolent model: if a slave is loyal to his/her first owner, how can anyone ever buy "used" slaves and expect loyalty from them? And what about people who were not reared as slaves?[39] Even within the benevolent model of slavery, there is an ineradicable concern that the slave's actions result from acting, that the slave maintains what Erving Goffman calls a "front" at all times for his or her master, while revealing his or her true intentions, thoughts, and motivations only "backstage," to other slaves.[40]

At the end of the play, Hegio is reunited with his son Philopolemus, he receives Philocrates graciously, and he sends for Tyndarus to be brought back from the mines, offering to return him to Philocrates at no cost (922–52). He then confronts Stalagmus, telling him to "speak clearly and honestly, although you have never done anything clearly and honestly" (960). Stalagmus scoffs at his impending punishment and tells Hegio that he sold his little boy to the father of Philocrates (961–73). Hegio realizes that Tyndarus is his long-lost son just as Tyndarus returns from the mines, loaded down with chains. Their recognition scene is the last scene in the play, and it is brief, almost rushed. Tyndarus enters, mingling complaints and jokes about his stint in the mines (998–1005); Philocrates relates the story of his abduction as a child by Stalagmus and tells him Hegio is his father; Tyndarus recalls that that was his father's name; Hegio announces he will have Tyndarus' heavy chains transferred to Stalagmus;[41] and they all exit (1006–21).

---

[37] Thalmann (1996) 128.

[38] This pattern suggests a taboo observed: no tricky slave is ever portrayed as deceiving *everyone*, just as tricky slaves do not usually perform their tricks in order to gain their freedom, but rather from the sheer joy of the trick; Segal (1987) 164–9, Parker (1989) 241. Taboos, of course, reveal social anxieties; no slave-owner would want to think that his slaves would betray him, although he might enlist their help in deceiving others. This is an antitheatrical anxiety, since it expresses a fear of appearances being manipulated to confuse reality.

[39] McCarthy (2000) 170–73, 187–8 discusses the "problem of a slave's loyalty" for the master, who wants to imagine that the slave both is and is not capable of such "humane" sentiments.

[40] Goffman (1959) ch. 3.

[41] On chains in this play as symbols of slavery and identity, and their circulation among the characters, see Ketterer (1986) 111–18.

Critics tend to comment on the unpleasantness of the reunion between father and son (in chains)[42] and on the churlishness and dramatic awkwardness of Stalagmus.[43] The rushed ending, the joyless reunion, and the poor motivation of Stalagmus as a character are all related. The play introduces Stalagmus as the paradigmatic "bad" slave just at the moment when the (impossibly) "good" slave Tyndarus is discovered to have "really" been a free man all along.[44] I place "really" in quotation marks because it is the ontological status of slavery that this play puts into question, only to resolve in the hastiest and most conservative way. Once the benevolent model of slavery has been demystified, the suspicious model returns and sorts out the "true" slaves from the "false" ones. Stalagmus, a cartoon villain, is "naturally" fit to be a slave, while Tyndarus, who seemed too noble to be a slave all along, turns out to have been acting according to his "real" nature as freeborn. (This explains, incidentally, why Tyndarus was not a very good actor in the insanity scene.) This recuperative ending attempts to silence the questions raised by the play, particularly the linkage of slavery with acting. If anyone can become a slave through misfortune, and if a tricky slave can successfully pass himself off as a free man, then how can any theory of slavery based on "natural" worth be justified? And how can a society differentiate between its slave and free members with any confidence?

The metatheatrical dimension of the *Captivi* further unsettles the picture, for the actors playing the roles of Tyndarus and Philocrates may well have been slaves themselves.[45] For a slave actor to play Tyndarus, the slave who passes as a free man, reinforces the threat of acting: acting in this play enables social mobility. Tyndarus' ability to pass as a free man threatens the foundation of Roman society, because it means that any reasonably

---

[42] Segal (1987) 210; Ketterer (1986) 113; Leach (1969) 292–3, 296.

[43] Duckworth (1994) 152, 159, 180; Leach (1969) 293.

[44] McCarthy (2000) 178, 199 sees Stalagmus as a "scapegoat" for the play's anxiety about slavery. Both McCarthy (2000) 175–6, 179, 200 and Hunter (1985) 117 compare the revelation of Tyndarus' secret identity as a freeborn youth in this play to the standard comic revelation of the *pseudo-meretrix*'s identity as a freeborn girl; McCarthy notes that both are bad at dissembling.

[45] Thalmann (1996) 129; Segal (1987) 212. On the other hand, Brown (2002) 235–6 traces out the possibility that during this period, the lead actor of a troupe – who would often play the tricky slave – might have been the only free member of the troupe. This possibility, however, would mean that in a performance of the *Captivi*, Philocrates would have been played by a slave: the same irony, but with a threat of *downward* social mobility.

skilled actor could do the same. The threat is neutralized by having him turn out to have "really" been free all along.[46] We will next examine how anxieties about the social status of actors play themselves out in the anecdotal tradition about the famous Republican actor Roscius, who did, in fact, experience significant social mobility during the course of his career.

ROSCIUS: A STUDY IN SELF-CONTROL

Quintus Roscius Gallus was born somewhere between 134 and 125 BCE near the town of Lanuvium, in Italy. His *cognomen*, Gallus, may suggest that his parents or ancestors were originally from Gaul, and may have been brought to Rome as slaves, but that Roscius himself was either free or a freedman.[47] He seems to have spent his entire career in Rome.[48] Roscius performed in both tragedy and comedy, although he is remembered primarily as a comic actor. One of his well-known comic roles was the pimp Ballio in Plautus' *Pseudolus*; he was also known for his performance of a famous passage in Ennius' tragedy *Andromacha*.[49] He became one of the most famous actors of his generation, and traveled in elite social circles: as a young man, he was admired by Catulus, who wrote erotic epigrams about him, while in his maturity, he was a friend of important political figures such as Sulla and Cicero. Roscius was promoted to equestrian rank by Sulla in the late 80s or early 70s BCE and thereafter had to stop charging fees for his performances.[50] Nevertheless, he was extremely wealthy, as Cicero attests in his defense of Roscius against a charge of fraud.[51] He wrote a handbook on acting, which has not

[46] McCarthy (2000) ch. 5 argues that Tyndarus' identity is never really in question for the audience because the Prologue reveals his free birth, and that therefore Tyndarus' seemingly incongruous nobility and his deception of Hegio would have proved reassuring, rather than anxiety-producing, to a Roman audience. I would argue that the fact that Plautus felt the need to present his audience with a prologue "explaining" Tyndarus' real identity suggests that there was a great deal of anxiety at stake.

[47] Lebek (1994) 36 suggests the later birth date; Dupont (1985) 103 suggests an earlier birth date and a servile ancestry.

[48] See Garton (1972) 260–61 (Appendix 1.128).

[49] Cic. *De or.* 109, *Sest.* 56, *Q. Rosc.* 20. See also Fantham (2002) 367 (excerpts from *Andromacha*). The evidence suggests that Roscius recited tragic speeches, rather than performing in entire tragedies; this was an emerging performance trend in the late Republic.

[50] Macrob. *Sat.* 3.14.13.

[51] Cic. *Q. Rosc.* 22–3.

survived. Roscius died around 63–2 BCE.[52] His name became a generic term for "a great actor" throughout the ages.[53]

There is a rich anecdotal tradition around Roscius. Many anecdotes are concerned with his use of gesture to express himself. Others concern his physical appearance, in particular his squint. Both themes reveal significant popular notions about Roscius in particular and, implicitly, about actors in general. As both an exemplary and an exceptional actor, Roscius is described in the anecdotal tradition as partaking in but also transcending, many stereotypes about actors.

The anecdotes about Roscius's use of gesture all credit him with complete control over his body. One story claimed that every gesture Roscius made on stage had been painstakingly rehearsed at home. Another story relates that, as a game, Roscius used to compete with Cicero to see which one of them could express an emotion or idea better, Roscius in gestures, Cicero in eloquent words.[54] In his (lost) treatise on gesture, Roscius supposedly compared gestures to speech in terms of expressiveness.[55] Roscius used to listen to the orations of Hortensius, a famous – and florid – orator, in order to imitate his gestures.[56] (This is the same Hortensius, incidentally, who was nicknamed "Dionysia" after a famous mime-actress.[57]) These anecdotes suggest that Roscius was famous, at least in part, for his gestures. They also stress the idea of rehearsal; far from being spontaneous expressions of feeling, the gestures he used were all carefully selected and practiced.[58] This, combined with the stories about his "game" with Cicero and his authorship of a treatise, suggests that Roscius' theory of acting involved control, distance, and analysis, that he saw acting as a skill that could be refined and perfected. We will see how this theory of acting differs from that implicit in anecdotes about Roscius' famous contemporary, the tragic actor Clodius Aesopus. For now, let us say that Roscius' theory of acting, at least as it is represented in the anecdotal tradition, conforms to Roman behavioral ideals of decorum, restraint, and self-control. Cicero claims, in the *Pro Roscio* and elsewhere,

---

[52] Cic. *Arch.* 17.
[53] See Garton (1972) ch. 9 and Appendix 3.
[54] See Dupont (2000) ch. 1. It is interesting to think about the professional and personal relationship between the two self-made men, both of whom achieved considerable success through the practice of similar skills of public speaking and display.
[55] Val. Max. 7.7.7; see Macrob. *Sat.* 3.14.12.
[56] Val. Max. 10.2. See Graf (1991); Dupont (1985) 33.
[57] Aulus Gellius 1.5.2.
[58] See Fantham (2002) 364–6.

that Roscius applied the same restraint and self-control to his life as to his work.[59]

As for his appearance, sources mention both his beauty and his squint.[60] The epigram by Catulus compares the young Roscius' beauty to Aurora, the dawn, in part by playing on Roscius' name, which resembles *roscidus*, "dewy," and *rosaceus*, "rosy," both common poetic epithets for dawn.[61]

> constiteram exorientem Auroram forte salutans,
> cum subito a laeva Roscius exoritur,
> pace mihi liceat, caelestes, dicere vestra,
> mortalis visus pulchrior esse deo.
> (Catulus fr.2 Courtney)

> I had come to a standstill, as it happened, paying reverence to
> the rising Dawn,
> when suddenly Roscius rose on the left.
> By your leave, heavenly ones, may I be allowed to say this:
> the sight of a mortal is more beautiful than a god.

Roscius rises like a second sun in the east; his beauty surpasses that of a god – or goddess.[62] (The combination of youthful beauty and an ability to transcend boundaries – between mortal and divine, between male and female, or between dramatic genres – should remind us of Agathon; Roscius is another cultural figure who opens up a "space of possibility.") A late testimonium about Roscius' appearance, on the other hand, claimed that Roscius invented the Roman theatrical mask to hide his squint, because he was only handsome enough to play the parasite![63] The anecdote of Diomedes seems to be working backwards, from a knowledge that Roscius specialized in playing parasites and pimps instead of romantic heroes to the inference that he must have specialized in these

---

[59] Cic. *Q. Rosc.* 19; *Quinct.* 76. See Fantham (2002) 367; Gunderson (2000) 118–20.

[60] See Dupont (2000) 70–71.

[61] See Weber (1996); see also Garton (1972) 60.

[62] *A laeva* refers to Roman augury, in which the omen-taker faced south, so that signs appearing on the left (the side of the rising sun) were considered auspicious. *Deo* has been taken to refer to Aurora in particular or, as Courtney prefers, to "any god": see Courtney (2003) 76–8.

[63] Diomedes p. 489 K. Cic. *De or.* 3.221 says that Roscius wore a mask. Wiles (1991) 132 argues against the assertions of some scholars, based on this passage, that Republican Roman actors wore wigs instead of full masks. Fantham (2002) 365 argues that masks were used in the time of Plautus and Terence, then fell into disuse, and were later reinstated. Dupont (1985) 81 argues that Roscius introduced the mask to hide his squint, which kept him from playing certain roles.

roles because of his appearance. This notion is based in the ideal that one's appearance should match, or reveal, one's character, and that the actor's appearance would therefore type-cast him – perhaps, even, that the actor's face in an unmasked dramatic tradition would function like a mask. In this anecdote, however, Roscius manages to break free from type-casting by inventing the mask; he introduces a discrepancy between the actor's *real* appearance and his appearance to the audience. In introducing a gap between appearance and reality, the anecdote implies, Roscius could have played romantic heroes, his squint safely concealed. In the social hierarchy of the stock characters, he enabled himself to "class up," to masquerade as a member of a higher class. This subtle insinuation recalls anxieties about actors and social class that we have traced in the *Captivi*, and recalls Roscius' actual elevation to the equestrian class.

Roscius differed from most Republican-era actors in several ways: he was free, he was born in Italy, and he performed both comedy and tragedy. His social elevation was made possible in part by his anomalous status, and in part by his carefully cultivated image of restraint, self-control, and skill.[64] It is interesting to note, for example, that Roscius is alleged to have modeled his gestures on an orator's gestures; even though the orator, Hortensius, was notoriously "stagy," he was still a respectable male citizen.[65] This would have been a reversal of the usual process by which orators surreptitiously modeled themselves on actors, and a reversal that emphasized Roscius' social aspirations. As a free Roman citizen, his promotion to the rank of *eques* was not as great a leap as it would have been for a foreigner or an ex-slave, and therefore not quite as remarkable. Because he was one of very few actors who appeared in both comic and tragic roles, and because of his reputation for hard work, his skill could be seen to merit recognition of some sort. His image, which fit rather than flouted Roman ideals of manhood, would also have helped ease anxiety about the social mobility of an actor. In addition to his other superlatives, Roscius was seen as the least threatening actor of his generation.[66] His

---

[64] There is anecdotal evidence of popular slave actors being freed because of great performances, although it seems to have been rare: Suet. *Tib.* 47; Cass. Dio 57.11; see Dupont (1985) 70.

[65] See Gunderson (2000) 127–32.

[66] In many ways, Roscius could be compared to David Garrick (usually referred to simply as "Garrick"), the most famous actor of eighteenth-century England. Both men distinguished themselves from their fellow actors by their "respectable" reputations, and audiences refused to identify them with the "low" characters they sometimes played. English audiences regularly perceived Garrick as satirizing the fops he played,

elevation to the equestrian class proves him the exception to the rule rather than the instigator of a disturbing trend. Cicero portrays him as such in his *Pro Roscio Comoedo*.

CICERO'S PORTRAIT OF ROSCIUS

Cicero's *Pro Q. Roscio Comoedo* (66 BCE) defends his friend Roscius, who was by then an extremely wealthy *eques*, in a complicated lawsuit involving the value of a deceased slave whom Roscius had trained as an actor. Cicero paints the plaintiff, Gaius Fannius Chaerea, as the villain, as is usual for Cicero; what is unusual about his portrayal of Fannius is that he inverts all of the standard criticisms of actors and applies them to Fannius instead.[67] This offensive strategy is also a good defensive maneuver against any attempt on Fannius' part to play on stereotypes of actors in accusing Roscius, for the plaintiff would still have to answer the charges against his own character that he was no better than an actor.

As far as we can tell from the fragmentary speech, the case involved a dispute over the value of a deceased slave, Panurgus, who had belonged to Fannius but had been trained as an actor by Roscius.[68] The slave apparently had been murdered fifteen years earlier by Quintus Flavius, and Roscius had initiated a suit against Flavius for the value of the slave. The two parties settled before the matter came to trial, however, and Roscius received a farm as his part of the settlement. After fifteen years, the farm was flourishing under Roscius' management. Fannius then initiated a suit against Roscius for half the value of the farm, claiming that it was owed to him as the equivalent for half the value of the slave who had been murdered and that Roscius had settled on behalf of the two of them with Flavius.

The name Panurgus, a transliteration of the Greek Πάνουργος, "Scoundrel," suggests the stock character of the tricky slave. Was the name given to him after his theatrical training? It hints at a conflation of the actor with the characters he might have played – or perhaps it announces the slave's "true identity," as many slave names did (such as

---

and one French audience member exclaimed, "Comment! Je ne le crois pas. Ce n'est pas Monsieur Garrick, ce grand homme!" Quotation from Boswell's *Life of Johnson*, quoted in Garton (1972) 172. On Garrick, see Straub (1992) 60–61.

[67] For a brief discussion of Republican and Imperial attitudes toward actors in terms of their perceived effeminacy, see Williams (1999) 70–71, 139–40, 175.

[68] One of the few studies of this speech is Klinger (1953), which analyzes this speech in terms of its place in the evolution of Cicero's prose style.

ethnic names such as Thrax, "Thracian," or function names such as Fax, "Torch.") Either way, it is a tantalizing shred of evidence.[69] Speaking of scoundrels, it is intriguing that this suit against a wealthy, successful actor – and one famous for playing scoundrels such as pimps and parasites at that – involves a charge of fraud. Moreover, the suit alleges fraud in withholding part of the value of a slave actor from one of his owners. Even off-stage, even in the case of an actor regarded as exceptionally trustworthy, the standard accusations against actors – that they are frauds, that their business is deception, that their value to society is hard to determine – come back to haunt this case.

The parts of Cicero's speech with which we are concerned give "character sketches" of the two men, the first describing Roscius alone, and the second contrasting Roscius with Fannius.[70] Both descriptions are saturated with acting imagery (as well as a good deal of histrionic emoting on Cicero's part) and deploy this imagery in fascinating ways. First, the description of Roscius:

> Roscius socium fraudavit! Potest hoc homini huic haerere peccatum? qui me dius fidius – audacter dico – plus fidei quam artis, plus veritatis quam disciplinae possidet in se, quem populus Romanus meliorem virum quam histrionem esse arbitratur, qui ita dignissimus est scaena propter artificium ut dignissimus sit curia propter abstinentiam. . . . Estne quisquam omnium mortalium de quo melius existimes tu? estne quisquam qui tibi purior, pudentior, humanior, officiosior liberaliorque videatur? (*Q. Rosc.* 6.17–8)

> Roscius cheated his partner! Is it possible to fasten this crime on this man here? A man who, honest to goodness – I dare say boldly – has in him more honesty than art, more truth than study, whom the Roman people esteem more highly as a man than as an actor, who is as worthy of the stage because of his skill as he is of the Curia because of his self-control. . . . Is there anyone in the whole world of whom you have a better opinion? Is there anyone who seems to you to be more chaste, more modest, more refined, more obliging, or more generous?

Even in such a short passage, we can gain some access to common stereotypes about actors, for Cicero methodically inverts them in order to praise his client. It is especially telling that Cicero tries to counter

---

[69] On Panurgus, see Lebek (1994).

[70] May (1988) 9 discusses the importance of character sketches as both "logical argument" and "proof" in Roman oratory.

Roscius' image as a diligent rehearser by insisting that he has "more honesty than art, more truth than study" in him. As we have seen with Demosthenes' public image, a reputation for practice and study could be read as a lack of sincerity in an orator, which was one of the fundamental objections of the antitheatrical prejudice.[71] Cicero's defense of Roscius proceeds by implied opposition, setting Roscius apart from the general mass of actors. If Roscius is honest, true, and worthy and possesses a great degree of self-control, then most actors are the opposite: they are crafty, insincere, intemperate creatures. They are unworthy of the Curia, and may be unworthy as human beings; the Roman people, it is implied, may value them as actors, but not as anything else. And they are greedy – the final adjective *liberaliorque* sneaks this term into the equation as well, suggesting that this may be a weak point in Roscius' defense (he was famously rich by this time, after all).

The positive qualities Cicero attributes to Roscius inversely define the stereotypical actor: he is *impurus, impudens, inhumanis, inofficiosus,* and *avarus.* Read straight, they are also the ideal qualities expected from a politician in the Republican period: he should be *purus, pudens, humanis, officiosus,* and *liberalis.* Cicero makes this explicit when he says that Roscius is worthy of the Curia as he is of the stage, because he has as much self-control (abstinentia) as skill (artificia). The categories of orator and actor, normally defined against each other in Roman culture, come together in the person of Roscius. Again, this is a bold statement for Cicero to make; he risks calling too much attention to the close and vexed relationship between oratory and acting.[72] Cicero's own rhetorical style in the speech takes this same risk, too, with its lists of adjectives, pairs of opposed terms, and frequent exclamations and rhetorical questions, all of which would require a rather animated delivery.[73] The client must have been exceptional to be worth the risk.[74]

---

[71] See my ch. 2, and Barish (1981) *passim*, especially ch. 2.

[72] On the conceptual distinction between orator and actor in Roman culture, and the ways in which the two categories are mutually implicated, see Fantham (2002); Gunderson (2000) ch. 4; Aldrete (1999) chs. 1–2, esp. 34–43, 67–73.

[73] Arist. *Rhet.* 3.1413b30–4 notes that *asyndeton* forces the person reading a passage aloud to perform it; see Sifakis (2002) 158; Handley (2002) 165–7.

[74] Fantham (1984) 304–5 (see also (2002) 365) suggests that Cicero had been a pupil of Roscius' and that defending him in this lawsuit was his means of repaying his debt to his former master. Aspiring orators in Republican and early Imperial Rome often did train (quietly) under actors: see Fantham (1984) and (2002).

After hinting at the contrast between Roscius and other actors, Cicero makes it explicit in the contrast he draws between the plaintiff and the defendant, whom Cicero makes to appear like an actor.

Oro atque obsecro vos qui nostis, vitam inter se utriusque conferte, qui non nostis, faciem utriusque considerate. Nonne ipsum caput et supercilia illa penitus abrasa olere malitiam et clamitare calliditatem videntur? non ab imis unguibus usque ad verticem summum, si quam coniecturam adfert hominibus tacita corporis figura, ex fraude, fallaciis, mendaciis constare totus videtur? qui idcirco capite et superciliis semper est rasis ne ullum pilum viri boni habere dicatur; cuius personam praeclare Roscius in scaena tractare consuevit, neque tamen pro beneficio ei par gratia refertur. Nam Ballionem illum improbissimum et periurissimum lenonem cum agit, agit Chaeream; persona illa lutulenta, impura, invisa in huius moribus, natura vitaque est expressa. Qui quam ob rem Roscium similem sui in fraude et malitia existimarit, mihi *vix* videtur, nisi forte quod praeclare hunc imitari se in persona lenonis animadvertit. Quam ob rem etiam atque etiam considera, C. Piso, quis quem fraudasse dicatur. Roscius Fannium! Quid est hoc? probus improbum, pudens impudentem, periurum castus, callidum imperitus, liberalis avidum? Incredibile est. Quem ad modum, si Fannius Roscium fraudasse diceretur, utrumque ex utriusque persona veri simile videretur, et Fannium per malitiam fecisse et Roscium per imprudentiam deceptum esse, sic, cum Roscius Fannium fraudasse arguatur, utrumque incredibile est, et Roscium quicquam per avaritiam appetisse et Fannium quicquam per bonitatem amisisse.

(*Q. Rosc.* 7.20–1)

I beg and beseech you: those of you who know them, to contrast their lives; those of you who do not know them, to contrast their faces. Doesn't *his* [Fannius'] head and those shaved-off eyebrows seem to completely stink of ill-will and to shout out craftiness? Doesn't *he* seem, from the tips of his toes to the top of his head – if it is possible to conjecture from the silent figures of men's bodies – to be completely made up of deceit, fraud, and lies? He keeps his head and eyebrows shaved for that reason, so that he may be said to have not a single hair of a good man on his head; Roscius has been accustomed to play *his* character brilliantly, yet he has not been repaid with thanks adequately for his kindness. For when he plays Ballio, that most shameless and dishonest pimp, he really plays Chaerea; that filthy, vile, hateful character was portrayed in *his* morals, inborn nature, and life.

That *he* would have thought that Roscius resembled *him* in deception and ill-will hardly seems likely to me, unless perhaps he noticed that Roscius here imitated him brilliantly in the character of the pimp. On account of which I ask you to consider and reconsider, C. Piso [the judge], which one of them is said to have defrauded the other. Roscius defrauded Fannius! What is this? A decent man defrauded a wicked one, a chaste man a shameless one, a virtuous man a lying one, a guile-less man a scheming one, a generous man a greedy one? It is beyond belief. Just as, if it were said that Fannius had cheated Roscius, it would seem likely of each one from the character of each, that Fannius had carried out trickery and that Roscius had been deceived through his ignorance, so it is that when Roscius is accused of having cheated Fan-nius, it is beyond belief for both of them, both that Roscius strove for anything out of greed and that Fannius lost anything out of his integrity.

We see the same inversion of adjectives as in our earlier passage, only now the negative terms are applied specifically to Fannius. It is Fannius who is wicked, shameless, deceitful, and greedy, Fannius who is like a (stereo)typical actor. Cicero undertakes something much more com-plicated and tricky than mere slander of his opponent in this passage, however: he introduces the idea of Roscius' actual stage roles.

Cicero tries to make the gap between appearance and reality, usually the source of trouble for actors, work here in Roscius' favor. Roscius' famous stage role as Ballio the pimp could suggest that Roscius is deceitful, either because he pretends to be what he is not (the stereotype of the dissembling actor) or because he is suited to playing a deceptive pimp (the stereotype of the typecast actor). If it is the case that he plays roles such as the pimp because he is good at pretending to be what he is not, then that suggests that he could have easily fooled his former business partner. If it is the case that he plays roles such as the pimp that match his real nature, then he is not only naturally deceptive, but naturally shameless and greedy as well. Instead of falling into either of these traps, though, Cicero argues that Roscius faithfully, accurately, and truthfully models his performance of Ballio on his former business partner. Roscius has made his reputation playing Ballio the pimp; Fannius *is* Ballio. Cicero makes the usual antitheatrical move of identifying actor with character, but he does it with Fannius in order to avoid doing it with Roscius. Roscius, then, is simply a hardworking, skilled actor who takes his models from nature – but not, in this case, from his own *natura*.

Anyone can tell the difference between Roscius and Fannius, Cicero claims, simply by looking at their faces: Fannius has the face of a pimp. "If it is possible to conjecture from the silent figures of men's bodies," Cicero says, then we can see written on Fannius' body that he is a lying, scheming, greedy *leno*. He not only is bald – the standard attribute of the pimp's mask – but shaves even his eyebrows so that it will be clear that he is not an honest man.[75] In his inmost nature (*natura*), Fannius is the character which Roscius plays, and that *natura* is written on his body and face. The body is the ground of personal identity, here as always in the ancient world, but that means it reveals the person's identity as a liar; Fannius' face has become the pimp's mask. Suddenly the ideal of an exact correspondence between inner essence and external appearance has been co-opted by Cicero in the service of making his opponent seem essentially deceitful and making an actor, by contrast, appear honest. It is a breathtakingly bold defense, and one that implicitly reaffirms the usual stereotypes of actors by insisting that Roscius is essentially not one of them.

This conception of Roscius as nobler than his profession will also appear when we compare the anecdotes about him with anecdotes about his most famous rival, the tragic actor Clodius Aesopus. For the moment, however, let us turn from Cicero's rhetoric in defense of an actor to Quintilian's theory of rhetoric, which attempts to defend the orator against charges of appearing too much like the actor.

QUINTILIAN'S *INSTITUTIO ORATORIA*: ACTORS VERSUS ORATORS

Roscius wrote a treatise on acting, now lost, which some scholars believe influenced Quintilian's handbook on oratory.[76] A century after Cicero and Roscius' friendly competitions between oratory and gesture, one of the preeminent handbooks on oratory circulating at Rome devotes an entire book to differentiating oratory from acting and the orator from the actor. It was a "common paradox" in Roman culture that the orator

---

[75] On the pimp's mask, see Poll. *Onom.* 143–54; Pickard-Cambridge (1988) 193–5; Csapo and Slater (1995) Appendix A. Cicero often uses the clothing, as well as the facial features, of plaintiffs or defendants to draw their characters: see Dyck (2001).

[76] Bieber (1961) 164 lists Quint. *Inst.* 11.3, 71, 73–4, 89, 91, 103, 111–12, 123, and 125 as being partly borrowed from Roscius or from Cicero on Roscius (*De or.* 3.59, 221). See also Fantham (2002) 365; Dupont (1985) 82–4; Garton (1972) 184 and n. 40.

could be difficult to distinguish from an actor.[77] The problem of rhetorical sincerity, which we first encountered in the fourth century BCE with Aeschines and Demosthenes, has not gone away. If anything, it has become more vexed in a culture that officially despised actors, yet drew on their abilities in an increasing variety of ways.

Quintilian's treatise in general gives the impression that "the delivery of the courtroom was coming closer to that of the stage" by the first century CE, and that he did not approve of this development.[78] His eleventh book is full of warnings to the aspiring orator to avoid certain "stagy" gestures in the pursuit of an effective, but not histrionic, style. The problem for Quintilian, and for the readers of his handbook, was that staginess often worked; often a dramatic performance in the courtroom or the Senate was quite effective. But using a histrionic style left the orator open to accusations of theatricality by his opponents.[79] Quintilian's usual advice to the aspiring orator is to walk a nearly impossible middle ground between boorish lack of polish and over-refined histrionics:

Quare norit se quisque, nec tantum ex communibus praeceptis sed etiam ex natura sua capiat consilium formandae actionis. neque illud tamen est nefas, ut aliquem vel omni vel plura deceant. huius quoque loci clausula sit eadem necesse est quae ceterorum est, regnare maxime modum: non enim comoedum esse, sed oratorem volo. quare neque in gestu persequemur omnis argutias nec in loquendo distinctionibus temporibus adfectionibus moleste utemur. ut si sit in scaena dicendum:

> quid igitur faciam? non eam ne nunc quidem,
> cum arcessor ultro? an potius ita me comparem,
> non perpeti meretricum contumelias?

hic enim dubitationis moras, vocis flexus, varias manus, diversos nutus actor adhibebit. aliud oratio sapit nec vult nimium esse condita: actione enim constat, non imitatione. quare non inmerito reprenditur pronuntiatio vultuosa et gesticulationibus molesta et vocis mutationibus resultans . . . sed iam recepta est action paulo agitatior et exigitur et quibusdam partibus convenit, ita tamen temperanda ne, dum actoris captamus elegentiam, perdamus viri boni et gravis auctoritatem.

(*Inst.* 11.3.180–84)

---

[77] Parker (1999) 167–8; see also Fantham (2002); Gunderson (2000) ch. 4; Purcell (1999) 185; Edwards (1993) 118–19; Graf (1991).

[78] Fantham (2002) 375.

[79] See Gunderson (2000) ch. 4; Aldrete (1999) 12, 36, 52–4, 56–7, 69–73.

Thus let each man know himself; let him take counsel on how to shape his performance not only from widely-held rules but also from his own nature. Nor is it forbidden that most or all things be becoming for a man. It is necessary that the conclusion of this section be the same as for the others, which is that the middle road rules over all. I do not want a man to be a comic actor, I want him to be an orator. Accordingly we will not seek out every subtlety in gesture nor will we employ pauses, beats, and emotions to the point of annoyance in speaking, as if one had to recite on stage:

> What, then, am I to do? Will I not go even now,
> when I am summoned, too? Or rather, will I prepare myself
> not to stomach the reproaches of prostitutes?

Here the actor will employ delays of hesitation, modulations of the voice, diverse hand movements, and distinct nods. An oration tastes different, and it does not want to be too spicy: it is based on deeds, not appearances. Thus one rightly reproaches an overly expressive delivery, annoying in its gestures, and jumping up and down with its shifts in voice ... But nowadays a delivery has been adopted and demanded that is a little more lively, and in some situations this is fitting; it must be moderated nevertheless, lest we lose the authority of the good and serious man while we pursue the finesse of the actor.

The actor is the orator's scare-figure; the orator must somehow avoid the staginess of the actor's gestures and delivery while availing himself of the power of gestures and delivery. We are reminded of Demosthenes' dependence on a rather histrionic style of delivery, which he got away with by deflecting criticism of his acting onto his rival, the former actor Aeschines. It is only by cultivating an image of restraint, decorum, and above all sincerity that the Roman orator is able to avoid accusations of histrionic effeminacy and servile debasement. While the Roman orator, like his Greek counterpart, is utterly dependent on the techniques of acting to be successful in the high-stakes world of elite male political competition, he must play only one role: that of the sincere, authoritative *vir bonus*.[80]

By the second half of the first century CE, then, oratory and acting were perceived as uncomfortably close by enough people that handbooks such as Quintilian's attempted to lay out "rules" separating oratorical delivery from theatrical performance. This suggests that a theatrical style

---

[80] See Gunderson (2000) ch. 2.

of oratorical performance was successful enough, and prevalent enough, to be perceived as a problem. It is telling that Quintilian has trouble quantifying the distinction between the orator and the actor; he relies instead on vague, generalizing maxims such as "the middle road is best." Quintilian's appeal to the individual orator's own nature (natura) to help determine his own authentic style is intriguing in this context: what if a given orator's nature tends toward the flamboyantly theatrical? Quintilian is not the first to raise the issue of different innate natures which can be expressed through acting; rather, he is continuing a dialogue on the subject that we also find expressed in the anecdotal tradition from the Republican period. We return to this tradition in our comparison of the first-century BCE contemporaries Roscius and Aesopus.

ROSCIUS AND CLODIUS AESOPUS: SKILL VERSUS POSSESSION

Where Roscius' public image had everything to do with self-control, the tragic actor Aesopus' had everything to do with loss of control, even with loss of self. The most famous, or infamous, anecdote about Aesopus is that while he was playing Atreus in either Ennius' *Thyestes* or Accius' *Atreus*, he got so "in character" that he struck a synagonist with his scepter and killed him onstage.[81] This story feeds into a theory of acting that goes back at least as far as Plato's *Ion*: acting as possession by the character being played. Another anecdote about Aesopus supports this association of acting with possession: "The tragic actor Clodius Aesopus was said to have staged a quasi-cannibalistic banquet out of birds that imitated the human voice, as though he were dining on the tongues of men."[82] This anecdote is highly suggestive, although indirect; the professional imitator eats imitative birds in a semimagical rite. His acting is strengthened by literally taking in other imitators. A third anecdote about Aesopus claims that he was accustomed to stare intently at his mask before putting it on, in order to be able to suit his voice and gestures to the *persona*.[83] Cicero describes (with some self-interest, to be sure) Aesopus' performances in

---

[81] Plut. *Vit. Cic.* 5.4. See Gunderson (2000) 142.

[82] Pliny. *NH* 10.141–2. The quotation is from Gowers (1993) 42, who has a fascinating discussion of mimetic foods and feasts. See also Dupont (2000) 188 on this anecdote.

[83] Fronto. *On Eloquence* 5.1.37; Wiles (1991) 110 reads this anecdote as evidence that "the actor, like the dramatist, regarded the mask as having a life of its own before the actor inhabits it."

Accius' tragedy *Eurysaces* and then in the *fabula praetexta Brutus* as moving the audience to tears, both because he interpreted each performance to refer to Cicero's own (post-exile) situation but also because he himself shed genuine tears:[84]

> histrio casum meum totiens conlacrimavit, cum ita dolenter ageret causam meam ut vox eius illa praeclara lacrimis impediretur. . . .
>
> *(Sest. 123)*

> The actor wept bitterly over my misfortune so many times, while he pled my case so sorrowfully, that his outstanding voice was choked with tears. . . .

Cicero describes Aesopus as wholly succumbing to the emotion of his character, his lines, and the extradramatic situation; the actor's performance was moving because he himself was moved.[85] It is a beautiful expression of the possession theory of acting. Interestingly, Aesopus was said to have watched Hortensius orate, as did Roscius, but this tradition seems to have done nothing to counter his reputation as an actor who "lost himself" in his roles.[86] He was as famous, as successful, and as rich as Roscius; when he died, Aesopus left an estate worth 20 million sesterces.[87]

Aesopus and Roscius thus embody the two major and opposed theories of acting from the ancient world: acting as possession, and acting as skill (what Plato refers to as *techne*). Each method of acting could be quite successful, as the testimonia reveal; both actors became immensely wealthy and famous. And each method had its drawbacks. If acting is possession by another self, then the actor is mad, and possibly dangerous; Aesopus, after all, supposedly killed someone onstage. If acting is a skill, on the other hand, then the actor is dangerously close to being a deliberate liar. We have seen how Cicero musters all his eloquence and force of assertion to divert this common accusation away from Roscius. Each theory of acting has the potential to reflect negatively on the self of the actor (as a madman or a liar), but in addition, each theory of acting poses a

---

[84] Cic. *Sest.* 120–23; see Erasmo (2004) 94–6; Fantham (2002) 368–9.

[85] This anecdote's focus on the actor's genuine sentiment is reminiscent of the famous story of Polos, the fourth c. BCE tragic actor who used his own son's funeral urn in his performance of Sophocles' *Electra*: see Duncan (2005a).

[86] See, e.g., Beacham (1991) 156.

[87] Macrob. *Sat.* 3.14.

potential risk to the self of the spectator. By applauding either a madman or a liar, the spectator is either mad himself, or swindled.

Both theories of acting were in play during the first century BCE at Rome, but the career of Roscius reveals that one was held to be more congenial to Roman values than the other. Roscius' public image tapped into the idealization of self-control and restraint in Roman culture, especially as evidenced in Roman oratorical theory, while Aesopus' public image tapped into Roman stereotypes about actors as dissolute, extravagant, unruly foreigners who needed to be disciplined. Aesopus' image had appeal for Roman audiences, obviously – his reputation for total submersion into his characters apparently aroused a great deal of interest and suspense – but it was Roscius, not Aesopus, who was awarded the gold ring of the equestrian class. That ring meant that at the end of his life, Roscius was allowed to sit in the reserved seats at the front of the theater[88]; he was promoted, in a sense, to the status of privileged spectator, rather than actor. Like Tyndarus in the *Captivi*, he was allowed to rise in the social order because he was revealed to have been better than his station all along.

---

[88] Garton (1972) 165; his n. 79 and n. 14 provide bibliography for the inference that the equestrian class had regained the front rows of theater seats by 68 or 67 BCE. See also Edwards (1993) 111.

CHAPTER SIX

EXTREME MIMESIS: SPECTACLE IN THE EMPIRE

I N ALL OF THE PERIODS WE HAVE DISCUSSED SO FAR, THE GAP BETWEEN appearance and reality that acting creates (or highlights) was a source of anxiety for many people. Both Greek and Roman actors aroused fears of excessive social mobility, although those fears originated in different social structures. Actors also aroused fears of gender instability, fears of deception, and fears of corruption. Various theories of acting arose, implicit in anecdotes about "possessed" or typecast actors, for example, or in the careful distance that orators maintained from actors, or in the behavior of certain stock characters within drama. All of these theories worked as ways of managing the threat to identity that mimesis was felt to pose, whether by diminishing the prestige of acting, diminishing the desire aroused by it, or associating acting with effeminacy, corruption, poverty, and deception. The actor was seen as someone who was able to re-create himself, if left unchecked.[1]

All this changed in the Empire: the anxiety that was aroused by the appearance-reality gap receded into the background. Dissembling became a survival strategy, and sincerity became dangerous. Instead, audiences became fascinated by the gap, and fascinated by the possibility of collapsing it. They flocked to spectacles that blurred, crossed, or even eliminated the line between mimesis and reality. And some audience members became fascinated by the possibility of becoming actors themselves. If until this point the history of attitudes toward acting in the ancient world was the story of a delicate oscillation between the audience's desire and disgust, then we could say that at this moment, desire won out over

---

[1] For a study of similar concerns about deliberate (and therefore suspicious) self-invention in an English setting, see Greenblatt (1980).

disgust. Audiences wished the spectacles were real – and they were made real, as much as possible.

There were several causes of this shift in cultural mentality. One was political: the experience of living under an Emperor who controlled great portions of the known world. Several emperors chose to make clear that their absolute power included the power to make fiction into reality; these were the "bad" emperors, Caligula and Nero and Domitian and their ilk, who, unsurprisingly, tended to show a great interest in theater and theatricality. As Nicholas Purcell puts it,

> The relationship of the emperor to the stage was a central structure of the literary analysis of imperial history. The theme is most celebrated in the portraits of Nero as tragic actor and Commodus as gladiator . . . this was not a new way of reflecting on the political and ethical philosophy of one-man rule.[2]

(We will return to this subject later.) Another reason was aesthetic: the weight of mythology, literature, theatrical tradition, and history, which by the time of the early Empire was quite heavy. This weight produced a sense of aesthetic sophistication in audiences that used to be called "decadence": a sense of having seen it all, a desire for novelty.[3] A less morally loaded and more useful term might be "belatedness," as the term is used in, for example, Vergilian studies to describe the author's sense that he is situated at the end of a long dialectical chain of tradition and innovation, and the author's impulse to insert himself innovatively into that tradition. We can expand the concept of belatedness to describe the audience as well as the author; the audiences of the early Imperial period seem to have desired a new balance between tradition

---

[2] Purcell (1999) 189. He argues that this was not simply a theme in the historiography of the period but the historians' reflection of a defining feature of early Imperial society.

[3] Gilman (1979) 15 offers a "tentative definition" of decadence as a cultural phenomenon: "a moribund or late – not necessarily 'last' – corrupted stage of one or another aspect of civilized existence, a stage, also, in its widest application, of a civilization itself. . . . Applied this way, the designation releases ideas of excess, loss of vigor, tyranny at the hands of the past (a despotism acquiesced in, however), a concern with manner at the expense of substance, a hunger for the deviant as a positive experience." See also Boyle (1997) 18–20 on late Julio-Claudian aesthetics as "baroque, post-classical" decadence; Barton (1993) ch. 2 on the early Imperial "quest for novelty," connected to political tyranny and empire; and Wiedemann (1992) 85–6 for the suggestion that "fatal charades" (see below) became popular in part through public demand for ever more artful and innovative spectacles.

and innovation. Yet another reason for the shift in cultural mentality was philosophical: the early Empire saw a fashion for religious and philosophical systems such as Stoicism, Epicureanism, Neoplatonism, and various salvation cults (including but not limited to early Christianity), which stressed turning inward and self-scrutiny.[4] These religious and philosophical systems, in other words, focused their attention on personal identity, especially on personal identity under extreme circumstances: the Stoic sage's self-control and integrity in the face of suffering and oppression; the Christian's conversion, chastity, and martyrdom; the fate of the soul or personal identity after death.[5] During the early Empire, all these factors – political absolutism, aesthetic sophistication, philosophical introspection – combined to produce a taste for "extreme mimesis." Audiences wanted to see identity in peril. That could mean bodily identity in peril, as in gladiatorial combat, military reenactments, and spectacular executions, or it could mean psychological identity in peril, the character threatening to consume the actor, as in "fatal charades."

As Florence Dupont says,

> Rome makes us discover a civilization where theatrical perception doesn't limit itself to the horizon at the end of the scene. Everything can become a spectacle: courtroom debates, battles in the civil war, a young pregnant woman or the execution of a criminal. This is because theater isn't the representation of the real but a different perception placed over reality which makes it unreal. Conversely, if the real can be perceived as a spectacle because theater isn't a lifeless image of the real, there is an effectiveness of theatrical speech and of setting the scene which make spectacle the complement of politics and rhetoric.[6]

Actors became more visible, more disreputable, and even more desired under the Empire. As performances of the traditional genres of tragedy and comedy dropped off and eventually stopped altogether, other genres and venues arose to take their places. Actors found work in a variety of settings, some "high," some "low"; at the same time, other kinds of entertainment (both "high" and "low") took on a more explicitly theatrical

---

[4] See Edwards (1993) 32, 56–7.

[5] In general, see Foucault (1986); see Kyle (2001) 243–8, Shaw (1996), and Potter (1993) on martyrs; Brown (1988) on chastity; Veyne (2003), Edwards (2002a) 387–93, Edwards (2002b), and Cagniart (2000) on Stoic responses to suffering and death; Bolton (1994) on Neoplatonism.

[6] Dupont (1985) 24.

tone, and so other kinds of entertainers came to resemble actors – gladiators, captives re-enacting famous battles, condemned criminals, even certain emperors. A particularly striking feature of the early Empire (roughly 50 BCE to 200 CE, from Julius Caesar's reign to the Antonines) is the extent to which entertainment pushed at the boundary between imitation and reality; I call this cultural trend "extreme mimesis." The effect of this trend was to put into cultural currency a revised conception of the self as a player of roles, a dissembler, an actor.[7] The old image of the self as the perfect match of soul and body remained as a nostalgic ideal, but poets, performers, and audiences experimented with reversing the valence of this ideal: the always-worrisome gap between appearance and reality (insincerity) was accepted by many as necessary for survival, and by way of contrast, complete harmony between appearance and reality (sincerity) was re-imagined as collapse, ruin, death.[8] In the reign of Tiberius, Mamercus Aemilius Scaurus composed a tragedy called *Atreus*; Tiberius, deciding the bloodthirsty tyrant of the play was supposed to be himself, said of the playwright, "I will make him Ajax," and forced him to commit suicide.[9]

The ancient historians who wrote about this period are helpful in tracing this shift in early Imperial culture. Tacitus' *Agricola*, for example, is obsessed with the question of how to maintain integrity in the face of a court culture that demands and rewards hypocrisy, dissembling, and outright lying; his answer is that one must speak as little as possible and avoid court as much as possible.[10] Tacitus' *Annals* locates possibly the low point in the scandalous life of Messalina, the Emperor Claudius' wife; in a quasi-judicial review of Messalina's ex-lovers, all of whom he will eventually have executed, Claudius encounters Mnester, a pantomime actor – and a slave.[11]

---

[7] See Edwards (2002a) and Fantham (2002) on Cicero's discussion of Panaetius' theory of the self's four *personae*.

[8] See Barton (1993) 39–40 (dissembling as a court strategy), 51–65 (boundaries between mimesis and reality). See also Coleman (1990) 68–73 on "realism" in theatrical spectacles as a taste developed during the early Empire.

[9] Dio Cassius 58.24.3–4; see Csapo & Slater (1995) 322. Cf. Tac. *Ann.* 6.29.4; Suet. *Tib.* 61.3. On forced suicide in the early Imperial period, see Plass (1995) part II.

[10] On Tacitus' *Agricola*, see Bartsch (1994) 33–5; see also Rubiés (1994) 38.

[11] On the Messalina episode in the *Annals*, see Joshel (1997). On Roman anxieties about elite women desiring low-status men, see Edwards (1993) 51–8.

Solus Mnester cunctationem attulit, dilaniata veste clamitans aspiceret verberum notas, reminisceretur vocis, qua se obnoxium iussis Messalinae dedisset: aliis largitione aut spei magnitudine, sibi ex necessitate culpam; nec cuiquam ante pereundum fuisse si Silius rerum poteretur. commotum his et pronum ad misericordiam Caesarem perpulere liberti ne tot inlustribus viris interfectis histrioni consuleretur: sponte an coactus tam magna peccavisset, nihil referre.   (*Ann.* 11.36)

Only Mnester received a stay [of execution]; tearing off his clothes, he called upon Claudius to look at the marks of the lash and to remember his words when he surrendered himself, obedient, to Messalina's commands. The guilt of others was due to gifts or grand promises, while his was due to necessity; nor would anyone else have had to die before him if Silius [Messalina's lover] had come to power. Caesar was moved by these things and was inclined to mercy, but his freedmen urged him not to let any indulgence be shown to an actor when so many illustrious citizens had been executed. They said it did not matter whether he had sinned so greatly by his own free will or under compulsion.

Ironically, it is the Empress who has been the dissembler, leading a double life in the Palace and the brothels, and it is the actor who tells the truth in this scene – one indication from Tacitus of how perverted court life under the Julio-Claudians has become. Mnester presents his body as the proof of his sincerity, just as we saw Aeschines do at the end of his speech against Demosthenes in Chapter 2. In both cases, the actor appeals to the audience to believe the truth of his account by offering up his vulnerable body as the ground of his identity. But in Mnester's case, his body is that of a slave, and it bears whip-marks, corroborating his story of compulsion, corroborating the *gap* between appearance (that he was just another of Messalina's willing lovers) and reality (that he had no choice). Tacitus reveals his nostalgia for the old definition of identity – having appearance match reality, soul match body – by demonstrating its conspicuous absence from the court of Claudius.

This nostalgia is not limited to Tacitus, however; other historians bear witness to the climate of dissembling, hypocrisy, and deceit that settled over the capital city and the upper classes during the Julio-Claudian and Flavian dynasties. Suetonius and Plutarch detail the sordid truths and theatrical pretenses of the more outrageous emperors such as Caligula and Nero.[12] Pliny's *Panegyricus* extols the sincerity of Trajan by contrasting

---

[12] On the biographical tradition about Nero, see Griffin (2000); Beacham (1999) ch. 5; Bartsch (1994) 1–62; Elsner and Masters (1994).

him with his infamous predecessor Domitian.[13] Over and over again, historians of this period describe a culture in which the emperor twists the truth to suit his purposes, and people near him must adopt a strategy of dissembling in order to survive. Tacitus summarizes the historian's challenge in recording the events of these difficult years:

> quicumque casus temporum illorum nobis vel aliis auctoribus noscent, praesumptum habeant, quoties fugas et caedes iussit princeps, toties grates deis actas, quaeque rerum secundarum olim, tum publicae cladis insignia fuisse. neque tamen silebimus si quod senatus consultum adulatione novum aut patientia postremum fuit. (*Ann.* 14.64)

Everyone who knows about the events of those times from me or from other authors, let them assume that as often as the Emperor [Nero] ordered banishments or murders, just so often the gods were thanked; and that events which were once considered favorable were now considered to be signs of a national disaster. Nevertheless, we shall not be silent if any senatorial decree reaches a new low point of flattery or submissiveness.

It is no surprise that this sort of culture was also crazy about theatrical performance, and interested in particular in seeing the line between pretense and reality crossed in aggressive and disturbing ways: identity in peril, "extreme mimesis." Paradoxically, it is also the case that in this culture of fear and dissembling, the theater offered one of the few venues for ordinary people to voice their real opinions: many Roman sources describe theatrical audiences seizing on lines delivered by actors that had an added resonance with regard to current events ("On, citizens: we lose our liberty!") and applauding them wildly, sometimes forcing the actors to repeat the lines over and over again.[14] As always, theater was such a prominent and flexible cultural institution that it could not be reduced to a wholly negative influence (sanctioning deceit) or a wholly

---

[13] On the *Panegyricus*, see Bartsch (1994) 148–87; Morford (1992). Edwards (1993) 28 has some cautionary remarks about taking the rhetoric of a return to decency under the Flavian emperors at face value.

[14] During the late Republic: Cic. *Att.* 2.19.2, 39.3, 357.2; *Sest.* 118, 120–23. During the early Empire: Dio 60.29.3; Suet. *Iul.* 84.2; *Aug.* 53.1, 68.1; *Tib.* 45.1; *Calig.* 27.4, 30.2; *Ner.* 39.3; *Galb.* 13; *Dom.* 10.4. See also Erasmo (2004) 6–7, 94–6; Richlin (2002) 202; Aldrete (1999) 91–2, 105, 107; Csapo & Slater (1995) 318–30; Flower (1995) 188–9; Bartsch (1994) 71–82; Edwards (1993) 116–19, 127–34. The quotation ("On, citizens!") is from a mime by the Roman *eques* Laberius, who was degraded from his rank by Julius Caesar and forced to perform in his own mime: Macrob. *Sat.* 2.7.2–5.

positive influence (licensing political protest). Both views were in play, just as multiple attitudes toward actors were in evidence at any given moment.

THEATER MADE REAL

PANTOMIME

During this period, traditional tragedy and comedy were more or less replaced by the genres of pantomime and mime, respectively. Pantomime was a craze especially among the emperors and the upper classes. It included several different types of performance, but seems to have featured solo actors who danced wordless impersonations of famous mythological characters; these actors were sometimes accompanied by musicians and a singer or chorus.[15] "In the time of Nero a pantomime 'danced' the adultery of Ares and Aphrodite. He had to play Sol, Hephaestus, Aphrodite, Ares, and other gods one after the other."[16] Part of the genre's appeal was the virtuosic ability of the pantomime actor to "become" a vast range of different characters in rapid succession; the anecdote mentioned in the Introduction about the barbarian's reaction to the pantomime dancer's multiple masks speaks to this fascination.[17] At the same time, pantomime dancers were perceived as a distinctive and recognizable type of person: competitive, attractive, effeminate, temperamental artists. Two famous pantomimes during Augustus' reign, Bathyllus and Pylades, gave their names to successive generations of pantomime dancers as professional names.[18]

Like their counterparts in tragedy and comedy (especially tragedy), pantomime actors seem to have had a reputation for arrogance.[19] Imperial pantomimes did not usually refer to themselves as παντομίμοι, but as "actors of tragic rhythmic movement," presumably because "all-mimes" made them sound too similar to mimes (on which, see below).[20] Riots broke out in Rome in 14 CE when one of the pantomime actors hired for the Augustalia refused to enter the theater and perform unless his pay was increased; the tribunes had to request an emergency meeting

---

[15] Hall (2002) 27–30; Jory (1996); Beacham (1991) 140–53.
[16] Lucian. *Salt.* 63; trans. Bieber (1961) 235.
[17] Lucian. *Salt.* 66; see pp. 7–8 above.
[18] Seneca. *Q. Nat.* 7.32.3; see also Potter (1999) 274; Beacham (1991) 142.
[19] For the origins of this stereotype in the Hellenistic period, see Lightfoot (2002) 210.
[20] Slater (1994b) 121.

of the Senate that very day in order to beg for an emergency disburse-ment.[21] Macrobius recounts several anecdotes about a pantomime actor interrupting performances to correct either his rival's performances or his audiences' reactions. In one story, the pantomime Pylades heckled his rival (and former pupil) Hylas, who was playing the blinded Oedipus, calling out "You're seeing!" as he danced the part. In another story, Pylades made a finger gesture at a heckling spectator.[22] And in a third story, Pylades was playing the insane Hercules when the spectators began to heckle him for using inappropriate gestures; Pylades supposedly pulled off his mask and said, "Fools, I am playing a madman!"[23]

Whether these anecdotes are historically accurate – and the fact that they all concern one famous pantomime suggests perhaps that they are not, that Pylades is being used to represent "all pantomime actors"[24] – they suggest that the public saw pantomimes as arrogant, competitive artists. They also suggest that pantomimes themselves were willing, even eager, to step out of the dramatic pretense of performance at heightened moments – to collapse the boundary between illusion and reality. It is possible that pantomimes felt they had something of a special license to act out in these ways; although Augustus supposedly banished Pylades for a time for insulting the spectator with his gesture, he did not choose to levy a heavier punishment on him when he might have – and pan-tomimes continued to act out, with Imperial license. The same Pylades, playing the role of Hercules in a performance of *Hercules Furens*, shot poisoned arrows into the audience. He repeated the act in a command performance of the play at a banquet given by Augustus.[25] We could have no clearer example of "extreme mimesis" as a distinctively and self-consciously Imperial phenomenon.[26]

In addition to being stereotypically arrogant and provocative in performance, pantomime actors were stereotypically effeminate and

[21] Dio Cassius 56.47.2; see Csapo & Slater (1995) 278; Slater (1994b). See Pliny, *NH* 7.128 on the fees pantomimes could command.

[22] Suet. *Aug.* 45.4. The gesture may or may not have been obscene, but it made the heckler conspicuous to everyone else, effectively turning the tables on him; see Purcell (1999) 188.

[23] Macrob. *Sat.* 2.7.15–17; see Jory (1986b) 149; Garton (1972) 25.

[24] See Easterling (2002) 333 for a discussion of the tendency of ancient anecdotes about actors to cluster around "paradigmatic figures."

[25] Macrob. *Sat.* 2.7.17; see Barton (1993) 60–61.

[26] It is possible also to see the popularity of pantomime as an index of Romanization in the provinces during this period: see Jory (2002).

"homosexual" in sexual inclination.[27] Many famous pantomime actors became consorts of emperors, such as the Bathyllus who was Maecenas' boyfriend, the Paris who was Nero's boyfriend, and the Pylades who was Trajan's boyfriend.[28] Caligula was obsessed with pantomime actors and even performed (most likely privately) as one himself.[29] But many sources also emphasize the sex appeal of pantomime actors to women: Juvenal (6.61–70) describes a female spectator squealing with delight and wetting her seat as she watches a pantomime perform, while Pliny (*Ep.* 7.24.4– 5) alleges that the elite woman Ummidia Quadratilla kept a troupe of pantomime actors and had a sexual interest in them, if not actual sexual dealings with them.[30] Interestingly, many sources stress the beauty of pantomime dancers, especially the beauty of their faces, despite the fact that they performed masked. This suggests both that pantomime dancers were valued as celebrities outside the moment of performance, and, perhaps, that there was a new interest in the actor "matching" his characters' appearances – most often beautiful women, heroic men, and gods.

MIME

Mime had been in existence throughout much of Republican history, but its popularity seems to have increased sharply during the early Empire. While pantomime tended to be patronized more by the upper classes, mime tended to be more popular among members of the lower classes; in fact, it has been argued that mime set itself up quite self-consciously and deliberately as opposing and debasing "high," official culture.[31] (This parodic element of mime extended "offstage" to the mime actors' union: barred from the Artists of Dionysus, possibly due to lingering snobbery about the hierarchy of the genres, mime actors created their own union, the Parasites of Apollo.[32]) Mime featured broad, crude comic sketches and bawdy humor; topics included daily life, especially in the famous "adultery mime," as well as travesties of mythology, and, in the later

---

[27] "Homosexuality," of course, is a keenly contested term in the scholarly literature; see Williams (1999) 4–8. On pantomimes as effeminate, see Williams (1999) 139–40; Jory (1996) 11–12, 18–19.

[28] Beacham (1991) 142; Bieber (1961) 236.

[29] Suet. *Calig.* 54; Beacham (1999) 169; Bellemore (1994).

[30] See also Auguet (1994) 166–7.

[31] Hunter (2002) 197.

[32] Pickard-Cambridge (1988) 302; see my ch. 3. Slater (1995) suggests that pantomimes as well were not admitted to the Artists for quite some time – probably not until about 180, when they were allowed to compete at the established Greek theatrical festivals (the Isthmian Games, etc.).

Empire, parodies of Christian rituals.[33] It was in mime performances that, for the first time in the ancient world, women appeared onstage.

Both male and female mime actors performed unmasked – another innovation, and one which seems connected to the stereotype that mime-actresses were, literally, whores. Unmasked women who performed scandalous mime routines, often with elements of striptease, were considered to be whores; the lack of a mask seems to have signified to the audience a conflation, or a collapse, of the actress' identity with the sexually suggestive character.[34] In a sense, however, this development in the history of ancient drama is a natural outgrowth of the complicated relationship between desiring and despising the displayed body that we have already explored in ch. 1 with the figure of Agathon and in ch. 4 with the stock character of the prostitute (as played by a man). Since desire had always been part of the ancient spectator's experience of watching drama, the substitution of actresses for actors in the Imperial period is another experiment with collapsing appearance and reality. In addition, the fact that mime tended to be performed outside of traditional dramatic contexts – on raised platforms in public spaces, rather than in theaters – and was often unscripted must have added to the sense that mime was pushing dramatic "realism," in a sense, as far as it could go.[35]

TRAGEDY

While pantomime and mime largely replaced tragedy and comedy in terms of audience popularity and frequency of performance, the traditional dramatic genres did not disappear altogether during the early Empire. Ovid and Seneca both wrote tragedies, and although Ovid's have not survived, seven of Seneca's have (*Agamemnon*, *Hercules Furens*, *Oedipus*, *Medea*, *Phaedra*, *Thyestes*, *Troades*). Seneca's tragedies are retreads of famous Greek tragedies, but they make interesting and significant changes to the myths they treat. They display a consistent tendency to increase the violence both off- and onstage, for example; images of dismemberment, maiming, and extreme suffering abound, and where these images or scenes replicate purple passages in Greek tragedies, they tend to be longer, more vivid, and much more gory than their Greek

---

[33] Puchner (2002) 316; Purcell (1999) 184; Csapo & Slater (1995) 371. See Wiseman (1999) for an attempt to reconstruct the plots of mimes performed by women at the *Ludi Florales*.

[34] Val. Max. 2.10.8 (set in the Republic); see French (1998); Barton (1993) 111 n. 26; Bieber (1961) 238; and, on mime-actresses in the later Roman Empire, Webb (2002).

[35] See Beacham (1991) 136–9.

counterparts.[36] Seneca's tragedies are highly influenced by rhetoric, with characters delivering long, highly wrought speeches and soliloquies.[37] Along with frequent soliloquies, his plays make much greater use of the aside than Greek tragedies, which produces the impression of "psychological interiority" in the characters.[38] In keeping with Seneca's Stoic cosmological beliefs, his tragedies tend to describe the entire universe, not simply the particular Greek *polis* of the play's setting, as falling into chaos as a result of human crimes.[39] And his tragedies offer extended meditations on the nature of kingship, reflecting his own experience of living under autocracy.[40] All of these factors combine to produce a drama that focuses (one might say obsessively) on identity *in extremis*, on the body and the soul – and indeed, the entire universe that reflects and mirrors the soul – at its limits.

Scholars have debated endlessly whether Seneca's dramas were written to be performed, were ever performed, or were even capable of being performed. The long, "undramatic" speeches in his plays are one reason that many scholars think they were simply impossible to stage;[41] the extreme violence in them is another reason. It is true that a scene like the augury in *Oedipus*, with its depiction of an extremely ill-omened sacrifice, would be virtually impossible to stage realistically as written: Manto reports to Tiresias, apparently describing the sacrifice she is performing,

> ... magna pars fibris abest
> et felle nigro tabidum spumat iecur,
> ac (semper omen unico imperio grave)
> en capita paribus bina consurgunt toris;
>
> (*Oed.* 357–60)

> A large part of the entrails is missing
> and the rotting liver oozes black bile,
> and look! (always a bad omen for sole rule)
> two heads rise up together with equal lobes. . . .

But many scenes that depict one character killing another onstage would have been stageable, according to the conventions of the time; blood-bags

---

[36] Varner (2000); Most (1992).

[37] See Boyle (1997) ch. 2; Pratt (1983) 132–63.

[38] Boyle (1997) 24–31 and 73–4, 78–81.

[39] Henry and Henry (1985) 40–54.

[40] Ibid., 157–76.

[41] See Erasmo (2004) 136–7 and Boyle (1997) 11–12 and n. 22 for a quick summary of the debate; Boyle comes down emphatically on the side of performance.

and retractable blades were standard stage properties.[42] And many other scenes detailing violent action, such as the death of Hippolytus in *Phaedra* or the sacrifice of the children in *Thyestes*, are actually traditional (if long) messenger speeches, with the messenger describing the offstage death or suffering of a character in literally gory detail. These scenes provide a sense of violence while remaining stageable. It is possible, moreover, that the great variation in the stageability of scenes in these plays was deliberate; John Fitch has argued that Seneca's dramas were written so that some scenes would be stageable and some – perhaps those with extended soliloquies or "difficult" violence – would be intended solely for reading aloud, as was in keeping with the fashions of the times for both reading aloud and staging "highlights."[43]

If we accept some version of the proposition that Seneca's tragedies were performed (or at least performable), then Seneca's tragedies partake in the culture of violent spectacle that is characteristic of the early Empire and that we will trace in the rest of this chapter.[44] And even if Seneca's tragedies were never staged, they speak to their historical moment's emphasis on *looking* at violence; the plays over and over again present us with characters looking on helplessly at desperate suffering, even as the audience does.[45] Amphitruo watches helplessly as Hercules slaughters his own wife and children in *Hercules Furens*; the ghost of Tantalus watches helplessly as Atreus murders, butchers, cooks, and serves Thyestes' children to him in *Thyestes*; Polyxena is described by the messenger in *Troades* as watching Pyrrhus plunge the sword into her throat.[46] Medea claims that her murder of her own children was not a crime because it was not witnessed by Jason.[47] Tragic characters have become spectators at performances of "real" violence, like the Roman citizens who attended arena spectacles such as "fatal charades" (see below) and gladiatorial combat. Cassandra describes Agamemnon's murder with language drawn

---

[42] Boyle (1997) 133–4; Sutton (1986), esp. Appendix I.

[43] Fitch (2000).

[44] On Seneca's metatheatrical emphasis on violence, voyeurism, and play-acting, see Boyle (1997) ch. 6.

[45] Varner (2000) argues that the Neronian era in particular saw an emphasis on vision, spectatorship, and voyeurism both in its literature, as represented by Seneca, and in its art, as represented by Fourth Style wall painting.

[46] On Amphitruo, see Varner (2000) 130; he notes that *Hercules Furens* and the *Troades* are both instances in which Seneca changes Euripides' plots. On the ghost of Tantalus, see Schiesaro (2003) 45–9. On Polyxena, see Erasmo (2004) 126–7.

[47] Erasmo (2004) 8, 81, 123–4.

from the arena: "he's had it; the deed is done!" (habet; peractum est, *Ag.* 901).[48]

Like various kinds of arena spectacle, Seneca's tragedies play with collapsing the boundaries between mimesis and reality, whether by actually sacrificing a cow onstage (*Oedipus*) or by having one character kill another onstage (*Hercules Furens, Medea*).[49] His plays also emphasize a distinctively Imperial inversion of values: the gap between appearance and reality is far more effective than a complete congruence between appearance and reality. There is virtually always one character in each tragedy who advocates an attitude of resignation to fate, temperance, steadfastness in suffering, avoidance of passionate emotion, renunciation of grand ambition – the attitude, in short, of a Stoic sage.[50] But this voice of Stoic reason is always overwhelmed by the violence of another character's passions, and often by violence itself.[51] And over and over, we see sincerity punished, and hypocrisy, insincerity, and deceit victorious (*Agamemnon, Medea, Thyestes, Phaedra, Troades*). When Atreus, dropping his mask of fraternal love and reconciliation, reveals the severed heads and hands of Thyestes' sons to Thyestes after his unwitting and unholy feast upon their flesh, he asks Thyestes if he recognizes his sons. Thyestes, who earlier praised the virtues of a simple, honest life in the forest, replies, "I recognize my brother" (agnosco fratrem, 1006). At the end of the play, Atreus the dissembler is triumphant, though we know his brother's curse will wreak further havoc in future generations of his family; Thyestes, the sincere penitent, the would-be Stoic sage, has seen his world collapse in ruin and the death of his sons.[52]

SPECTACULAR EXECUTIONS

The production of such spectacles as Kathleen Coleman has dubbed "fatal charades" is in a theatrical class by itself. Criminals condemned to death were costumed as tragic characters who died in myth or in tragedy; then

---

[48] Erasmo (2004) 128–9.

[49] On the sacrifice in *Oedipus*, see Fitch (2000) 9–11.

[50] Such as Thyestes (and the Attendant) in *Thyestes*, the Nurse in *Medea*, Hippolytus in *Phaedra*. In the other plays – *Hercules Furens, Agamemnon, Oedipus, Troades* – the Chorus voices these sentiments. See Henry and Henry (1985) 96–7.

[51] Moreover, the voice of Stoic reason within Seneca's plays is complicated by the fact that, as Edwards (2002a) 383 points out, Roman Stoicism required an audience for the Stoic sage's heroic actions in the face of death to be rendered meaningful; Stoicism itself became theatricalized, both inside and outside of the theater.

[52] On Atreus as both playwright- and actor-figure in the *Thyestes*, see Schiesaro (2003), esp. ch. 2.

those myths or tragedies, or at least the relevant death-scenes, would be enacted – only the criminal would actually be killed "onstage," in front of thousands of spectators.[53] We have evidence for the practice from the very late Republic:

νεωστὶ δ' ἐφ' ἡμῶν εἰς τὴν Ῥώμην ἀνεπέμφθη Σέλουρός τις, Αἴτνης υἱὸς λεγόμενος, στρατιᾶς ἀφηγησάμενος καὶ λεηλασίαις πυκναῖς καταδεδραμηκὼς τὰ κύκλῳ τῆς Αἴτνης πολὺν χρόνον, ὃν ἐν τῇ ἀγορᾷ μονομάχων ἀγῶνος συνεστῶτος εἴδομεν διασπασθέντα ὑπὸ θηρίων· ἐπὶ πήγματος γάρ τινος ὑψηλοῦ τεθεὶς ὡς ἂν ἐπὶ τῆς Αἴτνης, διαλυθέντος αἰφνιδίως καὶ συμπεσόντος κατηνέχθη καὶ αὐτὸς εἰς γαλεάγρας θηρίων εὐδιαλύτους ἐπίτηδες παρεσκευασμένας ὑπὸ τῷ πήγματι.   (Strabo 6.2.6–7)

And lately in my own time, a certain Selurus, called son of Etna, was sent up to Rome because he had been leading an army and had ravaged the area around Etna with frequent raids for a long time. I saw him torn asunder by wild animals at an organized gladiatorial contest in the agora [i.e., the Forum]; he was put onto some tall scaffold, as if he were on Etna, and suddenly it came apart and collapsed and he fell down with it into breakaway cages of wild beasts that had been set up underneath for that purpose.[54]

Strabo's description uses the language of stage machinery and props: *pegma*, the word used for the scaffolding upon which Selurus was placed, is the standard word for a stage machine, while the animals' cages are described as *eudialutous*, "deliberately easily broken," or "breakaway" in modern stage terms. Thus Strabo's account emphasizes the theatrical context of this execution: it is presented on a stage, with novel stage properties.

Most of the known examples of "fatal charades" date to the early Empire, however, especially to the reigns of Nero and Titus.[55] Most of these "performances" enact mythical punishments on real persons. At least two different criminals costumed as Hercules were burned alive on

---

[53] Coleman (1990). Barton (1993) 59–65 also discusses the phenomenon.

[54] See Csapo & Slater (1995) 387. Coleman (1990) 53 estimates a date of ca. 35 BCE for this event.

[55] Our best sources for "fatal charades" are concerned with the reigns of these two rulers for good reasons. The biographers of Nero collected material that emphasized his theatricality, and Martial's *Liber Spectaculorum* commemorated the extensive and novel *ludi* that Titus sponsored in 80 CE when he dedicated the Flavian Amphitheater (Colosseum). See Kyle (2001) 54; Coleman (1990) 62, 70.

separate occasions.[56] A woman costumed as Dirce was apparently tied to the horns of a bull and died (though it is unclear exactly how death resulted from this enactment of myth).[57] A man costumed as Attis was forced to castrate himself.[58] Suetonius and Martial both recount the story of a woman forced to play "Pasiphae" who was hidden in a wooden cow, or so the spectators believed, and mounted by a bull in the arena.[59] In the time of the emperor Trajan, a criminal costumed as Orpheus was torn apart by wild animals in the Flavian amphitheater – an ironic reversal of the Orpheus myth, in which his music soothed and tamed wild animals.[60] Roman legends were also enacted: a man costumed as Mucius Scaevola, the famous figure from early Roman history, had his left hand burned.[61] Sometimes, it seems, ordinary Roman punishments such as crucifixion were incorporated into dramatic settings: Suetonius records that "on the day when Caligula was murdered, the robber Laureolus in a mime was actually nailed to a cross and died before the eyes of the spectators."[62] (A robber would probably have been crucified anyway, possibly in the amphitheater, but Suetonius stresses that this was part of a *performance* of a crucifixion in the Laureolus-mime, popular during Caligula's reign.) And sometimes the end result of a theatrical performance was a "fatal charade," even if the intent was not to provide one: Suetonius mentions that a man costumed as Icarus fell to his death near the emperor Nero's box in the amphitheater, splattering it with his blood; the text implies that this was an accident.[63]

Clearly, one of the elements in these spectacular executions is the concept of *talio*, "fitting" punishment: the robber is crucified (a standard punishment for theft), the bandit nicknamed "son of Etna" is destroyed by animals under a fake Mt. Etna. Arsonists were typically burned alive.[64] Watching the condemned criminal receive, not merely punishment, but fitting punishment – poetic justice, we could say – was appealing to Roman spectators. The use of fitting punishment in these spectacular

---

[56] Lucillius. *Anthologia Palatina* 11.184; Tert. *Apol.* 15.4–5. See Coleman (1990) 60–61.

[57] Clement. *I Cor.* 6.2. Coleman (1990) 65–6.

[58] Tert. *Apol.* 15.5. Coleman (1990) 61.

[59] Suet. *Ner.* 12.2; Mart. *Lib. Spect.* 5; see Bartsch (1994) 53, 57; Coleman (1990) 68.

[60] Mart. *Lib. Spect.* 21; August. *Conf.* 6.8.13; see Coleman (1990) 62–3; Bieber (1961) 253.

[61] Mart. 8.30, 10.25. Coleman (1990) 61–2, 64–5.

[62] Suet. *Calig.* 57, trans. Bieber (1961) 238; Mart. *Lib. Spect.* 7. See Plass (1995) 24, 32, 54; Bartsch (1994) 52–5.

[63] Suet. *Ner.* 12.2; Coleman (1990) 68–9.

[64] Wiedemann (1992) 70–71; Coleman (1990) 46.

executions could also be seen as an extreme application of the longstand-ing idea that actors simply played themselves onstage. The adulteress plays Pasiphae; the madman plays Hercules; the arsonist plays himself.

All of these spectacles drew their power and their interest from the complete collapse of theater and reality into each other. "Fatal charades" were the supreme example of identity in peril. They also represent an end point for mimesis as traditionally defined in the ancient world: if the actor playing a dying character actually dies onstage, is this in any sense an *imitation* of real life? Is it theater? And yet, if the audience's interest consisted simply in wanting to watch people really die, why bother with costumes and mythological references? It was the combination of theatri-cal distancing and immediate suffering which gave "fatal charades" their novelty and their appeal.

REAL LIFE THEATRICALIZED

GLADIATORIAL COMBAT

Gladiatorial games had been in existence for centuries already, but they became wildly popular during this period, being produced on a previ-ously inconceivable scale.[65] The games had many features in common with theatrical performance, including the use of costumed stock char-acters with stage names, dramatic conflict, musical accompaniment, and intense fan involvement. One of the less obvious features that gladiatorial games and theatrical performance shared, interestingly, is the account of their origins: both gladiatorial combat and dramatic performance were imagined by the Romans to have been Etruscan inventions, imported to Rome at a later time.[66] (This seems a rather obvious attempt to dis-avow responsibility for the aspects of these "foreign" forms of entertain-ment that some Romans found distasteful.) In the early days of gladi-atorial combat, moreover, before the construction of permanent stone amphitheaters, gladiatorial shows were sometimes presented in the same venues as theatrical performances.[67]

Of course, there was one significant difference between gladiatorial combat and dramatic performance: the violence in the arena was real. Yet in light of our discussion of violence in Roman tragedy, we can

[65] For the testimonia, see Hopkins (1983) 4.
[66] See Beacham (1999) 14; Potter (1999) 305; Kyle (2001) 44–5; Edwards (1993) 101; Wiedemann (1992) 30–33.
[67] Jory (1986a).

see that stage violence and arena violence are related as expressions of a distinctively Imperial fascination with watching identity in peril. There is compelling evidence, moreover, to suggest that the majority of gladiatorial bouts were not fights to the death, as modern cinema would have us believe: professional gladiators were too highly trained and too expensive to be entirely disposable.[68] Under the early Empire, no one but the Emperor could sponsor a *munus sine missione*, a fight without the possibility of surrender;[69] in the provinces, special permission had to be obtained for gladiators to fight with sharp weapons.[70] Many bouts, it seems, would have been fought to the point of "first blood" and then stopped by a *missio*, or submission, from one of the combatants; there is even some evidence for the presence of umpires during bouts.[71] If we also consider the other theatrical features of gladiatorial combat discussed below, the picture that develops is of something closer to a combination of modern boxing and stage combat than death matches.

The most strikingly theatrical quality of gladiatorial combat is its use of stock characters with distinctive costumes like "net-and-trident men" (*retiarii*), "Samnians," and "Thracians."[72] I am not the first to note that there was a "fixed roster of types"[73] of gladiator, but scholars have not pursued the theatrical implications of this observation. There were a number of these stock characters, which are most conveniently grouped by armor type. Among the heavily armored types were the *murmillo*, the *hoplomachus*, the *provocator*, the Thracian (*thrax*), and the Samnite (*samnis*). These types were modeled on foot soldiers: the *murmillo* was modeled on the Roman infantryman, the *hoplomachus* was modeled on the Greek hoplite, and the "ethnic" types (the Thracian, the Samnite) were modeled, loosely, on the soldiers of those countries or enemy tribes as well. Among the medium-armored types were the *secutor*, the *eques*, or cavalryman, and the *essedarius*, or chariot-fighter. Among the lighter-armored types was the *retiarius*, or net-and-trident fighter.[74] While we do not know how fighters in the training schools were sorted into gladiator

---

[68] See Wiedemann (1992) 120–24.

[69] Suet. *Aug.* 45.3.

[70] See Potter (2004) 76–7.

[71] Wiedemann (1992) 15, 94, 96, 155; Ville (1981) 403–6.

[72] "The 'noble' *retiarius* carried the trident and net, weaponry of the most theatrical kind": Barton (1993) 26.

[73] Gunderson (1996) 133.

[74] See Junkelmann (2000); Gunderson (1996) 133 and n. 73; Barton (1993) 27–8.

types, it seems likely that these types were independent of a fighter's "true" identity: not all gladiators fighting as Thracians could have been exclusively ethnic Thracians, for example. These types were characters that the gladiators played.[75]

Spectators developed certain expectations of each gladiator type. One witness to this phenomenon is the second-century CE dream interpreter Artemidorus.[76] He has a lengthy passage in his *Interpretation of Dreams* (*Oneirocritica* 2.32) about dreams in which the dreamer is engaged in gladiatorial combat: interestingly, it usually signifies either an impending lawsuit or an impending marriage. The bulk of the passage goes into detail about how the type of gladiator one faces in the dream – *murmillo*, *essedarius*, Thracian, *secutor* – predicts the type of wife one will have:

οἷον εἰ μὲν θρᾳκὶ πυκτεύοι τις, λήψεται γυναῖκα πλουσίαν <καὶ> πανοῦργον καὶ φιλόπρωτον· πλουσίαν μὲν διὰ τὸ κατεσκεπάσθαι τοῖς ὅπλοις, πανοῦργον δὲ διὰ τὸ μὴ ὀρθὸν ἔχειν τὸ ξίφος, φιλόπρωτον δὲ διὰ τὸ ἐπιβαίνειν... διμάχαιρος δὲ καὶ ὁ λεγόμενος ἀρβήλας ἤτοι φαρμακὸν ἢ ἄλλως κακότροπον ἢ ἄμορφον εἶναι τὴν γυναῖκα σημαίνουσι.

For example, if [in a dream] someone fights with a Thracian, he will marry a wife who is rich, tricky, and fond of being first: rich, because the Thracian's body is entirely covered by armor; tricky, because his sword is not straight; and fond of being first, because he advances.... The two-sworded gladiator and the so-called *arbelas* gladiator[77] indicate that the wife will be a poisoner or an otherwise malicious or ugly woman.

[75] Junkelmann (2000) 37 notes that in the Republican period, there were several "ethnic" types: the Gallus, the Samnite, the Thracian. "As with the Samnites, the first representatives of these types must have been captured Celtic and Thracian warriors who were made to fight with their own kind of armour and in their own way, and then gradually developed into standardized gladiatorial categories." Wiedemann (1992) 114 lists the ethnic identities of various gladiators, based on inscriptional evidence, to demonstrate that they often fought as types that had nothing to do with their ethnic origin – including "a Thracian at Rome who fought as a Samnite, not as a Thracian: perhaps an example of double deracination."

[76] On Artemidorus as an unselfconscious means of access to "public perceptions" (in this case, gender customs), see Winkler (1990) 23–33, relying heavily on Foucault (1986) Pt. I.

[77] *Arbelas* is a *hapax legomenon* and has thus provoked confusion to interpreters of this passage: Pack (1957) 190 interprets it to be related to ἄρβηλος, a "semicircular" knife used to cut leather, and thus presumably a reference to the kind of weapon this gladiator type used. Carter (2001) convincingly supports Pack's thesis with visual evidence; he also argues that the *arbelas* gladiator is grouped with the two-sworded

For Artemidorus, and presumably for the ancient reader of his dream handbook, the armor and fighting styles of the different gladiators have developed into personality types. Marriage, often imagined (jokingly or not) as a battle, is here interpreted as a clash between gladiators; the best one can hope for is that the match pairs complementary and equally matched opponents. The worst one can expect is a "partner" who does not fight fair, like the two-sworded gladiator.

The stock types of gladiator were indeed paired up in standard combinations, which seem to have been established in order to pair opposed strengths and weaknesses. Examples might include a heavily armored fighter against a lighter-armed, highly mobile fighter, or a fighter whose armor mostly protected his upper body against a fighter whose armor mostly protected his lower body, or a fighter who carried a short sword and a large shield against a fighter who carried a long sword and a small shield. The *murmillo* usually faced the *hoplomachus* or the Thracian; the *retiarius*, who resembled a fisherman, fought the *secutor*, whose closed, smooth, visorless helmet resembled a fish's head; and the *equites* and *essedarii* fought only their own kind – horseman versus horseman, or chariot-fighter versus chariot-fighter – probably because of their unusual equipment.[78] In each pairing, we can read a dramatic subtext, whether Roman military conquest of its enemies (with the *murmillo* and his "ethnic" opponents[79]) or man versus nature (the *retiarius* and the *secutor*) or manly man versus effeminate man (the *secutor* and the *retiarius* again[80]). These pairings would have worked like the standard pairings of Roman comedy: the *miles gloriosus* and the parasite, the *adulescens* and the tricky slave, the young *pseudo-hetaira* with the old, cynical *lena*. There were dramatic subtexts in each comic pairing, usually that of the lower-status character (the parasite, the tricky slave, the *lena*) undercutting

gladiator because both fought with weapons in each hand, which is presumably why Artemidorus interprets them to signify treachery and duplicity.

[78] Junkelmann (2000) 45–64; Auguet (1994) 73–80. Junkelmann (2000) 63 notes that the visual evidence for the *essedarii* depicts them fighting on foot, and surmises that they may have entered the arena in chariots, then dismounted to fight.

[79] Junkelmann (2000) 55–7. Auguet (1994) 59 refers to the gladiatorial types based on enemies of Rome as a "composite gallery where, as if in a museum of antiquities, all the weapons and techniques of the peoples formerly conquered by Rome were to be found."

[80] So Gunderson (1996) 145–6 argues; he notes that the *retiarius* was the "effeminate" among the types and that he was always paired up in combat with heavily armed types, because "the subtext of male domination would be lost in a *retiarius–retiarius* contest."

the higher-status character's pretensions to grandeur, intelligence, or virtue.[81]

The comparison between stock characters and gladiator types is strengthened if we look at the tradition in both kinds of entertainment of producing terracotta figurines – we might as well call them "action figures" – which, presumably, enthusiastic fans could purchase. We do not know whether people purchased these action figures individually or in complete sets, although the former is more likely, based simply on cost; a fan who purchased one figure might purchase his or her favorite character type, while purchasing several different characters presumably allowed the fan to re-create the play or the fight at home, or to stage imaginary encounters. In the case of theatrical stock characters, many different examples of each of the character types have been found.[82] In the case of gladiators, we find many of the types represented, and some of the figures fashioned with extra features, like removable helmets.[83]

It is commonly believed that all types of gladiator (except the *retiarius*) wore full-head helmets not only for protection, but also for the purpose of hiding the gladiator's identity. This was felt to be necessary because gladiators were trained in schools (*ludi*), and gladiators from the same school might easily wind up fighting each other in the arena; thus they were depersonalized to each other, to make the job of killing easier.[84] At the same time, however, there is abundant evidence that spectators were very interested in the identities of particular gladiators, not just in the pairings of stock types. The detachable helmets of the terracotta action figures speak to this interest. Gladiators took "stage names" that spoke to their fierceness (Tiger, Killer, Ajax), their victories (Stephanus), and their erotic appeal (Hermes, Hyacinthus), names that emphasized the man's identification with his role as fighter/entertainer, and later, his identity as a sex symbol. These stage names hid the gladiator's real

---

[81] Lape (2004) 64: "In comedy, flattery often operates as a weapon of the weak that more than levels the playing field between rich and powerful braggart soldier and relatively powerless citizens and slaves."

[82] The figurines are of comic stock characters, and the earliest ones date to the fourth century BCE. See Bieber (1961) 39–43, 45–8 and figs. 133–79, 185–200; Green (1994) 37, 63. See Green (2002) 115–20 for an analysis of subtle differences among five figurines of the same stock character. It is interesting that no figurines representing tragic characters have been found.

[83] Junkelmann (2000) 46 fig. 29.

[84] Junkelmann (2000) 33.

identity while permitting the development of a fan base, something that is eloquently attested in ancient graffiti and other sources.[85] Both the gladiators' use of stage names and the audience's fascination with the faces behind the helmets have parallels with theatrical culture at this time; as mentioned earlier, pantomime dancers in particular are described in the ancient sources as surpassingly beautiful, and they adopted stage names.[86]

Gladiatorial bouts were fought to musical accompaniment, a fact sometimes mentioned by scholars but rarely dwelled on. Musicians played flutes, trumpets, and water-organs during the fight, and seem to have been used to highlight intense moments, much like a modern movie soundtrack.[87] This practice is analogous to the use of musical accompaniment in traditional Roman drama from the time (at least) of Plautus and Terence[88]; it seems possible that it was, in fact, inspired by the use of musical accompaniment in drama. Even if there is only a relationship to theater music by analogy, however, the use of musical accompaniment in gladiatorial combat would have had a theatricalizing – which is to say a distancing and aestheticizing – effect. Spectators wanted to see real violence, but real violence that proceeded according to very strict guidelines and had emotional cues: a script and a soundtrack.

Another way in which gladiators resembled theatrical performers is that gladiators depended on the spectators' approval in order to be successful.[89] Gladiators were expected to engage the spectators throughout their match, but the spectators had a chance to intervene in the match directly at the end, when the victorious fighter looked to the sponsor of the fight (the *editor*) to see whether he should slaughter or spare his

---

[85] Robert (1971) 297–301 provides dozens of examples of stage names ("soubriquets") from inscriptional evidence. On fan bases, see Kyle (2001) 83 and n. 40; Barton (1993) 48.

[86] Barton (1993) 80 notes the emphasis on physical beauty among those training and advertising gladiators; see also Sen. *Controv.* 10.4.18.

[87] Junkelmann (2000) 65–6; Ville (1981) 372–5. For visual evidence, see the mosaic from Zliten depicting a five-piece orchestra near a pair of fighting gladiators, reproduced in Auguet (1994) fig. 3, and the terracotta lamp shaped like a water-organ, reproduced in Junkelmann (2000) fig. 69. Anyone who doubts the impact of musical accompaniment on the spectator's experience should try watching a film that has no music whatsoever, such as Robert Duvall's "4 Tomorrow" (1972).

[88] Hall (2002) 24–7 (tragedy), 31–5 (comedy); Wilson (2002) 64–7; see also Moore (1998) 93–4.

[89] On the interdependence of gladiators and the audience: Barton (1993) 19–25, 32, 34–5.

defeated opponent – popularized in countless images from films as the "thumbs up/thumbs down" moment.[90] The *editor*, in turn, was expected to take the wishes of the crowd into consideration. Thus the crowd could vote, in a sense, on the fallen gladiator's fate – though they could also be overruled. This sort of audience intervention is also documented in sources on theatrical performance in the early Empire. Gladiatorial combat was a kind of theatrical performance, though with the obvious and crucial difference that the participants could actually die. The fact that large crowds of Roman spectators enjoyed and enthusiastically participated in this kind of spectacular violence has disturbed many people ever since Seneca's famous letter (*Ep.* 7.2–5):

Nihil vero tam damnosum bonis moribus quam in aliquo spectaculo desidere; tunc enim per voluptatem facilius vitia subrepunt. quid me existimas dicere? avarior redeo, ambitiosior, luxuriosior? immo vero crudelior et inhumanior, quia inter homines fui. casu in meridianum spectaculum incidi, lusus expectans et sales et aliquid laxamenti quo hominum oculi ab humano cruore adquiescant. contra est: quidquid ante pugnatum est misericordia fuit; nunc omissis nugis mera homicidia sunt. nihil habent quo tegantur, ad ictum totis corporibus exposit numquam frustra manum mittunt. hoc plerique ordinariis paribus et postulaticiis praeferunt. quidni praeferant? non galea, non scuto repellitur ferrum. quo munimenta? quo artes? omnia ista mortis morae sunt. mane leonibus et ursis homines, meridie spectatoribus suis obiciuntur. interfectores interfecturis iubent obici et victorem in aliam detinent caedem; exitus pugnatium mors est. ferro et igne res geritur. haec fiunt, dum vacat harena. 'sed latrocinium fecit aliquis, occidit hominem.' quid ergo? quia occidet, ille meruit ut hoc pateretur; tu quid meruisti miser ut hoc spectes? 'occide, verbere, ure! quare tam timide incurrit in ferrum? quare parum audacter occidit? quare parum libenter moritur? plagis agatur in vulnera, mutuos ictus nudis et obviis pectoribus excipiant.' intermissum est spectaculum: 'interim iugulentur homines, ne nihil agatur.'

Nothing indeed is so pernicious to good habits as sitting idle at some spectacle. Then vices steal over us more easily through pleasure. What do you think I am saying? I return home [from the games] greedier,

---

[90] Scholars disagree over whether *pollice verso* meant "thumbs up" or "thumbs down," and whether the term meant the defeated gladiator should be spared or killed; see Junkelmann (2000) 68 (arguing that *pollice verso* meant "thumbs up" and that it indicated a vote for death); Aldrete (1999) 90–91; Potter (1999) 316 (arguing that *pollice verso* could mean either "up" or "down," and that it indicated a vote for death).

more ambitious, more decadent, basically more cruel and inhumane because I have been with humans. By chance, I went to the midday spectacles, hoping for some entertainment and wit and something relaxing, where human eyes could take a break from human gore; it was exactly the opposite. However the games were fought before, there was mercy. Now, with these trifles omitted, the games are unvarnished murder. The men have nothing covering them, and with their entire bodies exposed to blows, no blow is wasted. Many prefer this to the ordinary bouts and request matches. Who wouldn't prefer it? No helmet or shield repels the sword. What need of armor? What need of skill? All these things are delays to death. In the morning hours men are thrown to lions and bears, at midday to the spectators. They demand that the murderers be thrown to future murderers to be killed and they keep the winner for other slaughter. The only escape from the fights is death; by fire and sword it is done. These things all take place while the arena is empty. "But someone committed a robbery, someone killed a man." What of it? Since he killed a man he deserves to suffer this, but what has made you, poor man, deserve to watch it? "Kill him, whip him, burn him. Why does he charge the sword so timidly? Why does he die with so little daring? Why does he die with so little pleasure? Let him be urged on with lashes to his wounds. Let them take matching blows on exposed, bare chests." There is an intermission at the spectacles: "Meanwhile, let men have their throats cut so there is something happening."

Seneca is unfavorably contrasting the practice of forcing criminals to fight each other to the death with gladiatorial combat in this passage; what he misses in these thinly theatricalized executions is the skill and panache of a gladiatorial bout. As other scholars have noted, moreover, Seneca's concern in this passage is not for the victims of violence themselves, but for the spectators, who become debased by watching violence.[91] Recent scholarship has emphasized the ways in which Roman spectacular violence was arranged to create a sense of community among the spectators, who were encouraged to identify not with the victims of violence – criminals, war captives, gladiators, and other social outcasts – but rather, with

---

[91] Cagniart (2000) 611–12; Varner (2000) 126; Kyle (2001) 3–4. Cagniart and Kyle point out that Seneca elsewhere holds up the gladiator as a model for the Stoic facing death. Barton (1993) 24–5 points out that what Seneca objects to in this passage is the absence of a theatrical veneer of bravery and voluntary self-sacrifice: "The absence of cooperation between the actors and the audience turned the witnesses of this uplifting miracle into perpetrators of a sordid spectacle, ugly and nasty for themselves as well as their victims (both clearly and emphatically exposed now as victims)."

the Roman state which punished those victims justly.[92] Seneca's letter, therefore, is not an early expression of "humanitarian" horror at theatricalized executions (or gladiatorial combat, for that matter) as cruel, but rather an expression through negation of what Romans found appealing about gladiatorial combat. Carlin Barton has argued that one way to understand the mentality that could enjoy gladiatorial combat is to realize that "the arena, which seems to epitomize Roman 'decadence' when seen through modern eyes, also offered a stage on which might be reenacted a lost set of sorely lamented values."[93] In other words, when Roman spectators watched gladiators fight (ostensibly) to the death, they saw socially low, despised men – slaves, criminals, and the desperate – forced to duel each other, but they also saw what they imagined their warrior ancestors to have been like;[94] they saw men bravely facing death in a way they hoped to face it eventually as well;[95] they saw, possibly, a model of resistance to absolute political power that both embraced and defied coercion.[96] Roman spectators saw theatrical, philosophical, and political qualities in gladiators that they admired, and imaginatively projected themselves into.[97]

This brings us to the fourth point of similarity between gladiators and theatrical performers: the desire gladiators aroused in their spectators. Spectators felt a desire for them, as well as a desire to impersonate them. The gladiator became a sex symbol in the early Empire, just like the pantomime actor. Literary sources refer to the gladiator's appeal to female fans.[98] Juvenal's sixth satire, for example, rants against female spectators aroused by gladiators (6.82–113):

Qua tamen exarsit forma, qua capta iuventa
Eppia? quid vidit propter quod ludia dici

---

[92] Coleman (1990); Kyle (2001); Shelton (2000).
[93] Barton (1993) 33.
[94] Like the Roman tradition at aristocratic funerals in which actors were hired to impersonate the deceased's illustrious ancestors, wearing the *imagines* (death masks) of those ancestors. See Sumi (2002); Purcell (1999) 182; Flower (1995), esp. ch. 4. Flower speculates that the *imagines* could have come to represent stock characters to Roman spectators: "the wise old censor, the young warrior, the famous senator, or the learned judge" (115). See also Wiles (1991) 127–49.
[95] See Wiedemann (1992) 34–8.
[96] See Barton (1993) 19–25, 39–40.
[97] Barton (1993) 16 and n. 16 observes that in an age when the Roman elite males did not experience combat firsthand in the army, their model for military virtue and behavior became the gladiator rather than the solider.
[98] Juv. 6; Petron. 126; Mart. 5.24.10 and others; Tert. *De spect.* 22.

sustinuit? nam Sergiolus iam radere guttur
coeperat et secto requiem sperare lacerto;
praeterea multa in facie deformia, sicut
attritus galeae mediisque in naribus ingens
gibbus et acre malum semper stillantis ocelli.
sed gladiator erat. facit hoc illos Hyacinthos,
hoc pueris patriaeque, hoc praetulit illa sorori
atque viro. ferrum est quod amant. hic Sergius idem
accepta rude coepisset Veiento videri.

(Juv. 6.103–13)

And what appearance did Eppia burn for, by what youthful beauty
was she captivated? What did she see, that she endured to be called
a female gladiator? For her Sergius had already begun to shave
his neck and to hope for retirement, since his arm had been wounded;
moreover, he had a number of disfigurements on his face, for example
a place rubbed by his helmet, and a huge hump on his nose,
and a bitter humor constantly dripping from his eye.
But he was a gladiator! This makes those fellows into Hyacinthuses,
this she chose instead of children and country, sister
and husband: the sword is what women love. This same Sergius
would have begun to seem like Veientus, if he had received his
wooden sword.[99]

Archaeological evidence also attests to the gladiator's erotic appeal: the
stone sculpture from the first century CE of a gladiator (a *hoplomachus*)
leaning on a statue of Priapus, the perfume bottle from the third century
CE shaped like the helmet of a *secutor*.[100] Graffiti from Pompeii testify to
the gladiator's status as a sex symbol as well as to his fan base.[101]

Scholars have located the source of this appeal in the gladiator's mix-
ture of admirable and despicable qualities: his courage, skill, strength, and
valor, combined with his degraded social status and brutal occupation.[102]

---

[99] The *rudis*, or wooden sword, was awarded to gladiators when they retired and were
freed.

[100] Ewigleben (2000) 133 figs. 147, 149.

[101] *CIL* 4.4342 and 4353; see Hopkins (1983) 21.

[102] See Kyle (2001) 85; Gunderson (1996) 136–42; Barton (1993) 25–31; Wiedemann
(1992) 26 and ch. 3; Hopkins (1983) 21–3; Ville (1981) 339–44; see also the discussion
in Auguet (1994) 166–70, which, although dated, is still relevant. Much has been made
of the skeleton of a woman adorned with expensive jewelry found in the gladiatorial
barracks at Pompeii, which has been interpreted as everything from the remains of
an elite woman who was having an affair with a gladiator to the remains of a female
gladiator: see Auguet (1994) 179; Barton (1993) 81; Hopkins (1983) 23; and even a

The gladiator, in this reading, was the original "bad boy," the ruggedly masculine man who combines positive personal qualities with the status of a social outcast. But there was another component to the gladiator's sex appeal, and it had to do with his role as a public performer. He was desirable because he was looked at by thousands and thousands of spectators, because he was on stage. Juvenal's female fans of gladiators do not overlook their scars and wounds in their attraction to their despised status; rather, they focus fetishistically on the gladiator's scars and wounds as the visual markers of their status. Eppia would not desire Sergius as a *retired* gladiator, Juvenal says; she wants a man who is watched by thousands as he actively fights in the arena. The spectator's desire for the gladiator is reminiscent of the kind of desire we have already seen operating in theatrical performance, in the representation of Agathon in Aristophanes' *Thesmophoriazousai*, and in the stock character of the prostitute in Greek New Comedy and Roman comedy. These figures onstage inspire an ambivalent desire in the spectators, a volatile combination of contempt and attraction.

The early Empire was also witness to a small-scale, if much-ballyhooed, phenomenon: people of high, even aristocratic status, degrading themselves in order to appear in the arena.[103] Laws against this practice were passed repeatedly, suggesting their ineffectiveness. Even the occasional emperor was struck by this desire, Commodus most famously.[104] In an era in which aristocratic men might rarely, if ever, see military action, watching gladiators fight allowed spectators to imagine themselves as brave warriors. The move from sympathetic identification to literal identification, from wanting to be like the gladiator to entering the arena as one, was a leap in terms of social status, but in a way, it was a small step in the Roman imagination. And if we consider the much broader phenomenon of the volunteer gladiator in this time period, a free man of low to middling status who chose to fight in the arena, then literal identification with the gladiator was a considerable phenomenon. It was

---

historical novel, *Gladiatrix* (Zoll 2002). Of all these, Kyle (2001) 85 and n. 64 is the most cautious; he suggests she may have simply taken refuge in the barracks during the ash storm.

[103] Suet. *Tib.* 35.2; Tac. *Hist.* 2.62.2; see Kyle (2001) 87–90; Cagniart (2000) 609; Csapo & Slater (1995) 282; Auguet (1994) 155–9; Barton (1993) 13–14, 25–31; Wiedemann (1992) 102–12; Hopkins (1983) 20–21. Kyle (2001) 81 argues that the recent emphasis on volunteer gladiators in the scholarly literature is a revisionist attempt to make Roman violent spectacle "less offensive to us."

[104] Herodian 1–2.

another way in which identity was collapsed in the culture of "extreme mimesis" – and again, this collapse led to death.

Like other kinds of performance in the early Empire, gladiatorial combats played on the line between making mimesis real and maintaining the distinction between appearance and reality. On the one hand, the different types of gladiators could easily be seen as stock characters in a bloody drama; on the other hand, the end of this drama was sometimes the very real end of one of the performers. Not every match was fought to the death, contrary to popular images in films; some gladiators, and some matches, were more valuable than others.[105] But when a match was fought to the death, measures were taken to ensure there was no theatrical fakery; it was apparently a common practice for fallen gladiators to be "tested" with hot irons to make sure they were not merely *playing* dead.[106]

MILITARY REENACTMENTS

Another kind of theatricalized, often violent spectacle was the large-scale reenactment of famous land or even naval battles by casts of hundreds or thousands of people, usually prisoners of war or condemned criminals. Some of these naval battles were performed complete with sinking ships, pillaging, and wholesale slaughter.[107] Julius Caesar began the practice in 46 BCE with 4,000 oarsmen and 2,000 soldiers fighting as "Tyrians" and "Egyptians"; so many people came to watch the show that some spectators were trampled to death.[108] The emperor Claudius staged a naval battle between "Sicilians" and "Rhodians" on the Fucine Lake in which 19,000 people were killed.[109] Many emperors after Julius Caesar produced large-scale naval battles, including Augustus, Claudius, Nero, Titus, and Domitian; as they became customary spectacles, each successor tried to outdo his predecessor's efforts with a larger cast, more expensive and exotic costumes, or a more improbable setting.[110] Some battles were not so much historical reenactments (the Greeks vs. the Persians) as stagings of imaginary battles between legendary sea powers (the Egyptians vs. the Tyrians). As far as we know, none of these large-scale, violent

[105] Junkelmann (2000) 67–8; Potter (1999) 307, 315–16.
[106] Tert. *Apol.* 15.5.
[107] See Coleman (1993); Wiedemann (1992) 89–90; Coleman (1990) 70–72; Hopkins (1983).
[108] App. *BC* 2.102; Suet. *Jul.* 39.4; see Coleman (1990) 71.
[109] Suet. *Claud.* 21.6; Tac. *Ann.* 12.56.2; see Coleman (1990) 71.
[110] Coleman (1990) 68.

reenactments featured famous battles from Roman history; we have no record of anyone staging a "Battle of Actium," appealing as it would seem. The reason seems to be that the outcome of even a reenacted battle was unpredictable (the Greeks could lose the Battle of Salamis, for example), and presumably, no one in Rome wanted to see the Romans lose, even if it were only war captives playing Romans.[111] Gambling on the outcomes of the battles may also have been quite widespread, which would provide another incentive to make sure the outcome was not predictable.

Other kinds of military reenactments replayed recent Roman history, and thus downplayed bloodshed. The emperor Claudius staged a reenactment of his conquest of the Britons, with representative captive Britons in faux British "villages" on the Campus Martius "surrendering" to him in costume – that is, wearing his military cloak.[112] It is tempting to view this sort of military reenactment as a large-scale version of the *fabula praetexta*, the Republican-era dramatic genre of serious plays about Roman history.[113]

As with mime, the extension of these dramatic spectacles into public spaces beyond the theater suggests a developing theatricalization of "ordinary" public space and "real life." The Fucine Lake becomes another flooded Colosseum, where specially created ships and slave combatants engage in gladiatorial-style violence on a mass scale. The Campus Martius, previously used for real military drills, becomes a stage on which to mime recent military victories. In the Imperial period, history was felt to be available for dramatic treatment, but at a distance, and with the occasional twist of real carnage before the spectators. The gap between appearance and reality (staging deliberately artificial and bloodless "battles") is used to preserve Rome's history and military victories intact, while the collapse of appearance and reality (causing real carnage

---

[111] Coleman (1990) 69–72 discusses possible reasons for the avoidance of reenacting naval battles from Roman history, while presenting tentative evidence that this may have happened on rare occasions; she concludes, however, that it would have been easier to present battles where the outcome was not rigged if neither of the "sides" involved was Roman.

[112] Suet. *Claud.* 21.6; see Coleman (1993) 49; (1990) 71–2. Auguet (1994) 70–71 says that "This nonsense of a prince 'triumphing,' if one may so call it, at a theatrical performance cannot be attributed entirely to mental derangement" but rather to the "tendency to play with reality which became one of the characteristic aspects of the spectacles under the Empire."

[113] On the *fabula praetexta*, see Erasmo (2004) ch. 3; Manuwald (2001); Flower (1995); Sumi (2002) 579; Purcell (1999) 184–5.

at fake battles) is interesting to Roman spectators when the combatants' identities are not Roman.

THE EMPEROR'S SHOW

Certain emperors could not resist the temptation to "get into the act." Nero was the most infamous example, but Caligula, Commodus, and a host of other rulers all played at being actors, singers, pantomimes, or even gladiators.[114] Suetonius' lurid biography of Nero relates that Nero performed in both female and male roles, playing a range of characters from Canace in labor to Hercules driven mad; he also connects Nero's roles (e.g., Orestes) to his "real life" crimes (e.g., matricide).[115] Most tantalizingly for our purposes, Suetonius adds that Nero acted in tragedies wearing a mask of his own face.[116] With this detail, we see how the "mad" emperor apparently collapses the distinction between actor and character, mimesis and identity – but the collapse is only apparent; Nero wearing a mask of Nero is not at all the same as Nero acting without a mask. (Although one scholar has hypothesized that the change in hairstyle visible in Nero's various portraits through time was influenced by Nero's association with theater; he may have been attempting to make his own hair look like the *ogkos*, the tall, stylized hairdo of the tragic mask.[117]) As Mary Beard has commented, "In Roman imperial ideology one of the characteristics of monstrous despots is that they *literalize* the metaphors of cultural politics – to disastrous effect: Elagabalus responded to the religious metaphors of ambivalent gendering in his eastern cult

---

[114] Barton (1993) 66 lists Caligula, Titus, Hadrian, Lucius Verus, Commodus, Didius Julianus, Caracalla, and Geta as all having "'played' gladiator in and out of the arena." Garton (1972) 156–7 lists Sulla, Verres, Catiline, Mark Antony, and Commodus as having spent time in the company of actors. On Commodus as a gladiator, see Kyle (2001) 224–8; Gunderson (1996) 146. On Nero as an actor, see Erasmo (2004) 117–21; Griffin (2000) 160–63; Beacham (1999) ch. 5; Gunderson (1996) 131–2; Bartsch (1994) ch. 2; Edwards (1994); Edwards (1993) 134–6. On Caligula as an actor, see Gunderson (1996) 130; Bellemore (1994).

[115] Suet. *Ner.* 10, 21, 47; cf. Cass. Dio 63.10.2; see Bieber (1961) 234.

[116] Suet. *Ner.* 21.3; Cass. Dio 63.9.5. On how the "mad" emperors exploited the boundaries between mimesis and reality most effectively, see Gunderson (1996) 130, 149; Barton (1993) 55–9; see also Dupont (2000) 155–7; Edwards (1993) 135. In an interesting argument, Slater (1996) reads this anecdote as revealing that Nero performed wearing the *imagines* usually reserved for funeral processions (here, of himself and his dead wife Poppaea). While I am not convinced by his argument at the literal level, at the symbolic level I find fascinating his idea that Nero wearing a mask of his own face is anticipating his own death.

[117] Sande (1996).

by 'really' attempting to give himself a vagina; Commodus sought the charisma of the arena by literally jumping over the barrier to make himself a gladiator."[118]

This impulse to literalize the metaphor, as Beard puts it, or to collapse the gap between appearance and reality, as I have put it, is something that does not originate with the histrionic emperors. Rather, as I have tried to argue throughout this chapter, it is an impulse widely diffused throughout the culture of the early Imperial era; the histrionic emperors are the emperors who, like their fellow private citizens who became volunteer gladiators, chose to enact this impulse rather than simply applauding it in others.

CONCLUSION

As seen in all of these spectacles, it was the line between mimesis and reality that fascinated audiences in this period. There was a *frisson*, a thrill of transgression, perhaps even danger, in blurring or crossing this line. Sometimes crossing the line was literally dangerous for the performer, as in the gladiatorial games or the compulsory "performances" of "fatal charades"; sometimes crossing the line could be dangerous for the audience, as when the pantomime actor shot poisoned arrows into the audience during his performance of the insane Hercules. The real danger, paradoxically, is what makes the performance enjoyable *as a performance*. The stage and the arena have become nearly indistinguishable from the "real world," and the members of the audience have become actors.[119] In this context, the old ideal of personal identity as a congruence between appearance and reality was inadequate at best and dangerous at worst; the new conception of personal identity saw the self as a player of roles, an actor. The extreme forms of mimesis in the early Roman Empire suggested (or revealed) that the old stereotype about actors was true – only it was true about everyone: we are all merely playing ourselves onstage.

---

[118] Beard (2003) 39.
[119] In this context, see Leach (2004) ch. 3 on the early Imperial taste among the elite for painting rooms of their villas to resemble Roman stage sets.

BIBLIOGRAPHY

TEXTS, COMMENTARIES, AND TRANSLATIONS

Aelian. *Varia Historia*, ed. and trans. N. G. Wilson. Loeb Classical Library, 1997.

Aeschines. *Orationes*, ed. Mervin R. Dilts. Teubner, 1997.

Agathon. In *Tragicorum Graecorum Fragmenta*, vol. I, ed. Bruno Snell. Vandenhoeck & Ruprecht: Göttingen, 1971.

Aristophanes. *Comoediae*, vol. I, eds. F. W. Hall and W. M. Geldart. Oxford Classical Texts, 1988.

Aristophanes. *Comoediae*, vol. II, eds. F. W. Hall and W. M. Geldart. Oxford Classical Texts, 1988.

Aristotle. *Ars Rhetorica*, ed. W. D. Ross. Oxford Classical Texts, 1975.

Aristotle. *Ethica Nicomachea*, ed. I. Bywater. Oxford Classical Texts, 1890.

Aristotle. *Poetics*, ed. and trans. Stephen Halliwell; Longinus, *On the Sublime*, trans. W. Hamilton Fyfe, revised by Donald Russell; Demetrius, *On Style*, ed. and trans. Doreen C. Innes, based on the translation by W. Rhys Roberts. Loeb Classical Library, 1995.

Aristotle. *Problems*, vol. II, ed. W. S. Hett. Loeb Classical Library, 1936.

Athenaeus. *Deipnosophistae*, vol. III, ed. and trans. Charles Burton Gulick. Loeb Classical Library, 1927.

Athenaeus. *Deipnosophistae*, vol. V, ed. and trans. Charles Burton Gulick. Loeb Classical Library, 1933.

Catulus fr. 2 in *The Fragmentary Latin Poets*, edited with commentary by Edward Courtney. Oxford University Press: Oxford, 2003.

Cicero. *Pro Q. Roscio Comoedo*, in *Orationes*, ed. Albert Curtis Clark. Oxford Classical Texts, 1962.

Demosthenes. *Orationes*, vol. I, ed. M. R. Dilts. Oxford Classical Texts, 2002.

Demosthenes. *Private Orations*, vol. III, ed. and trans. A. T. Murray. Loeb Classical Library, 1936.

Epicharmus. *Hope or Wealth* fr. 35–37 Kaibel, in Athenaeus, *Deipnosophis-tae*, vol. III, ed. and trans. Charles Burton Gulick. Loeb Classical Library, 1927.

Henderson, Jeffrey, ed. and trans. *Three Plays by Aristophanes: Staging Women.* Routledge: New York and London, 1996.

Homer, *Ilias*, vol. I, ed. Martin L. West. Teubner, 1998.

Juvenal, *Saturae*, ed. A. E. Housman. Cambridge University Press, 1938.

Lucian, *De saltatione*, in *Opera* vol. III, ed. M. D. Macleod. Oxford Classical Texts, 1980.

Menander. *Reliquiae Selectae*, ed. F. H. Sandbach. Oxford Classical Texts, 1972.

Plato. *Symposium*, in *Opera*, vol. II, ed. John Burnet. Oxford Classical Texts, 1991.

Plautus. *Comoediae*, vol. I, ed. W. M. Lindsay. Oxford Classical Texts, 1963.

Plautus. *Comoediae*, vol. II, ed. W. M. Lindsay. Oxford Classical Texts, 1963.

Plutarch. *Lives*, ed. and trans. Bernadotte Perrin, vol. I. Loeb Classical Library, 1914.

Plutarch. *Lives*, ed. and trans. Bernadotte Perrin, vol. V. Loeb Classical Library, 1914.

Plutarch. *Lives*, ed. and trans. Bernadotte Perrin, vol. VII. Loeb Classical Library, 1914.

Plutarch. *Lives*, ed. and trans. Bernadotte Perrin, vol. VIII. Loeb Classical Library, 1914.

Plutrach, *Moralia*, vol. I, ed. and trans. Frank Cole Babbitt. Loeb Classical Library, 1927.

Quintilian, *Institutio Oratoria*, vol. II, ed. M. Winterbottom. Oxford Classical Texts, 1970.

Segal, Erich. trans. *Plautus: Four Comedies*. Oxford University Press: Oxford, 1996.

Seneca, *Epistulae Morales*, vol. I, ed. L. D. Reynolds. Oxford Classical Texts, 1965.

Seneca, *Tragoediae*, ed. Otto Zwierlein. Oxford Classical Texts, 1986.

Sommerstein, Alan H., ed., trans. and notes *Aristophanes: Thesmophoriazusae.* Aris & Phillips Ltd: Warminster, 1994.

Strabo, *Geography*, vol. III, ed. and trans. Horace Leonard Jones. Loeb Classical Library, 1927.

Tacitus, *Annalium Libri*, ed. C. D. Fisher. Oxford Classical Texts, 1951.

Terence. *Comoediae*, eds. Robert Kauer and Wallace M. Lindsay. Oxford Classical Texts, 1961.

Theophrastos. *Characteres*, ed. Hermann Diels. Oxford Classical Texts, 1961.

Xenophon. *Commentarii*, ed. E. C. Marchant. Oxford Classical Texts, 1934.

BOOKS AND ARTICLES

Adams, J. N. "Words for 'Prostitute' in Latin." *Rheinisches Museum für Philologie* 126 (1983) 321–58.

Alcorn, Marshall W., Jr. "Self-Structure as a Rhetorical Device: Modern *Ethos* and the Divisiveness of the Self," in Ethos: *New Essays in Rhetorical and Critical Theory*, eds. James S. Baumlin and Tita French Baumlin. Southern Methodist University Press: Dallas, 1994.

Aldrete, Gregory S. *Gestures and Acclamations in Ancient Rome.* The Johns Hopkins University Press: Baltimore, 1999.

Anderson, Benedict. *Imagined Communities: Reflections on the Origin and Spread of Nationalism.* Verso: London and New York, 1991.

Anderson, William S. *Barbarian Play: Plautus' Roman Comedy.* University of Toronto Press: Toronto, Buffalo, and London, 1996.

Anderson, William S. "Love Plots in Menander and His Roman Adapters." *Ramus* 13, (1984) 124–34.

Anton, John P. "The Agathon Interlude." *Greek Roman and Byzantine Studies* 37 (1996) 209–35.

Arieti, James A. *Interpreting Plato: The Dialogues as Drama.* Rowman & Littlefield Publishers: Savage, MD, 1991.

Arnott, Peter D. *Greek Scenic Conventions in the Fifth Century B.C.* The Clarendon Press: Oxford, 1962.

Auerbach, Erich. Mimesis: *The Representation of Reality in Western Literature*, trans. Willard R. Trask. Princeton University Press: Princeton, NJ, 1974.

Auguet, Roland. *Cruelty and Civilization: The Roman Games.* Routledge: London and New York, 1994.

Bacon, Helen. "Socrates Crowned." *Virginia Quarterly Review* 35 (1959) 415–30.

Badian, E. "The Road to Prominence," in *Demosthenes: Statesman and Orator*, ed. Ian Worthington. Routledge: London and New York, 2000.

Bain, David. *Actors & Audience: A Study of Asides and Related Conventions in Greek Drama.* Oxford University Press: Oxford, 1977.

Baker, Susan. "Personating Persons: Rethinking Shakespearean Disguises." *Shakespeare Quarterly* 43 (1992) 303–17.

Baldwin, Barry. *Studies in Aulus Gellius.* Coronado Press: Lawrence, KS, 1975.

Barish, Jonas. *The Antitheatrical Prejudice.* The University of California at Berkeley Press: Berkeley, 1981.

Barton, Carlin A. *The Sorrows of the Ancient Romans: The Gladiator and the Monster.* Princeton University Press: Princeton, NJ, 1993.

Bartsch, Shadi. *Actors in the Audience: Theatricality and Doublespeak from Nero to Hadrian.* Harvard University Press: Cambridge, MA, 1994.

Bassi, Karen. *Acting like Men: Gender, Drama, and Nostalgia in Ancient Greece.* The University of Michigan Press: Ann Arbor, 1998.

Bassi, Karen. "Male Nudity and Disguise in the Discourse of Greek Histrionics." *Helios* 22 (1995) 3–22.

Baumlin, James S. and Baumlin, Tita French, eds. *Ethos: New Essays in Rhetorical and Critical Theory*. Southern Methodist University Press: Dallas, 1994.

Beacham, Richard C. *Spectacle Entertainments of Early Imperial Rome*. Yale University Press: New Haven and London, 1999.

Beacham, Richard C. *The Roman Theatre and Its Audience*. Harvard University Press: Cambridge, MA, 1991.

Beard, Mary. "The Triumph of the Absurd: Roman Street Theatre," in *Rome the Cosmopolis*, eds. Catharine Edwards and Greg Woolf. Cambridge University Press: Cambridge, 2003.

Beck, M. "Anecdote and the Representation of Plutarch's *Ethos*," in *Rhetorical Theory and Praxis in Plutarch: Acta of the IVth International Congress of the International Plutarch Society, Leuven, July 3–6, 1996*. Leuven, 2000.

Bellemore, Jane. "Gaius the Pantomime." *Antichthon* 28 (1994) 65–79.

Bers, Victor. "Dikastic *Thorubos*," in *CRUX: Essays Presented to G.E.M. de Ste. Croix on his 75th Birthday*, eds. P. A. Cartledge and F. D. Harvey. Imprint Academic: Exeter, 1985.

Bieber, Margarete. *The History of the Greek and Roman Theater*, revised edition. Princeton University Press: Princeton, NJ, 1961.

Blondell, Ruby. *The Play of Character in Plato's Dialogues*. Cambridge University Press: Cambridge, 2002.

Bobrick, Elizabeth. "The Tyranny of Roles: Playacting and Privilege in Aristophanes' *Thesmophoriazusae*," in *The City as Comedy: Society and Representation in Athenian Drama*, ed. Gregory W. Dobrov. The University of North Carolina Press: Chapel Hill and London, 1997.

Bolton, Robert. *Person, Soul and Identity: A Neoplatonic Account of the Principle of Personality*. Minerva Press: Washington and London, 1994.

Boswell, John. *Christianity, Social Tolerance, and Homosexuality: Gay People in Western Europe from the Beginning of the Christian Era to the Fourteenth Century*. The University of Chicago Press: Chicago, 1980.

Bourdieu, Pierre. *Outline of a Theory of Practice*, trans. Richard Nice. Cambridge University Press: Cambridge, 1977.

Boyle, A. J. *Tragic Seneca: An Essay in the Theatrical Tradition*. Routledge: London and New York, 1997.

Bradley, Keith R. *Slavery and Rebellion in the Roman World, 140 B.C.–70 B.C.* Indiana University Press: Bloomington and Indianapolis, and B. T. Batsford: London, 1989.

Bradley, Keith R. *Masters and Slaves in the Roman Empire: A Study in Social Control*. Oxford University Press: New York and Oxford, 1987.

Braund, David. "Strattis' *Kallipides*: The Pompous Actor from Scythia?" in *The Rivals of Aristophanes: Studies in Athenian Old Comedy*, eds. David Harvey and John Wilkins. Swansea, 2000.

Brown, Peter. *The Body and Society: Men, Women and Sexual Renunciation in Early Christianity*. Columbia University Press: New York, 1988.

Brown, Peter G. McC. "Actors and Actor-Managers at Rome in the Time of Plautus and Terence," in *Greek and Roman Actors: Aspects of an Ancient Profession*, eds. Pat Easterling and Edith Hall. Cambridge University Press: Cambridge, 2002.

Brown, Peter G. McC. "Menander, Frr. 745 and 746 K-T, Menander's *Kolax*, and Parasites and Flatterers in Greek Comedy." *Zeitschrift für Papyrologie und Epigraphik* 92 (1992) 91–107.

Brown, Peter G. McC. "Plots and Prostitutes in Greek New Comedy." *Papers of the Leeds International Latin Seminar*, 6 (1990) 241–66.

Buckler, John. "Aeschines and Demosthenes," in *Demosthenes: Statesman and Orator*, ed. Ian Worthington. Routledge: London and New York, 2000.

Butler, Judith. *Gender Trouble: Feminism and the Subversion of Identity*. Routledge: New York, 1990.

Cagniart, Pierre. "The Philosopher and the Gladiator." *Classical World* 93 (2000) 607–18.

Carlson, Marvin. *Theories of the Theatre: A Historical and Critical Survey, from the Greeks to the Present*, expanded edition. Cornell University Press: Ithaca and London, 1993.

Carnes, Jeffrey S. "This Myth Which Is Not One: Construction of Discourse in Plato's *Symposium*," in *Rethinking Sexuality: Foucault and Classical Antiquity*, eds. David H. J. Larmour, Paul Allen Miller, and Charles Platter. Princeton University Press: Princeton, NJ, 1998.

Carrithers, M., Collins, S., and Lukes, S., eds. *The Category of the Person: Anthropology, Philosophy, History*. Cambridge University Press: Cambridge, 1985.

Carter, M. "Artemidorus and the ΑΡΒΗΛΑΣ Gladiator." *Zeitschrift für Papyrologie und Epigraphik* 134 (2001) 109–15.

Cawkwell, G. L. "Demosthenes," in *The Oxford Classical Dictionary*, eds. Hornblower and Spawforth, Third Edition. Oxford University Press: Oxford, 1996.

Cawkwell, G. L. "The Crowning of Demosthenes." *Classical Quarterly* 19 (1969) 163–80.

Clay, Diskin. "The Tragic and Comic Poet of the *Symposium*," in *Essays on Ancient Greek Philosophy* II, eds. John P. Anton and Anthony Preus. SUNY Press: Albany, 1983.

Cohen, David. *Law, Sexuality, and Society: The Enforcement of Morals in Classical Athens*. Cambridge: Cambridge University Press, 1991.

Cohen, Edward E. *Athenian Economy and Society: A Banking Perspective*. Princeton University Press: Princeton, NJ, 1992.

Coleman, K. M. "Launching into History: Aquatic Displays in the Early Empire." *Journal of Roman Studies* 83 (1993) 48–74.

Coleman, K. M. "Fatal Charades: Roman Executions Staged as Mythological Enactments." *Journal of Roman Studies* 80 (1990) 44–73.

Compton-Engle, Gwendolyn. "Control of Costume in Three Plays of Aristophanes." *American Journal of Philology* 124 (2003) 507–35.

Connors, Catherine. "Monkey Business: Imitation, Authenticity, and Identity from Pithekoussai to Plautus." *Classical Antiquity* 23.2 (2004) 179–207.

Cooper, Craig. "Philosophers, Politics, Academics: Demosthenes' Rhetorical Reputation in Antiquity," in *Demosthenes: Statesman and Orator*, ed. Ian Worthington. Routledge: London and New York, 2000.

Csapo, Eric. "Kallipides on the Floor-Sweepings: The Limits of Realism in Classical Acting and Performance Styles," in *Greek and Roman Actors: Aspects of an Ancient Profession*, eds. Pat Easterling and Edith Hall. Cambridge University Press: Cambridge, 2002.

Csapo, Eric, and Slater, William J. *The Context of Ancient Drama*. The University of Michigan Press: Ann Arbor, 1995.

Culham, Phyllis. "The *Lex Oppia*." *Latomus* 41 (1982) 769–83.

D'Ambra, Eve. "The Calculus of Venus: Nude Portraits of Roman Matrons," in *Sexuality in Ancient Art: Near East, Egypt, Greece, and Italy*, ed. Natalie Boymel Kampen, with Bettina Bergman, Ada Cohen, Eva Stehle. Cambridge University Press: Cambridge, 1996.

Damon, Cynthia. *The Mask of the Parasite: A Pathology of Roman Patronage*. The University of Michigan Press: Ann Arbor, 1997.

Damon, Cynthia. "Greek Parasites and Roman Patronage." *Harvard Studies in Classical Philology* 97 (1995) 181–95.

Davidson, James. *Courtesans and Fishcakes: The Consuming Passions of Classical Athens*. St. Martin's Press: New York, 1998.

Dean-Jones, Lesley. "Literacy and the Charlatan in Ancient Greek Medicine," in *Written Texts and the Rise of Literate Culture in Ancient Greece*, ed. Harvey Yunis. Cambridge University Press: Cambridge, 2003.

Dean-Jones, Lesley. "The Politics of Pleasure: Female Sexual Appetite in the Hippocratic Corpus." *Helios* 19.$^1\!/_2$ (1992) 72–91.

Dearden, C. W. *The Stage of Aristophanes*. Athlone Press: London, 1976.

De Quiroga, Pedro Lopez. "Freedman Social Mobility in Roman Italy." *Historia* 44.3 (1995) 326–48.

Dessen, Cynthia S. "Plautus' Satiric Comedy: The *Truculentus*." *Philological Quarterly* 56 (1977) 145–68.

Di Vito, Robert A. "Old Testament Anthropology and the Construction of Personal Identity." *Catholic Biblical Quarterly* 61 (1999) 217–38.

Dollimore, Jonathan. *Sexual Dissidence: Augustine to Wilde, Freud to Foucault*. Clarendon Press: Oxford, 1991.

Douglas, Mary. *Purity and Danger: An Analysis of the Concepts of Pollution and Taboo*. ARK Paperbacks: London and New York, 1984.

Dover, K. J. *Greek Homosexuality*, Updated and with a New Postscript. Harvard University Press: Cambridge, MA 1989.

Dover, K. J. "Anecdotes, Gossip, and Scandal," in *The Greeks and their Legacy: Collected Papers II.* Oxford University Press: Oxford, 1988.

Dover, K. J. "Portrait-Masks in Aristophanes," in *ΚѠΜѠΙΔΟΤΡΑΓΗΜΑΤΑ: Studia Aristophanea viri Aristophanei: W.J.W. Koster in honorem*, ed. Boerma. Amsterdam, 1976.

Dover, K. J. *Greek Popular Morality in the Time of Plato and Aristotle.* Basil Blackwell: Oxford, 1974.

Dover, K. J. *Aristophanic Comedy.* The University of California Press: Berkeley and Los Angeles, 1972.

Duckworth, George E. *The Nature of Roman Comedy: A Study in Popular Entertainment*, Second Edition, with a Foreword and Bibliographical Appendix by Richard Hunter. University of Oklahoma Press: Norman, 1994.

Dumont, Jean Christian. *Servus: Rome et l'esclavage sous la république.* École Française de Rome: Palais Farnèse, 1987.

Duncan, Anne. "Gendered Interpretations: Two Fourth-Century Performances of Sophocles' *Electra.*" *Helios* 32.1 (2005a).

Duncan, Anne. "Infamous Performers: Female Prostitutes and Actors at Rome," in *Prostitutes and Courtesans in the Ancient World*, ed. C. A. Faraone and L. McClure. University of Wisconsin Press: Madison (2005b).

Duncan, Anne. "Agathon, Essentialism, and Gender Subversion in Aristophanes' *Thesmophoriazusae.*" *European Studies Journal* 17 & 18 (2000–01) 25–40.

Dupont, Florence. *L'orateur sans visage: Essai sur l'acteur romain et son masque.* Paris, 2000.

Dupont, Florence. *L'acteur-roi, ou le théâtre dans la Rome antique.* Société d'Édition ≪Les Belles Lettres≫: Paris, 1985.

Dyck, Andrew R. "Dressing to Kill: Attire as a Proof and Means of Characterization in Cicero's Speeches." *Arethusa* 34 (2001) 119–30.

Dyck, Andrew R. "The Function and Persuasive Power of Demosthenes' Portrait of Aeschines in the Speech *On the Crown.*" *Greece & Rome* 32.1 (1985) 42–8.

Easterling, Pat, and Hall, Edith, eds. *Greek and Roman Actors: Aspects of an Ancient Profession.* Cambridge University Press: Cambridge, UK, 2002.

Easterling, Pat. "Actor as Icon," in *Greek and Roman Actors: Aspects of an Ancient Profession*, eds. Pat Easterling and Edith Hall. Cambridge University Press: Cambridge, 2002.

Easterling, Pat. "Actors and Voices: Reading between the Lines in Aeschines and Demosthenes," in *Performance Culture and Athenian Democracy*, eds. Simon Goldhill and Robin Osborne. Cambridge University Press: Cambridge, 1999.

Easterling, Pat. "The End of an Era? Tragedy in the Early Fourth Century," in *Tragedy, Comedy and the Polis: Papers from the Greek Drama Conference,*

Nottingham, 18–20 July 1990, eds. Alan H. Sommerstein, Stephen Halliwell, Jeffrey Henderson, and Bernhard Zimmerman. Levante Editori: Bari, 1993.

Ebbeler, Jennifer. "Caesar's Letters and the Ideology of Literary History." *Helios* 30.1 (2003) 3–20.

Edmonds III, Radcliffe G. "Socrates the Beautiful: Role Reversal and Midwifery in Plato's *Symposium*." *Transaction of the American Philological Association* 130 (2000) 261–85.

Edwards, Catharine. "Acting and Self-Actualisation in Imperial Rome: Some Death Scenes," in *Greek and Roman Actors: Aspects of an Ancient Profession*, eds. Pat Easterling and Edith Hall. Cambridge University Press: Cambridge, 2002a.

Edwards, Catharine. "The Suffering Body: Philosophy and Pain in Seneca's Letters," in *Constructions of the Classical Body*, ed. James I. Porter. The University of Michigan Press: Ann Arbor, 2002b.

Edwards, Catharine. "Unspeakable Professions: Public Performance and Prostitution in Ancient Rome," in *Roman Sexualities*, eds. Judith P. Hallett and Marilyn Skinner. Princeton University Press: Princeton, NJ, 1997.

Edwards, Catharine. "Beware of Imitations: Theatre and the Subversion of Imperial Identity," in Elsner, Jas, and Masters, Jamie, eds. *Reflections of Nero: Culture, History, & Representation*. The University of North Carolina Press: Chapel Hill, 1994.

Edwards, Catharine. *The Politics of Immorality in Ancient Rome*. Cambridge University Press: Cambridge, 1993.

Else, Gerald. "On the Origin of ΤΡΑΓѠΔΙΑ." *Hermes* 85 (1957) 17–46.

Elsner, Jas, and Masters, Jamie. eds. *Reflections of Nero: Culture, History, & Representation*. The University of North Carolina Press: Chapel Hill, 1994.

Enders, Jody. *Death by Drama and Other Medieval Urban Legends*. The University of Chicago Press: Chicago, 2002.

Erasmo, Mario. *Roman Tragedy: Theatre to Theatricality*. The University of Texas Press: Austin, 2004.

Evans, Elizabeth Cornelia. "Roman Descriptions of Personal Appearance in History and Biography." *Harvard Studies in Classical Philology* 46 (1935) 43–84.

Ewigleben, Cornelia. "'What These Women Love Is the Sword': The Performers and Their Audiences," in *Gladiators and Caesars*, eds. Eckart Köhne and Cornelia Ewigleben. British Museum Press: London, 2000.

Fantham, Elaine. "Orator and/et Actor," in *Greek and Roman Actors: Aspects of an Ancient Profession*, eds. Pat Easterling and Edith Hall. Cambridge University Press: Cambridge, 2002.

Fantham, Elaine. "Roman Experience of Menander in the Late Republic and Early Empire." *Transactions of the American Philological Association* 114 (1984) 299–309.

Fantham, Elaine. "Sex, Status, and Survival in Hellenistic Athens: A Study of Women in New Comedy." *Phoenix* 29 (1975) 44–74.

Ferrari, Gloria. *Figures of Speech: Men and Maidens in Ancient Greece*. The University of Chicago Press: Chicago and London, 2002.

Ferris, Lesley. *Acting Women: Images of Women in Theatre*. New York University Press: Washington Square, 1989.

Fineman, Joel. "The History of the Anecdote: Fiction and Fiction," in *The New Historicism*, ed. H. Aram Veeser. Routledge: New York, 1989.

Fishelov, David. *Metaphors of Genre: The Role of Analogies in Genre Theory*. The Pennsylvania State University Press: University Park, 1993.

Fisher, Nick. "Symposiasts, Fish-Eaters and Flatterers: Social Mobility and Moral Concerns," in *The Rivals of Aristophanes: Studies in Athenian Old Comedy*, eds. David Harvey and John Wilkins. Duckworth and The Classical Press of Wales: Swansea, 2000.

Fitch, John. "Playing Seneca?" in *Seneca in Performance*, ed. George W. M. Harrison. Duckworth: London, 2000.

Flemming, Rebecca. "*Quae Corpore Quaestum Facit*: The Sexual Economy of Female Prostitution in the Roman Empire." *Journal of Roman Studies* 89 (1999) 38–61.

Flower, Harriet I. *Ancestor Masks and Aristocratic Power in Roman Culture*. Oxford University Press: Oxford, 1996.

Flower, Harriet I. "*Fabulae Praetextae* in Context: When Were Plays on Contemporary Subjects Performed in Republican Rome?" *Classical Quarterly* 45 (1995) 170–90.

Ford, Andrew. *The Origins of Criticism: Literary Culture and Poetic Theory in Classical Greece*. Princeton University Press: Princeton, NJ and Oxford, 2002.

Foucault, Michel. *The History of Sexuality, vol. 3: The Care of the Self*, trans. Robert Hurley. Vintage Books: New York, 1986.

Foucault, Michel. *The History of Sexuality, vol. 2: The Use of Pleasure*, trans. Robert Hurley. Random House: New York, 1985.

Frangoulidis, S. A. "Counter-Theatricalization in Plautus' *Captivi* III.4." *Mnemosyne* 42 (1996) 144–58.

Frangoulidis, S. A. "The Soldier as a Storyteller in Terence's *Eunuchus*." *Mnemosyne* 47 (1994) 586–95.

Franko, George Frederic. "*Fides*, Aetolia, and Plautus' *Captivi*." *Transactions of the American Philological Association* 125 (1995) 155–76.

French, Dorothea R. "Maintaining Boundaries: The Status of Actresses in Early Christian Society." *Vigiliae Christianae* 52 (1998) 293–318.

Fuss, Diana. *Essentially Speaking: Feminism, Nature, & Difference*. Routledge: New York and London, 1989.

Gagarin, Michael. "The Torture of Slaves in Athenian Law." *Classical Philology* 91 (1996) 1–18.

Gagarin, Michael. "Socrates' *Hybris* and Alcibiades' Failure." *Phoenix* 31 (1977) 22–37.

Gallagher, Catherine, and Greenblatt, Stephen. *Practicing New Historicism*. The University of Chicago Press: Chicago and London, 2000.

Garber, Marjorie. *Vested Interests: Cross-Dressing & Cultural Anxiety*. Routledge: New York and London, 1992.

Gardner, Jane F. *Women in Roman Law & Society*. Croom Helm: London & Sydney, 1986.

Garton, Charles. *Personal Aspects of the Roman Theatre*. Hakkert: Toronto, 1972.

George, Lisa. "Domination and Duality in Plautus' *Bacchides*." 2001. Available at www.stoa.org/diotima. Accessed 3.25.02.

Ghiron-Bistagne, Paulette. *Recherches sur les acteurs dans la Grèce antique*. Société d'Édition ≪Les Belles Lettres≫: Paris, 1976.

Gill, Christopher. "The Question of Character-Development: Plutarch and Tacitus." *Classical Quarterly* 33.2 (1983) 469–87.

Gilman, Richard. *Decadence: The Strange Life of an Epithet*. Farrar, Straus and Giroux: New York, 1979.

Gilula, D. "The Concept of the *Bona Meretrix*: A Study of Terence's Courtesans." *Rivista di Filologia* 108 (1980) 142–65.

Gleason, Maud W. *Making Men: Sophists and Self-Presentation in Ancient Rome*. Princeton University Press: Princeton, NJ, 1995.

Goffman, Erving. *Frame Analysis: An Essay on the Organization of Experience*. Harper & Row: New York, 1974.

Goffman, Erving. *The Presentation of Self in Everyday Life*. Doubleday Anchor Books: Garden City, 1959.

Goldberg, Sander M. *Understanding Terence*. Princeton University Press: Princeton, NJ, 1986.

Goldberg, Sander M. *The Making of Menander's Comedy*. The University of California Press: Berkeley and Los Angeles, 1980.

Golden, Leon. *Aristotle on Tragic and Comic Mimesis*. Scholars Press: Atlanta, 1992.

Golden, Mark. "Demosthenes and the Social Historian," in *Demosthenes: Statesman and Orator*, ed. Ian Worthington. Routledge: London and New York, 2000.

Goldhill, Simon, and Osborne, Robin, eds. *Performance Culture and Athenian Democracy*. Cambridge University Press: Cambridge, 1999.

Gowers, Emily. "The Anatomy of Rome from Capitol to Cloaca." *Journal of Roman Studies* 85 (1995) 23–32.

Gowers, Emily. *The Loaded Table: Representations of Food in Roman Literature*. Clarendon Press: Oxford, 1993.

Graf, Fritz. "Gestures and Conventions: The Gestures of Roman Actors and Orators," in *A Cultural History of Gesture*, eds. Jan Bremmer and Herman Roodenburg. Cornell University Press: Ithaca, NY, 1991.

Green, Richard. "Towards a Reconstruction of Performance Style," in *Greek and Roman Actors: Aspects of an Ancient Profession*, eds. Pat Easterling and Edith Hall. Cambridge University Press: Cambridge, 2002.

Green, Richard. *Theatre in Ancient Greek Society*. Routledge: London and New York, 1994.

Greenblatt, Stephen. *Renaissance Self-Fashioning: From More to Shakespeare*. University of Chicago Press: Chicago and London, 1980.

Griffin, Miriam T. *Nero: The End of a Dynasty*. Routledge: New York, 2000.

Groupe de Recherches sur l'Afrique Antique. *Les Flavii de Cillium: Étude Architecturale, Épigraphique, Historique et Littéraire du Mausolée de Kasserine (CIL VIII, 211–16)*. Collection de l'École Française de Rome 169: Rome, 1993.

Gruen, Erich S. *Culture and National Identity in Republican Rome*. Cornell University Press: Ithaca, NY, 1992.

Gunderson, Erik. *Staging Masculinity: The Rhetoric of Performance in the Roman World*. The University of Michigan Press: Ann Arbor, 2000.

Gunderson, Erik. "The Ideology of the Arena." *Classical Antiquity* 15 (1996) 113–51.

Gwatkin, William E., Jr. "The Legal Arguments in Aischines' *Against Ktesiphon* and Demosthenes' *On the Crown*." *Hesperia* 26.2 (1957) 129–41.

Hall, Edith. "The Singing Actors of Antiquity," in *Greek and Roman Actors: Aspects of an Ancient Profession*, eds. Pat Easterling and Edith Hall. Cambridge University Press: Cambridge, 2002.

Hall, Edith. "Lawcourt Dramas: The Power of Performance in Greek Forensic Oratory." *Bulletin of the Institute of Classical Studies* 40 (1995) 39–58.

Halliwell, Stephen. *The Aesthetics of Mimesis: Ancient Texts and Modern Problems*. Princeton University Press: Princeton, NJ, 2002.

Halliwell, Stephen. *Aristotle's Poetics*. The University of North Carolina at Chapel Hill Press: Chapel Hill, 1986.

Halperin, David. "Plato and the Erotics of Narrativity," in *Methods of Interpreting Plato and His Dialogues*, eds. J. C. Klagge and N. Smith. Clarendon Press: Oxford, 1992.

Halperin, David. *One Hundred Years of Homosexuality: And Other Essays on Greek Love*. Routledge: New York and London, 1990.

Halperin, David, Winkler, John J., and Zeitlin, Froma I., eds. *Before Sexuality: The Construction of Erotic Experience in the Ancient World*. Princeton University Press: Princeton, NJ, 1990.

Handley, Eric. "Acting, Action, and Words in New Comedy," in *Greek and Roman Actors: Aspects of an Ancient Profession*, eds. Pat Easterling and Edith Hall. Cambridge University Press: Cambridge, 2002.

Harding, Phillip. "Demosthenes in the Underworld: A Chapter in the *Nachleben* of a *rhētōr*," in *Demosthenes: Statesman and Orator*, ed. Ian Worthington. Routledge: London and New York, 2000.

Harris, Edward M. *Aeschines and Athenian Politics*. Oxford University Press: Oxford, 1995.

Harvey, D. "*Dona Ferentes*: Some Aspects of Bribery in Greek Politics," in *CRUX: Essays Presented to G.E.M. de Ste. Croix on his 75th Birthday*, eds. P. A. Cartledge and F. D. Harvey. Imprint Academic: Exeter, 1985.

Heiden, Bruce. "Emotion, Acting, and the Athenian *ethos*," in *Tragedy, Comedy and the Polis: Papers from the Greek Drama Conference, Nottingham, 18–20 July 1990*, eds. Alan H. Sommerstein, Stephen Halliwell, Jeffrey Henderson, and Bernhard Zimmerman. Levante Editori: Bari, 1993.

Henry, Denis and Henry, Elisabeth. *The Mask of Power: Seneca's Tragedies and Imperial Rome*. Aris & Phillips Ltd. and Bolchazy-Carducci Publishers: Warminster and Chicago, 1985.

Henry, Madeline. *Menander's Courtesans and the Greek Comic Tradition. Studien zur klassisichen Philologie*, vol. 20. Verlag Peter Lang: Frankfurt am Main, Bern, and New York, 1985.

Holford-Strevens, Leofranc. *Aulus Gellius: An Antonine Scholar and His Achievement*, rev. ed. Oxford University Press: Oxford, 2003.

Hollis, Martin. "Of Masks and Men," in *The Category of the Person: Anthropology, Philosophy, History*, eds. M. Carrithers, S. Collins, and S. Lukes. Cambridge University Press: Cambridge, 1985.

Hopkins, Keith. *Death and Renewal: Sociological Studies in Roman History*, vol. II. Cambridge University Press: Cambridge, 1983.

Hopkins, Keith. *Conquerors and Slaves: Sociological Studies in Roman History*, vol. I. Cambridge University Press: Cambridge, 1978.

Hopkins, Keith. "Élite Mobility in the Roman Empire," in *Studies in Ancient Society*, ed. M. I. Finley. Routledge and Kegan Paul: London and Boston, 1974.

Howard, Jean E. *The Stage and Social Struggle in Early Modern England*. Routledge: London and New York, 1994.

Hubbard, T. K. "Popular Perceptions of Elite Homosexuality in Classical Athens." *Arion* 6.1 (1998) 48–78.

Hunter, Richard. "'Acting Down': The Ideology of Hellenistic Performance," in *Greek and Roman Actors: Aspects of an Ancient Profession*, eds. Pat Easterling and Edith Hall. Cambridge University Press: Cambridge, 2002.

Hunter, Richard. *The New Comedy of Greece and Rome*. Cambridge University Press: Cambridge, 1985.

Jones, John. *On Aristotle and Greek Tragedy*. Oxford University Press: New York, 1962.

Jory, John. "Gladiators in the Theatre." *Classical Quarterly* 36 (1986a) 537–8.

Jory, John. "Continuity and Change in the Roman Theatre," in *Studies in Honour of T. B. L. Webster* vol. I, eds. J. H. Betts, J. T. Hooker, and J. R. Green. Bristol Classical Press: Bristol, 1986b.

Jory, John. "The Masks on the Propylon of the Sebasteion at Aphrodisias," in *Greek and Roman Actors: Aspects of an Ancient Profession*, eds. Pat Easterling and Edith Hall. Cambridge University Press: Cambridge, 2002.

Jory, John. "The Drama of the Dance: Prolegomena to an Iconography of Imperial Pantomime," in *Roman Theater and Society*, ed. William J. Slater. The University of Michigan Press: Ann Arbor, 1996.

Joshel, Sandra. "Female Desire and the Discourse of Empire: Tacitus's Messalina," in *Roman Sexualities*, eds. Judith P. Hallet and Marilyn Skinner. Princeton University Press: Princeton, NJ, 1997.

Junkelmann, Marcus. "*Familia Gladiatoria*: The Heroes of the Amphitheatre," in *Gladiators and Caesars*, eds. Eckart Köhne and Cornelia Ewigleben. British Museum Press: London, 2000.

Ketterer, Robert C. "Stage Properties in Plautine Comedy II: Props in Four Plays of Exchange." *Semiotica* 59 − $^1/_2$ (1986) 93−135.

Kindstrand, Jan Fredrik. *The Stylistic Evaluation of Aeschines in Antiquity*. Almqvist & Wiksell International: Stockholm, 1982.

Klinger, Friedrich. "Ciceros Rede für den Schauspieler Roscius: Eine Episode in der Entwicklung seiner Kunstprosa." *Sitzungsberichte der Bayerischen Akademie der Wissenschaften Philosophisch-historische Klasse* Heft 4 (1953) 1−15.

Knorr, Ortwin. "The Character of Bacchis in Terence's *Heautontimoroumenos*." *American Journal of Philology* 116 (1995) 221−35.

Konstan, David. "Between Courtesan and Wife: Menander's *Perikeiromene*." *Phoenix* 41 (1987) 122−39.

Konstan, David. *Roman Comedy*. Cornell University Press: Ithaca, NY and London, 1986.

Kyle, Donald G. *Spectacles of Death in Ancient Rome*. Routledge: London and New York, 2001.

Lada-Richards, Ismene. "The Subjectivity of Greek Performance," in *Greek and Roman Actors: Aspects of an Ancient Profession*, eds. Pat Easterling and Edith Hall. Cambridge University Press: Cambridge, 2002.

Lada-Richards, Ismene. *Initiating Dionysus: Ritual and Theatre in Aristophanes' Frogs*. Clarendon Press: Oxford, 1999.

Lada-Richards, Ismene. "'Estrangement' or 'Reincarnation'? Performers and Performance on the Classical Athenian Stage." *Arion* 5.2 (1997a) 66−107.

Lada-Richards, Ismene. "Drama and the Actor: Fifth Century Perceptions of Performers and Performance," in *Acta: First Panhellenic and International Conference on Ancient Greek Literature (23−26 May 1994)*, ed. J.-Th. A. Papademetriou. Athens, 1997b.

Lamberton, Robert. *Plutarch*. Yale University Press: New Haven and London, 2001.

Lane Fox, R. J. "Theophrastus' *Characters* and the Historian." *Proceedings of the Cambridge Philological Society* 42 (1996) 127−70.

Lape, Susan. *Reproducing Athens: Menander's Comedy, Democratic Culture, and the Hellenistic City*. Princeton University Press: Princeton, NJ and Oxford, 2004.

Leach, Eleanor Winsor. *The Social Life of Painting in Ancient Rome and on the Bay of Naples*. Cambridge University Press: Cambridge, 2004.

Leach, Eleanor Winsor. "Ergasilus and the Ironies of the *Captivi.*" *Classica et Mediaevalia* 30 (1969) 263–96.

Lebek, W. D. "Moneymaking on the Roman Stage," in *Roman Theater and Society: E. Togo Salmon Papers I*, ed. William Slater. The University of Michigan Press: Ann Arbor, 1994.

Lefkowitz, Mary. *Lives of the Greek Poets.* The Johns Hopkins University Press: Baltimore, 1981.

Leppin, Hartmut. *Histrionen: Untersuchungen zur sozialen Stellung von Bühnenkünstlern im Westen des Römischen Reiches zur Zeit der Republik und des Principats.* Dr. Rudolf Habelt GmbH: Bonn, 1992.

Lévêque, Pierre. *Agathon.* Société d'Édition ≪Les Belles Lettres≫: Paris, 1955.

Levine, Laura. *Men in Women's Clothing: Anti-theatricality and Effeminization, 1579–1642.* Cambridge University Press: Cambridge, 1994.

Lightfoot, Jane L. "Nothing to Do with the *technitai* of Dionysus?" in *Greek and Roman Actors: Aspects of an Ancient Profession*, ed. Pat Easterling and Edith Hall. Cambridge University Press: Cambridge, 2002.

Lowe, J. C. B. "Plautus' Parasites and the Atellana," in *Studien zur vorliterarischen Periode im frühen Rom*, ed. Gregor Vogt-Spira. Gunter Narr Verlag: Tübingen, 1989.

Ludwig, Paul W. *Eros and Polis: Desire and Community in Greek Political Theory.* Cambridge University Press: Cambridge, 2002.

Ludwig, Paul W. "Politics and Eros in Aristophanes' Speech: *Symposium* 191E–192A and the Comedies." *American Journal of Philology* 117 (1996) 537–62.

Manuwald, Gesine. *Fabulae praetextae: Spuren einer literarischen Gattun der Römer.* Munich, 2001.

May, James M. *Trials of Character: The Eloquence of Ciceronian Ethos.* University of North Carolina Press: Chapel Hill, 1988.

MacDowell, Douglas. "The Meaning of ἀλαζών," in *"Owls to Athens": Essays on Classical Subjects Presented to Sir Kenneth Dover*, ed. E. M. Craik. Oxford University Press: Oxford, 1990.

MacMullen, Ramsay. *Roman Social Relations: 50 B.C. to A.D. 284.* Yale University Press: New Haven, CT, 1974.

McCarthy, Kathleen. *Slaves, Masters, and the Art of Authority in Plautine Comedy.* Princeton University Press: Princeton, NJ and Oxford, 2000.

McGarrity, T. J. "Reputation vs. Reality in Terence's *Hecyra.*" *Classical Journal* 76 (1980–81) 49–56.

McGinn, Thomas. *Prostitution, Sexuality, and the Law in Ancient Rome.* Oxford University Press: Oxford, 1998.

Mirhady, David C. "Demosthenes as Advocate: The Private Speeches," in *Demosthenes: Statesman and Orator*, ed. Ian Worthington. Routledge: London and New York, 2000.

Momigliano, A. "Marcel Mauss and the Quest for the Person in Greek Biography and Autobiography," in *The Category of the Person: Anthropology, Philosophy,*

History, eds. M. Carrithers, S. Collins, and S. Lukes. Cambridge University Press: Cambridge, 1985.

Montserrat, Dominic. "Unidentified Human Remains: Mummies and the Erotics of Biography," in *Changing Bodies, Changing Meanings: Studies on the Human Body in Antiquity*, ed. Dominic Montserrat. Routledge: London and New York, 1998.

Mooney, T. Brian. "The Dialectical Interchange between Agathon and Socrates: *Symposium* 198b–201d." *Antichthon* 28 (1994) 16–24.

Moore, Timothy J. *The Theater of Plautus: Playing to the Audience*. University of Texas Press: Austin, 1998.

Morford, Mark P. O. "*Iubes Esse Liberos*: Pliny's *Panegyricus* and Liberty." *American Journal of Philology* 113 (1992) 575–93.

Most, Glenn W. "*Disiecti membra poetae*: The Rhetoric of Dismemberment in Neronian Poetry," from *Innovations of Antiquity*, eds. Ralph Hexter and Daniel Selden. Routledge: New York, and London, 1992.

Muecke, Frances. "Plautus and the Theater of Disguise." *Classical Antiquity* 5 (1986) 216–29.

Muecke, Frances. "Names and Players: The Sycophant Scene of the 'Trinummus' (*Trin.* 4.2)." *Transactions of the American Philological Association* 115 (1985) 167–86.

Muecke, Frances. "A Portrait of the Artist as a Young Woman." *Classical Quarterly* 32 (1982) 41–55.

Murnaghan, Sheila. *Disguise and Recognition in the Odyssey*. Princeton University Press: Princeton, NJ, 1987.

Murray, Penelope. "Bodies in Flux: Ovid's *Metamorphoses*," in *Changing Bodies, Changing Meanings: Studies on the Human Body in Antiquity*, ed. Dominic Montserrat. Routledge: London and New York, 1998.

Naddaff, Ramona A. *Exiling the Poets: The Production of Censorship in Plato's Republic*. The University of Chicago Press: Chicago and London, 2002.

Nehamas, Alexander. *Virtues of Authenticity: Essays on Plato and Socrates*. Princeton University Press: Princeton, NJ, 1999.

North, Helen. "The Use of Poetry in the Training of the Ancient Orator." *Traditio* 8 (1952) 1–33.

Ober, Josiah. *The Athenian Revolution: Essays on Ancient Greek Democracy and Political Theory*. Princeton University Press: Princeton, NJ, 1996.

Ober, Josiah. *Mass and Elite in Democratic Athens: Rhetoric, Ideology, and the Power of the People*. Princeton University Press: Princeton, NJ, 1989.

O'Connor, John Bartholomew. *Chapters in the History of Actors and Acting in Ancient Greece: Together with a Prosopographia Histrionum Graecorum*. Diss. Princeton. The University of Chicago Press: Chicago, 1908.

Pack, Roger. "Textual Notes on Artemidorus Daldianus." *Transactions of the American Philological Association* 88 (1957) 189–96.

Parker, Holt N. "The Observed of All Observers: Spectacle, Applause, and Cultural Poetics in the Roman Theater Audience," in *The Art of Ancient Spectacle*, eds. Bettina Bergmann and Christine Kondoleon. Yale University Press: New Haven, CT and London, 1999.

Parker, Holt N. "Loyal Slaves and Loyal Wives: The Crisis of the Outsider-Within and Roman *exemplum* Literature" in *Women & Slaves in Greco-Roman Culture: Differential Equations*, eds. Sheila Murnaghan and Sandra R. Joshel. Routledge: London and New York, 1998.

Parker, Holt N. "The Teratogenic Grid," in *Roman Sexualities*, eds. Judith P. Hallett and Marilyn Skinner. Princeton University Press: Princeton, NJ, 1997.

Parker, Holt N. "Crucially Funny or Tranio on the Couch: The *Servus Callidus* and Jokes about Torture." *Transactions of the American Philological Association* 119 (1989) 233–46.

Parry, Noel, and Parry, José. *The Rise of the Medical Profession: A Study of Collective Social Mobility*. Croom Helm: London, 1976.

Pearson, Lionel. *The Art of Demosthenes*. Verlag Anton Hain: Meisenheim am Glan, 1976.

Pelling, Christopher. *Literary Texts and the Greek Historian*. Routledge: London and New York, 2000.

Pelling, Christopher. "Plutarch's Adaptation of His Source-Material," in *Essays on Plutarch's* Lives, ed. Barbara Scardigli. Clarendon Press: Oxford, 1995.

Pelling, Christopher. "The Question of Character Development: Plutarch and Tacitus." *Classical Quarterly* 33.2 (1983) 469–87.

Perelman, S. "Quotation from Poetry in Attic Fourth-Century Orators." *American Journal of Philology* 85 (1964) 155–72.

Pickard-Cambridge, Sir Arthur. *The Dramatic Festivals of Athens*, 2nd ed., revised by J. Gould and D. M. Lewis. Clarendon Press: Oxford, 1988.

Pickard-Cambridge, Sir Arthur. *The Dramatic Festivals of Athens*. Clarendon Press: Oxford, 1953.

Pitcher, Seymour Maitland. "The 'Anthus' of Agathon." *American Journal of Philology* 60.2 (1939) 145–69.

Plass, Paul. *The Game of Death in Ancient Rome: Arena Sport and Political Suicide*. The University of Wisconsin Press: Madison, 1995.

Potter, David S. "Gladiators and Blood Sport," in *Gladiator: Film and History*, ed. Martin M. Winkler. Blackwell Publishing: Malden, Oxford, and Victoria, 2004.

Potter, David S. "Entertainers in the Roman Empire," in *Life, Death, and Entertainment in the Roman Empire*, eds. D. S. Potter and D. J. Mattingly. The University of Michigan Press: Ann Arbor, 1999.

Potter, David S. "Martyrdom as Spectacle," in *Theater and Society in the Classical World*, ed. Ruth Scodel. The University of Michigan Press: Ann Arbor, 1993.

Pratt, Norman T. *Seneca's Drama*. The University of North Carolina Press: Chapel Hill and London, 1983.

Pucci, Pietro. *Hesiod and the Language of Poetry*. Johns Hopkins University Press: Baltimore, 1977.

Puchner, Walter. "Acting in the Byzantine Theater: Evidence and Problems," in *Greek and Roman Actors: Aspects of an Ancient Profession*, eds. Pat Easterling and Edith Hall. Cambridge University Press: Cambridge, 2002.

Purcell, Nicholas. "Does Caesar Mime?" in *The Art of Ancient Spectacle*, eds. Bettina Bergmann and Christine Kondoleon. Yale University Press: New Haven, CT and London, 1999.

Rawson, Elizabeth. *Roman Culture and Society: Collected Papers*. Oxford University Press: Oxford, 1991.

Rei, Annalisa. "Villains, Wives, and Slaves in the Comedies of Plautus," in *Women & Slaves in Greco-Roman Culture: Differential Equations*, eds. Sheila Murnaghan and Sandra R. Joshel. Routledge: London and New York, 1998.

Richlin, Amy. "Cicero's Head," in *Constructions of the Classical Body*, ed. James I. Porter. University of Michigan Press: Ann Arbor, 2002.

Richlin, Amy. "Not before Homosexuality: The Materiality of the Cinaedus and the Roman Law against Love between Men." *Journal of the History of Sexuality* 3.4 (1993) 523–73.

Robert, Louis. *Les gladiateurs dans l'Orient grec*. Adolf M. Hakkert: Amsterdam, 1971.

Roberts, W. Rhys. "Aristophanes and Agathon." *Journal of Hellenic Studies* 20 (1900) 44–56.

Rorty, Amélie Oksenberg, ed. *Essays on Aristotle's Poetics*. Princeton University Press: Princeton, NJ, 1992.

Rorty, Amélie Oksenberg, ed. *The Identities of Persons*. University of California Press: Berkeley, 1976.

Rowe, Galen O. "The Portrait of Aeschines in the *Oration on the Crown*." *Transactions of the American Philological Association* 97 (1966) 397–406.

Rubiés, Joan-Pau. "Nero in Tacitus and Nero in Tacitism: The Historian's Craft," in Elsner, Jas, and Masters, Jamie, eds. *Reflections of Nero: Culture, History, & Representation*. Chapel Hill: The University of North Carolina Press, 1994.

Russell, D. A. "On Reading Plutarch's *Lives*," in *Essays on Plutarch's Lives*, ed. Barbara Scardigli. Clarendon Press: Oxford, 1995.

Saïd, Suzanne. "Travestis et travestissements dans les comédies d'Aristophane." *Cahiers du groupe interdisciplinaire du théâtre antique* 3 (1987) 217–48.

Saller, Richard. "Anecdotes as Historical Evidence for the Principate." *Greece & Rome* 27 (1980) 69–83.

Sande, Siri. "Qualis Artifex! Theatrical Influences on Neronic Fashions." *Symbolae Osloenses* 71 (1996) 135–46.

Scafuro, Adele C. *The Forensic Stage: Settling Disputes in Graeco-Roman New Comedy.* Cambridge University Press: Cambridge, 1997.

Schiesaro, Alessandro. *The Passions in Play: Thyestes and the Dynamics of Senecan Drama.* Cambridge University Press: Cambridge, 2003.

Scodel, Ruth, ed. *Theater and Society in the Classical World.* The University of Michigan Press: Ann Arbor, 1993.

Scullard, H. H. *From the Gracchi to Nero: A History of Rome from 133 B.C. to A.D. 68,* 5th ed. Methuen: London and New York, 1984.

Segal, Erich. *Roman Laughter: The Comedy of Plautus,* 2nd ed. Oxford University Press: New York and Oxford, 1987.

Sealey, Raphael. *Demosthenes and His Time: A Study in Defeat.* Oxford University Press: New York and Oxford, 1993.

Sedgwick, Eve Kosovsky. *Epistemology of the Closet.* University of California Press: Berkeley, 1990.

Sellén, Francisco. *La muerte de Demósthenes, tragedia.* Habana, 1926.

Shaw, Brent. "Body/Power/Identity: Passions of the Martyrs." *Journal of Early Christian Studies* 4.3 (1996) 269–312.

Shelton, Jo-Ann. "The Spectacle of Death in Seneca's *Troades*," in *Seneca in Performance,* ed. George W. M. Harrison. Duckworth: London, 2000.

Sidwell, Keith. "Aristotle, *Poetics* 1456a25-32.1," in *Eklogai: Studies in Honour of Thomas Finan and Gerard Watson,* ed. Kieran McGroarty. Maynooth: Department of Ancient Classics, 2001.

Sifakis, Gregory M. "Looking for the Actor's Art in Aristotle," in *Greek and Roman Actors: Aspects of an Ancient Profession,* eds. Pat Easterling and Edith Hall. Cambridge University Press: Cambridge, 2002.

Slater, Niall W. "Nero's Masks." *Classical World* 90 (1996) 33–40.

Slater, Niall W. "From Ancient Performance to New Historicism," in *DRAMA: Beiträge zum antiken Drama und seiner Rezeption,* Band 2: *Intertextualität in der griechisch-römischen Komödie,* eds. Niall W. Slater and Bernhard Zimmerman. Metzlerschen & Pöschel: Stuttgart, 1993.

Slater, Niall W. "The Idea of the Actor," in *Nothing to Do with Dionysos? Athenian Drama in its Social Context,* eds. John J. Winkler and Froma I. Zeitlin. Princeton University Press: Princeton, NJ, 1990.

Slater, Niall W. *Plautus in Performance: The Theatre of the Mind.* Princeton University Press: Princeton, NJ, 1985.

Slater, William. "The Pantomime Tiberius Julius Apolaustus." *Greek Roman and Byzantine Studies* 36.3 (1995) 263–92.

Slater, William. "Actors and Their Status in the Roman Theatre in the West." *Journal of Roman Archaeology* 7 (1994a) 364–8.

Slater, William. "Pantomime Riots." *Classical Antiquity* 13 (1994b) 120–44.

Stallybrass, Peter, & White, Allon. *The Politics and Poetics of Transgression.* Cornell University Press: Ithaca, NY, 1986.

Stehle, Eva. "The Male Body in Aristophanes' *Thesmophoriazusae*: Where Does the Costume End?" *American Journal of Philology* 123.3 (2002) 369–406.

Stohn, Günther. "Zur Agathonszene in den 'Thesmophoriazusen' des Aristophanes." *Hermes* 121 (1993) 196–205.

Storey, Ian. "Poets, Politicians, and Perverts: Personal Humour in Aristophanes." *ClIre* 5 (1998) 85–134.

Straub, Kristina. *Sexual Suspects: Eighteenth-Century Players and Sexual Ideology.* Princeton University Press: Princeton, NJ, 1992.

Sumi, Geoffrey. "Impersonating the Dead: Mimes at Roman Funerals." *American Journal of Philology* 123.4 (2002) 559–85.

Sutton, Dana Ferrin. *Seneca on the Stage.* E. J. Brill: Leiden, 1986.

Swearingen, C. Jan, "*Ethos*: Imitation, Impersonation, and Voice," in James S. Baumlin and Tita French Baumlin, eds. *Ethos: New Essays in Rhetorical and Critical Theory.* Southern Methodist University Press: Dallas, 1994.

Swift Riginos, Alice. *Platonica: The Anecdotes Concerning the Life and Writings of Plato.* E. J. Brill: Leiden, 1976.

Taaffe, Lauren. *Aristophanes and Women.* Routledge: London and New York, 1993.

Taplin, Oliver. *The Stagecraft of Aeschylus: The Dramatic Use of Exits and Entrances in Greek Tragedy.* Clarendon Press: Oxford, 1977.

Tarrant, Dorothy. "Plato as Dramatist." *Journal of Hellenic Studies* 75 (1955) 82–9.

Taylor, Rabun. "Two Pathic Subcultures in Ancient Rome." *Journal of the History of Sexuality* 7 (1997) 319–71.

Thalmann, William G. "Versions of Slavery in the *Captivi* of Plautus." *Ramus* 25 (1996) 112–45.

Todd, Stephen. "The Use and Abuse of the Attic Orators." *Greece & Rome* 37 (1990) 159–78.

Too, Yun Lee. *The Rhetoric of Identity in Isocrates: Text, Power, Pedagogy.* Cambridge University Press: Cambridge, 1995.

Trilling, Lionel. *Sincerity and Authenticity.* Harvard University Press: Cambridge, MA, 1972.

Tylawsky, Elizabeth Ivory. *Saturio's Inheritance: The Greek Ancestry of the Roman Comic Parasite.* Artists and Issues in the Theatre, vol. 9. Peter Lang: New York, 2002.

Ubersfeld, Anne. "Notes sur la dénégation théâtrale," in *La relation théâtrale*, ed. Régis Durand. Presses Universitaires de Lille, 1980.

Ussher, R. G. "Old Comedy and 'Character': Some Comments." *Greece & Rome* 24 (1977) 71–9.

Vansina, Jan. *Oral Tradition as History.* The University of Wisconsin Press: Madison, 1985.

Varner, Eric R. "Grotesque Vision: Seneca's Tragedies and Neronian Art," in *Seneca in Performance*, ed. George W. M. Harrison. Duckworth: London, 2000.

Veyne, Paul. *Seneca: the life of a stoic*, trans. David Sullivan. Routledge: New York, 2003.

Ville, Georges. *La gladiature en Occident des origines à la mort de Domitien*. Ecole Française de Rome: Palais Farnèse, 1981.

Von Blanckenagen, Peter H. "Stage and Actors in Plato's *Symposium*." *Greek Roman and Byzantine Studies* 33 (1992) 51–68.

Vout, Caroline. "The Myth of the Toga: Understanding the History of Roman Dress." *Greece & Rome* 43 (1996) 204–20.

Wallace-Hadrill, Andrew. "Patronage in Roman Society: From Republic to Empire," in *Patronage in Ancient Society*, ed. Andrew Wallace-Hadrill. Routledge: London and New York, 1989.

Weaver, P. R C. "Social Mobility in the Early Roman Empire: The Evidence of the Imperial Freedmen and Slaves," in *Studies in Ancient Society*, ed. M. I. Finley. Routledge and Kegan Paul: London and Boston, 1974.

Webb, Ruth. "Female Entertainers in Late Antiquity," in *Greek and Roman Actors: Aspects of an Ancient Profession*, eds. Pat Easterling and Edith Hall. Cambridge University Press: Cambridge, 2002.

Weber, C. "Roscius and the *roscida dea*." *Classical Quarterly* 46 (1996) 298–302.

Weineck, Silke-Maria. "Talking about Homer: Poetic Madness, Philosophy, and the Birth of Criticism in Plato's *Ion*." *Arethusa* 31 (1998) 19–42.

Wiedemann, Thomas. *Emperors and Gladiators*. Routledge: London and New York, 1992.

Wiles, David. *Greek theatre performance: an introduction*. Cambridge University Press: Cambridge and New York, 2000.

Wiles, David. *The Masks of Menander: Sign and meaning in Greek and Roman Performance*. Cambridge University Press: Cambridge, 1991.

Wilkins, John. *The Boastful Chef: The Discourse of Food in Ancient Greek Comedy*. Oxford University Press: Oxford, 2000.

Williams, Craig A. *Roman Homosexuality: Ideologies of Masculinity in Classical Antiquity*. Oxford University Press: New York and Oxford, 1999.

Wilson, Peter. "The Musicians among the Actors," in *Greek and Roman Actors: Aspects of an Ancient Profession*, eds. Pat Easterling and Edith Hall. Cambridge University Press: Cambridge, 2002.

Wilson, Peter. *The Athenian Institution of the Khoregia*. Cambridge University Press: Cambridge, 2000.

Winkler, John J. *The Constraints of Desire: The Anthropology of Sex and Gender in Ancient Greece*. Routledge: New York and London, 1990.

Winkler, John J., and Zeitlin, Froma I., eds. *Nothing to Do with Dionysos? Athenian Drama in Its Social Context*. Princeton University Press: Princeton, NJ, 1990.

Wise, Jennifer. *Dionysus Writes: The Invention of Theatre in Ancient Greece*. Cornell University Press: Ithaca and London, 1998.

Wiseman, T. P. "The Games of Flora," in *The Art of Ancient Spectacle*, eds. Bettina Bergmann and Christine Kondoleon. Yale University Press: New Haven, CT and London, 1999.

Woodruff, P. "Aristotle on *Mimēsis*," in *Essays on Aristotle's* Poetics, ed. Amélie Oksenberg Rorty. Princeton University Press: Princeton, NJ, 1992.

Wooten, Cecil W. "A Few Observations on Form and Content in Demosthenes." *Phoenix* 31.3 (1977) 258–61.

Worthington, Ian. "Introduction: Demosthenes, Then and Now," in *Demosthenes: Statesman and Orator*, ed. Ian Worthington. Routledge: London and New York, 2000a.

Worthington, Ian. ed. *Demosthenes: Statesman and Orator*. Routledge: New York, 2000b.

Xanthakis-Karamanos, G. *Studies in Fourth Century Tragedy*. Athens, 1980.

Zagagi, Netta. *The Comedy of Menander: Convention, Variation & Originality*. Indiana University Press: Bloomington and Indianapolis, 1995.

Zeitlin, Froma I. *Playing the Other: Gender and Society in Classical Greek Literature*. University of Chicago Press: Chicago, 1996.

Zoll, Amy. *Gladiatrix: The True Story of History's Unknown Woman Warrior*. Berkeley Publishing Group, 2002.

INDEX